Shamrock and Sword

San Patricio Commemorative Medal

Shamrock and Sword

The Saint Patrick's Battalion in the U.S.–Mexican War

by Robert Ryal Miller

UNIVERSITY OF OKLAHOMA PRESS : NORMAN AND LONDON

BY ROBERT RYAL MILLER

For Science and National Glory: The Spanish Scientific Expedition to America, 1862–1866 (Norman, 1968)
Arms Across the Border: United States Aid to Juárez During the French Intervention in Mexico (Philadelphia, 1973)
Chronicle of Colonial Lima: The Diary of Josephe and Francisco Mugaburu, 1640–1697 (Norman, 1975)
Latin America (with John Francis Bannon and Peter M. Dunne) (Encino, Calif., 1977 and Minneapolis, Mn. 1982)
Mexico: A History (Norman, 1985)
Shamrock and Sword: The Saint Patrick's Battalion in the U.S.–Mexican War (Norman, 1989)

Library of Congress Cataloging-in-Publication Data

Miller, Robert Ryal.
    Shamrock and sword : The Saint Patrick's Battalion in the U.S.-Mexican War / by Robert Ryal Miller.
        p.   cm.
    Bibliography: p.
    Includes index.
    ISBN 0-8061-2204-8 (hardcover, alk. paper)
    ISBN 0-8061-2964-6 (paperback, alk. paper)
    1. Mexico. Ejército. Batallón de San Patricio—History.
2. United States—History—War with Mexico, 1845–1848—
Regimental histories—Mexico. 3. United States—History—War
with Mexico, 1845–1848—Desertions. 4. Defectors—United
States—History—19th century. 5. Defectors—Mexico—History—
19th century. I. Title.
E409.8.M55   1989
973.6′24—dc19   89-5252
                                                                         CIP

The paper in this book meets the guidelines for permanence and durability of the Committee on Production Guidelines for Book Longevity of the Council on Library Resources, Inc. ∞

2   3   4   5   6   7   8   9   10   11

Contents

Illustrations

Maps

Tables

Preface

HISTORIANS AND GENERAL readers on both sides of the Rio Grande continue to be fascinated by the United States–Mexican War of 1846 through 1848. That transcontinental struggle involved American naval blockades in the Gulf and Pacific, as well as army campaigns from Texas to California that extended south into the heartland of Mexico. Besides tracing the origins, principal battles, conclusion, and significance of the Mexican War, this book tells for the first time the interrelated story of the rise and fall of the Saint Patrick's Battalion (Battallón de San Patricio), a unique unit of the Mexican army. What made this outfit exceptional was that it was composed almost entirely of deserters from the United States Army who, after defecting, fought on the Mexican side in five major battles. The battalion also had a brief history in the months after the war ended.

Having studied and taught Mexican history for more than thirty years, I have long been aware of the existence of the Saint Patrick's Battalion. Yet, except for two romantic novels, one in Spanish by Patricia Cox and the other by the American writer Carl Krueger, there was no book about it. A play, *A Flag to Fly,* in 1986 by Chris Matthews, was first staged in Santa Cruz, California, by the Bill Motto Post of the Veterans of Foreign Wars. Several published articles in American magazines and journals have highlighted some aspects of the "legion of deserters," but the dramatic quality of the story and the controversial nature of the subject seemed to deserve a scholarly volume. Furthermore, the truth about this unusual military contingent is even more fascinating than its published fictional accounts.

Searching American sources for clues to the history

of the Saint Patrick's Battalion, I examined government
documents and many books about the Mexican War, some
of which mentioned the military unit, but only briefly. At
the Navy and Old Army Branch of the National Archives
in Washington, staff member Elaine C. Everly was extremely helpful in locating records of the enlistment, desertion, court-martial, and punishment of scores of the
San Patricios—the Mexican name of the defectors. She
also pointed out that surnames of some soldiers had variant spellings (Newer and Neuer, for example) in different
army files.

Information about American arms and military organization came from several sources. My own military experience in the U.S. Army Air Corps during World War II gave
me some familiarity with army terminology, command
structure, discipline, and court-martial proceedings. For
suggestions and documentation about nineteenth-century
army pay, desertion rates, executions, and other matters,
I am indebted to John J. Slonaker, Chief of Historical Reference, Army Military History Institute, Carlisle Barracks,
Pennsylvania. At the United States Military Academy,
Curator Michael J. McAfee and other staff members
searched the West Point Museum collections to locate rele-
vant information about weapons, uniforms, trophies, and
illustrations.

In the Hemeroteca Nacional periodical library in Mexico City, I carefully read one-half-dozen wartime newspapers, including those published in 1847–48 by American occupation forces, where I found a number of articles
about the San Patricios. During various visits to Mexico,
my attempts to check military records in the National Defense Archive were frustrated—that repository is closed to
virtually all civilian historians, Mexican or foreign. Nor
would the director of that archive provide microfilm or
photocopies of documents listed in a guide. Nevertheless,
a number of key documents, as well as records of pay,
promotion, and retirement of certain individuals, were
printed in the official newspaper of the Mexican govern-

ment, and a few of the microfilmed records were found in
American libraries.

Great Britain's Public Record Office yielded some important data for this story, including six letters written by
John Riley, an Irishman who first organized the Saint Patrick's unit. When Riley and other British-born renegades
were in trouble in Mexico, they wrote to Her Majesty's diplomatic and consular agents in that country, affirming
their loyalty to Great Britain and appealing for assistance.
The diplomatic correspondence shows that the minister
and consuls talked with some of the San Patricios, gave
them a small amount of money, and helped a few of them
eventually return to Great Britain. Published dispatches
from the Mexico City correspondent of *The Times* of London were another important British source for this study.

Despite searches in Ireland, I was unable to locate additional biographical information about several of this story's
chief characters who were born in the Emerald Isle. Unfortunately, many vital statistics records in Dublin were destroyed in an 1882 fire, and some official papers were lost
during disturbances accompanying the Irish independence
movement between 1919 and 1922. Checking baptismal
and other records maintained by Roman Catholic parish
priests in Ireland was not possible because exact birth
dates and parish affiliations are unknown for the Irish-
born San Patricios.

In addition to the helpful archival personnel mentioned
above, I wish to acknowledge the assistance and encouragement of others. Virtually all books used to research this
subject were found in The Bancroft Library at the University of California, Berkeley, where the staff kindly provided study space and located pertinent books and microfilmed documents. Also, for their encouragement, as well
as suggestions about specific sources and ways to approach
this study, I wish to thank Ferol Egan, Richard Dillon,
George Rascoe, and Thaddeus Holt.

Berkeley, California   ROBERT RYAL MILLER

Shamrock and Sword

CHAPTER 1

Bloodshed on the Rio Grande

MEXICANS REVERE JOHN RILEY, a tall, blue-eyed Irishman who fought in their army; yet Americans north of the Rio Grande vilify this same man as a traitor. Riley was a soldier of fortune who served under three different national flags in the nineteenth century. Born in County Galway, Ireland, he seems to have first served in the British army, from which he deserted while stationed in Canada. He then went to Michigan, where he enlisted in the United States Army in 1845. Only seven months later, while based on the Rio Grande in Texas, he defected to the Mexican army. In this last service he attained the permanent rank of major and brevet rank as colonel.[1]

Riley achieved notoriety during the United States–Mexican War of 1846–48 because he organized a special unit of the Mexican army that came to be known as the Saint Patrick's Battalion (Batallón de San Patricio, in Spanish). Named for the patron saint of Ireland, the battalion's members were called San Patricios (Saint Patricks). Riley also designed the unit's shamrock flag and personally recruited more than one hundred fifty men to serve under him.[2] This outfit was unique in that it was composed primarily of deserters from the United States Army, virtually all of whom defected during the Mexican War. Representing a cross section of the American army at that time, most of these turncoats were foreign-born, and the greatest number were Irish. The story of Saint Patrick's Battalion is intertwined with the war that erupted on the Rio Grande in 1846.

The Mexican War was a culmination of competing forces that had been set in motion centuries earlier. After

Columbus' historic discovery, Spaniards, Frenchmen, and Englishmen contended for North America, where they eventually founded New Spain, New France, New England, and other beachheads on the Atlantic and Gulf coasts. Their colonial descendants—explorers, missionaries, trappers, traders, soldiers, and settlers—gradually moved toward the center of the continent and toward each other. Anglo-French rivalry culminated in war, after which the French withdrew from North America in 1763. A new contender appeared when the United States of America achieved its independence from Great Britain and acquired as its western boundary the Mississippi River, beyond which was Spanish Louisiana (until 1800 when the area was retroceded to France).

During the nineteenth century an increasing number of Yankees crossed the Mississippi and migrated west, stimulated by a growing sentiment called "Manifest Destiny"—the belief that divine providence had given the United States a moral mission to occupy and develop western lands. When, in 1803, the United States purchased from France the large, undefined territory known as Louisiana, it doubled the existing size of the country and moved the frontier much farther west. Meriwether Lewis and William Clark traversed the northern part of the new territory from Missouri to the Continental Divide and on to the Pacific. Another American explorer, Zebulon Montgomery Pike, moved south along the Rocky Mountains to the southern boundary until he was arrested in 1807, by Spanish soldiers in New Mexico. Conducted as a prisoner to Santa Fe, El Paso, and Chihuahua, Pike eventually was released and returned to St. Louis where he suggested the possibility of trade with Santa Fe. Subsequently, other Americans penetrated the entire Southwest. Spain was eliminated from the continent when it ceded Florida to the United States in 1819 and lost its colony of New Spain (Mexico) two years later.

After Mexico broke away from Spain and set up its own government in 1821, conflict with the United States developed along the extended frontier from Texas to California. Although many Mexican leaders admired their northern neighbor, especially its form of government and its economic progress, they were apprehensive about America's expansionist tendencies. Officials in Mexico City reacted negatively to proposals by United States agents who tried to purchase California or other parts of northern Mexican territory, and they fretted about the growing number of American trappers, traders, explorers, and settlers in California, New Mexico, and Texas.[3]

Affairs in Texas dominated Mexican-American problems of that era. Having first claimed title to Texas as part of the Louisiana Purchase, the United States relinquished that claim by signing the Adams-Onís Treaty of 1819, ratified two years later, which defined the border between Texas and Louisiana: the Sabine River north to the Red River, then westward in a zigzag line along the Red and Arkansas rivers to the crest of the Rocky Mountains.

After Mexican independence in 1821, a considerable number of Americans, some with black slaves, migrated as colonists to Texas, where they became Mexican citizens. They were attracted primarily by the abundance of cheap, arable land suitable for cotton cultivation and by exemption of taxation for ten years. By 1834 the English-speaking residents numbered 20,700 and the Spanish-speaking sector 4,000. The newcomers, joined by some Spanish-surnamed Texans, quarrelled with the government in Mexico City over issues such as black slavery, which was officially abolished in Mexico in 1829, but not totally enforced; import-export duties and regulations; restrictions on additional immigration of *gringos* (Anglo-Americans); and the location of the state capital. Moreover, they vehemently opposed the centralized dictatorship established in 1835, which abolished Mexico's federal constitution of 1824 (patterned on that of the United States). A Mexican army's movement into Texas in the autumn of 1835 led to hostilities at the Alamo and elsewhere, and to a declaration of independence by Texans,

The Texas Frontier, 1836–1848. Map by R. R. Miller

who won their freedom on the battlefield. In the final battle at San Jacinto in April, 1836, the Texans captured General Antonio López de Santa Anna, who was also president of Mexico.[4] By terms of a law proposed by the first congress of the Republic of Texas, the new nation's southwestern boundary was the Rio Grande (Rio Bravo y Grande del Norte) from its mouth to its source, thereby shifting the line many miles southwest of the Nueces River, the traditional Texas boundary. This exaggerated claim not only tripled the size of the old Spanish and Mexican Texas, it put the eastern half of New Mexico, including Santa Fe and Albuquerque, into the Lone Star Republic, as Texas was popularly called. It is true that a boundary not to extend beyond the Rio Grande had been acknowledged by General Santa Anna when he signed the peace treaty with Texas; however, he was at that time a Texan prisoner of war trying to save his own life.

After the battle of San Jacinto the Mexican government ousted Santa Anna (temporarily), repudiated the treaty he had signed, refused to recognize the independence of Texas, and scorned the Rio Grande boundary claim. Frequently during the next few years various Mexican leaders threatened to reconquer their lost province of Texas, and they backed two military strikes against San Antonio. However, internal unrest and foreign threats to Mexico prevented any major northern campaign. Between 1836 and 1845, Texas maintained its own sovereignty and was recognized as an independent nation by the United States, Great Britain, France, and other countries—but not by Mexico.[5]

More than once during the nine years of Texas independence, emissaries from that new republic asked for annexation to the United States. The issue provoked heated controversy in Washington and elsewhere. Northern antislavery forces did not want to add another slave state to the Union, but southern planters favored annexation, as did Americans who believed that the destiny of the United States was to subdue the continent from sea to sea. An annexation treaty was rejected by the Senate in June, 1844. Meanwhile, Santa Anna and other Mexican officials accused the United States of complicity with Texas in its independence war, and they declared that annexation of the territory "would mean war with Mexico."[6]

American moves to acquire Texas came to a head in 1845. At the end of February, just before the inauguration of President James K. Polk, who had campaigned for acquisition of Texas and Oregon, a joint congressional resolution invited Texas to join the Union, if the Texans themselves ratified the agreement. A week later the Mexican minister in Washington, claiming that the resolution was "an act of aggression," broke off diplomatic relations and returned home. In mid-March the Mexican foreign minister protested the American congressional action, noting that his government had previously declared that it would look upon such an act as warlike, and, "as a consequence of this declaration, negotiation was by its very nature at an end, and war was the only recourse of the Mexican government."[7] When notified about the rupture of relations, the United States minister to Mexico closed the embassy there.

In midsummer of 1845, a popular convention in Austin, Texas, formally accepted the annexation offer, and five months later the American Congress officially declared Texas the twenty-eighth state in the Union. Meanwhile, as soon as Texas agreed to annexation, President Polk sent a naval squadron to the Texas coast and an occupation army to western Texas to protect the new American state against a threatened Mexican attack. Some of Polk's contemporaries and several historians have asserted that the president sent the large military force to the Texas frontier hoping to provoke an attack by Mexico, after which the United States would retaliate by seizing California and other Mexican territory.[8]

Besides Texas and Oregon, Polk did want California, by purchase if possible, or by gradual occupation. Reports indicated that leading citizens in California were alienated from the Mexican government and had talked of becoming a protectorate of Great Britain, France, or the United States. To forestall European domination of California and Oregon, Polk invoked the Monroe Doctrine, and he hoped that time and geography would favor American control of those desirable areas.[9] As for Texas, the American president was determined that the United States flag should fly over that land; if the Mexicans would not agree to that, they would have to pay for their intransigence, perhaps with additional land.

Brevet Brigadier General Zachary Taylor, best known as a hero of the Seminole War, headed the United States Army of Occupation in Texas. He had been an army officer for thirty-seven years, most of them spent at military posts on the western frontier from Minnesota to Louisiana. Raised in Kentucky with only a rudimentary education, Taylor was a typical backwoodsman—strong in character and body, unkempt in dress, and ungrammatical in speech. Although he lacked intellectual qualifications and was a poor administrator, he was a brave and inspiring leader on the battlefield. Moreover, he was solicitous of the well-being of his troops and treated them warmly; they called him "Old Rough and Ready."[10]

In the summer of 1845, Taylor accompanied his seaborne army from New Orleans to an encampment on the west bank of the Nueces River near its mouth at Corpus Christi, Texas. In mid-October, the Fifth Regiment of Infantry, including Private John Riley, joined Taylor's forces, which then totaled 3,900 men—almost half of the American army. Foreign-born soldiers made up almost 50 percent of the enlisted men; the Irish totaled 24 percent, Germans were 10 percent, English 6 percent, Scottish 3 percent, and another 4 percent came from Western Europe or Canada.[11]

In their diaries and letters home, a number of American soldiers complained about the rough living conditions in Texas. They were housed in tents that gave little protection from the searing heat of summer or the drench-

General Zachary Taylor. Courtesy The Bancroft Library

ing rains and icy cold of winter. Thornbush or mesquite wood for campfires was scarce on the sandy plains, and the drinking water was brackish, "unless qualified with brandy." Men of the Seventh Infantry reported that they had killed 114 rattlesnakes in one day. The small trading post at the head of Corpus Christi Bay changed radically after Taylor's army camped nearby. One account says that in five months this settlement of fifty people mushroomed to two thousand, "most of the inhabitants being adventurers. There are no ladies, and very few women. . . . Drinking, horse-racing, gambling, theatrical amusements are the order of the day."[12]

Taylor's army was in Texas to guarantee the annexation of that state, but his presence also underscored American monetary claims against Mexico. These claims were for repudiated bonds, revoked concessions, and damages to American property that had occurred during past civil wars in Mexico. Similar claims by France had led to a Franco-Mexican war in 1838. The Mexican government had ratified a convention in 1843 to pay the adjusted American debt of just over $2 million, but the following year it suspended payments because of its almost bankrupt condition.[13]

In November, 1845, Polk dispatched a special envoy, John Slidell, to Mexico with an offer to assume the unpaid monetary claims in exchange for Mexican recognition of the Rio Grande as the southern boundary of Texas and of the United States. Slidell also carried instructions to purchase northern California for $25 million, if possible. Although the Mexican government earlier had agreed to receive a commissioner, it refused to accept Slidell because, as one official said, "an American army was camped on Mexican territory." Slidell's title as minister plenipotentiary also displeased Mexican officials, who reasoned that his reception would mean restoration of normal relations and might imply acceptance of the loss of Texas. While the American diplomat was waiting to present his credentials, a revolution in late December, 1845, toppled the govern-

U.S. Army Camp at Corpus Christi. Courtesy The Bancroft Library

ment in Mexico City. The new president was Major General Mariano Paredes y Arrillaga, an unyielding nationalist who refused to see Slidell and who vowed to uphold the integrity of Mexican territory, not only to the Nueces, but all the way to the Sabine River, the Texas-Louisiana boundary.[14]

Mexican public opinion overwhelmingly supported national claims to Texas, but attitudes about waging war against the United States were divided. A large and very vocal body of public opinion, fanned by major newspapers, favored war. As early as the spring of 1845, the editor of the important Federalist party newspaper *El Siglo Diez y Nueve* espoused war and insisted that Mexico enjoyed excellent prospects of success. The opposition Centralist paper *El Defensor de las Leyes* agreed; so did *La Voz del Pueblo,* which boasted: "We have more than enough strength to make war. Let us make it, then, and victory will perch upon our banners." Some Mexicans predicted that if war broke out, black slaves and Indian tribes in the United States would take advantage of the situation and rise up to revenge their oppressors. A few Mexican leaders acknowledged two serious negative factors affecting their side—the nation's near bankruptcy, and political factionalism, which had caused internal revolts and might preclude successful prosecution of a foreign war.[15]

At this time the minister of war and a number of Mexican military officers felt confident that they could prevail if a war should develop on the northern border. Their army of about 25,000 men was more than three times larger than the American force, and many of their officers had gained field experience during the past decade when there were half a dozen civil uprisings, as well as a limited war with France. Mexico's cavalry was especially strong; each mounted man was armed with an *escopeta* (carbine), pistol, and sabre, plus an unconventional weapon, the lasso. Some cavalrymen wielded a long lance—an outmoded but effective arm. Mexican officers were well outfitted in resplendent uniforms, but their military qualifications were uneven. Although some officers were serious students of military tactics, others lacked professional training and skills, and many were in the military service because of its social and political advantages.[16]

The weakest part of the Mexican army was the ranks of the infantry, which were filled by conscripts drafted for a six-year term. All able-bodied single men, childless married men, and married men not living with their wives, were subject to the military draft. Lots were drawn on the last Sunday of each October, and those selected were obliged to enter the army the following December 15. Exemptions were granted to seminary students, attorneys with offices, men formally engaged to be married, and other categories. In general, those conscripted were poor, illiterate peasants, who, upon becoming soldiers, were "poorly clothed, worse fed, and seldom paid."[17]

A contemporary New York newspaper printed a sketch of the Mexican army giving the table of organization for the three branches: infantry, cavalry, and artillery. This account also contrasted the qualifications, pay, and uniforms of generals and privates. It ended with the following statement:

Let us say something about the private soldiers of the Mexican army. . . . The soldiers, when in garrison, cater for themselves [there are no mess halls]. Once a year they are supplied with a new suit of uniform. . . . About three-fourths of the Mexican troops are pure Indians—the rest *Mestizos,* or half-breeds. There are very few negroes amongst them. . . .

The Mexican soldier has one or two useful qualities. He is obedient to his officers, and he endures the greatest privations without a murmur. His strength is in his legs. He can march distances which even a Spanish soldier might fail to accomplish. . . . Detachments of Mexican infantry have been known to keep up with their mounted officers, though they (the officers) were going at a trot![18]

When the Mexican military president, confident in his army, rebuffed Polk's agent, Slidell, the American president ordered General Taylor to advance to the Rio Grande, where he was to take up a defensive position on the left bank. Reconnaissance of potential forward bases and acquisition of transport for supplies took some time. Then, early in March, 1846, the old camp was broken and the Americans, including Private John Riley, moved south across the virtually empty sandy plains of south Texas. A small force was detailed to establish a supply base at Point Isabel near the mouth of the "Great River," while the bulk of the army marched to an encampment twenty-five miles upriver.

American soldiers griped about the harsh living conditions at the makeshift bases on the lower Rio Grande. One

Georgian complained about the abundance of flies, centipedes, and other insects:

This country is distinguished, above all other particulars by its myriads of crawling, flying, stinging and biting things. Every thing you touch has a spider on it. We are killing them all day in our tents. We never draw on a boot or pull on a hat or garment without a close search for some poisonous reptile or insect crouching in their folds or corners. It is wonderful that we are not stung twenty times a day. . . . I would willingly forego the possession of all the rich acres I have seen to get back from this land of half-bred Indians and full-bred bugs.[19]

For his principal forward base, Taylor selected a bluff on the left bank of the Rio Grande, just opposite the Mexican town of Matamoros. There, at the end of March, American soldiers began construction of a five-sided fortress with earthen walls nine feet high and fifteen feet thick. Those soldiers who worked on the "fatigue detail" received a gill (four ounces) of whiskey per day as extra compensation. First named Fort Texas, the stronghold was later renamed Fort Brown (the present site of Brownsville).[20] Here, a few disgruntled Yankee soldiers deserted by simply crossing the river into Mexico, and some of them, like John Riley, joined the Mexican army in Matamoros. This provocative post also set the stage for a showdown between the two armies that faced each other.

Alerted about the American encampment opposite Matamoros, Major General Pedro de Ampudia, commander of the Mexican Army of the North, hurried there with a force of 2,400 reinforcements. Born in Havana, Cuba, in 1803, Ampudia had been an officer in the Mexican army for twenty-five years, serving much of that time on the northern frontier. As an artilleryman he had participated in the siege of the Alamo in San Antonio, Texas, and in 1842 he forced the surrender of a group of Texans who had attacked the Mexican city of Mier.[21] Even before his arrival in Matamoros, he ordered the printing in English

General Pedro de Ampudia. Courtesy The Bancroft Library

of handbills, which were scattered along the roads and smuggled into the American camp. These leaflets urged American soldiers to desert.

Addressed "To the English and Irish under the Orders of the American General Taylor," Ampudia's broadside dated April 2 1846, alleged foreign condemnation of United States' aggression:

Know ye: That the Government of the United States is committing repeated acts of barbarous aggression against the magnanimous Mexican Nation; that the Government which exists under "the flag of the stars" is unworthy of the designation of Christian. Recollect that you were born in Great Britain; that the American Government looks with coldness upon the powerful flag of St. George, and is provoking to a rupture the warlike people to whom it belongs; President Polk boldly manifesting a desire to take possession of Oregon, as he had already done of Texas. Now, then, come with all confidence to the Mexican ranks, and I guarantee to you, upon my honor, good treatment, and that all your expenses shall be defrayed until your arrival in the beautiful capital of Mexico.[22]

A subsequent paragraph called on Germans, French, Poles, and individuals of other nations to "separate yourselves from the Yankees."

When General Ampudia arrived at Matamoros on April 12, he ordered the Americans to decamp at once and return to the other side of the Nueces. If the withdrawal were not begun within twenty-four hours, he warned, it would "clearly result that arms, and arms alone, must decide the question; and in that case, I advise you that we accept the war to which, with so much injustice on your part, you provoke us. . . ."[23] General Taylor replied that he regretted the alternative of war, the responsibility of which would rest on those who should commence hostilities, and that his instructions did not permit a withdrawal.

Twelve days later, Major General Mariano Arista, who had been ordered to replace Ampudia, arrived in Matamoros with additional reinforcements. A native of San

Luis Potosi, Arista was forty-two years old, redheaded, and had lived in Cincinnati for some years. Like Ampudia, he had been commanding general of the Division of the North, and he had served as governor of one of the northern frontier states. He also smuggled handbills into the American camp, one of which appealed to the soldiers to abandon their "desperate and unholy cause . . . throw away your arms and run to us, and we will embrace you as true friends and Christians." The surrender leaflets also promised that land would be given to deserters, based on their rank—privates to receive the minimum amount of 320 acres. It was not specifically stated, but in order to be eligible for land grants, deserters would have to join the Mexican army, and the land would be distributed after the war ended.[24]

General Arista arrived in Matamoros with presidential instructions to attack the United States military force on the Rio Grande, which had, from the Mexican viewpoint, invaded their territory. His orders read: "It is indispensable that hostilities be commenced, yourself taking the initiative against the enemy."[25] Arista immediately sent a column of sixteen hundred mounted soldiers across the river with orders to cut the Yankee supply line to Fort Brown.

Hostilities began on April 25, 1846, when an American scouting party was ambushed by a Mexican cavalry unit in the disputed territory on the left bank of the Rio Grande. In that engagement, eleven Yankees were killed, six wounded, and sixty-three taken prisoner. Taylor rushed this news to Washington where President Polk already had considered asking Congress for a declaration of war. Announcing news of the armed clash, Polk told the legislators, "Mexico had passed the boundary of the United States, has invaded our territory and shed American blood upon the American soil. . . . A war exists, and notwithstanding all our efforts to avoid it, exists by the act of Mexico herself. . . ." Influenced by these assertions and other arguments such as unpaid claims, the overwhelming majority of legislators voted, on May 13, to declare war on

General Mariano Arista. Courtesy The Bancroft Library

Mexico—the vote was 174 to 14 in the House, and 40 to 2 in the Senate. Mexico's congress delayed its declaration of war until July 2, and a week later it was announced publicly by President Mariano Paredes.[26]

After congressional declaration of war in Washington, there were enthusiastic public demonstrations throughout the United States. Thousands of people gathered for mass meetings in New York, Philadelphia, Louisville, Cincinnati, Richmond, New Orleans, and other cities. Highlighted by torchlight parades, martial music, and patriotic oratory by local political figures, these gatherings generated support for the war and stimulated army enlistments. Speakers emphasized the popular belief that liberation of the Mexican people from domination by an outworn aris-

tocracy, an elite military clique, and the dead hand of the
Roman Catholic Church was the right and even the duty
of Americans.[27]

Overall war strategy of the United States, outlined in
cabinet meetings and military headquarters in Washington, was for naval units to blockade Mexico's principal Gulf
and Pacific ports, while land forces seized territory west and
south of Texas. Eventually, five separate American armies
invaded Mexico. General Zachary Taylor's Army of Occupation was ordered to cross the Rio Grande and attack
Monterrey; General John Wool's Central Division marched
southwest from San Antonio to Saltillo for an eventual
linkup with Taylor; General Stephen Kearny left Fort
Leavenworth and conquered New Mexico before moving
on to the occupation of California; one column of Kearny's
army under Colonel Alexander Doniphan marched south
from New Mexico to Chihuahua and Saltillo; and an amphibious force under General Winfield Scott was destined
to land at Veracruz and follow Hernán Cortés' footsteps to
Mexico City.

When the Mexican War began, the United States Army
was relatively small, and except for Indian wars, had not
been engaged for thirty years. Yet, long years of frontier duty had forced the professional soldiers to be self-
sufficient and prepared them to cope with feeble supply
and communication lines in Mexico. On the eve of the war
the authorized strength of the regular army was 734 officers and 7,885 enlisted men, but because the regiments
were not full, the actual total strength was only 6,562.
There were eight regiments of infantry, two of dragoons
(mounted infantry), and four of artillery, plus the staff
corps, and department personnel. Nine months later, in
February, 1847, Congress voted to create an additional
nine regiments of regular infantry and one of dragoons.[28]

In addition to the regular army, there were state militias,
which could be called into federal service for six months.
Because of a constitutional question about whether mili-
tiamen could be used outside the United States, those des-

tined for Mexico had to volunteer for that service. At the time of the declaration of war, Congress authorized 50,000 volunteers to serve for twelve months or for the duration of the war, at the discretion of the president. The volunteer units were composed of militia companies and larger tactical groups that were organized according to militia laws of the various states. Generally their officers were elected, but some were political appointees.[29]

In the United States, enthusiasm for the Mexican War varied from region to region. In the southern and western states closest to the battle front, the war was extremely popular—the Mississippi Valley and Texas furnished 49,000 army volunteers who dreamed of finding gold and glory in Mexico and who were eager to "revel in the Halls of the Montezumas." Enlistments languished in parts of New England where many civil leaders emphatically opposed the war. Some opponents were pacifists. Others were abolitionists or against the expansion of slavery. They viewed the war as "a plot to extend the slavocracy of the South." And there were those who objected to the cost of the war—financial as well as human. Naturalist-writer Henry David Thoreau protested the war by refusing to pay a poll tax; to justify his action he wrote "Civil Disobedience," an essay that later inspired other peoples who felt oppressed by their governments.[30]

Some Americans believed that grievances with Mexico had not been sufficient to justify a war, or that the differences could have been resolved through negotiated settlement rather than by arms. A few felt that the timing was wrong because of the possibility of war with Great Britain over the Oregon Country, but that argument ceased with the signing of the Oregon Treaty in mid-June of 1846. Still others opposed the war on political grounds—Whigs called it "Mr. Polk's war," or the Democratic party's war. Protesters aired their complaints through speeches, town meetings, letters to editors, and appeals to their elected representatives.

Although the great majority of American legislators

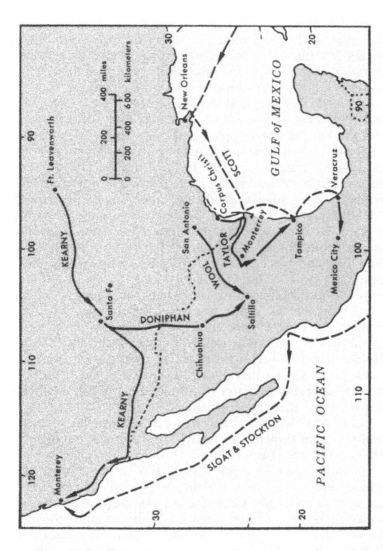

Campaigns of the U.S.–Mexican War. Map by Robert E. Winter

favored the Mexican War and voted funds to pursue it, a number of others were vehemently opposed. Senator Thomas Corwin of Ohio asked to be shown the area on the map where American blood was spilled on American soil. His colleague, Daniel Webster, declared in a speech: "We are, in my opinion, in a most unnecessary and therefore most unjustifiable war. . . . I hold it to be a war unconstitutional in its origin. I hold it to be a war founded upon pretexts."[31] The same theme was reiterated by freshman congressman Abraham Lincoln, who said that the war had been unnecessarily begun by the chief executive, whose justification for the war, he said, was "the sheerest deception."[32]

John Quincy Adams, the former president who served in Congress for seventeen years, was the most vociferous and bitterest American legislative opponent of the war. He voted against the original war bill, asserting that Polk had started the war to extend slavery. Then, after the war began, he said he hoped that military officers would resign their commissions and soldiers would desert rather than fight in such an "unrighteous war." He presented petitions calling for peace with Mexico on generous terms. Adams regularly voted against measures to honor and decorate the war's heroes; indeed, while opposing one such measure, he had a fatal stroke and slumped comatose over his desk in the House of Representatives.[33]

Dissent by American civilians had its counterpart in dissatisfaction among United States soldiers, many of whom deserted from their military units. Although desertion was also a problem in peacetime, the Mexican War desertion rate of more than 8 percent was the highest of any American foreign war. An examination of military records reveals that the number of enlisted deserters was 9,207 out of a total force of 111,063 (40,934 regular soldiers plus 70,129 volunteers). None of the 1,653 army officers deserted, but 8 of the 548 marines who accompanied the army in Mexico did desert. Approximately 13 percent of the regular army soldiers deserted, while only 6 percent of the wartime volunteers were listed as deserters.[34] Of those soldiers who deserted during the Mexican War, about 4,000 "went over the hill" in Mexico, but only a small percentage of them subsequently joined the Mexican military forces.

Like most armies elsewhere in that era, the ranks of the United States Army were filled by men from the less-favored strata of society. However, two groups at the bottom were precluded from military service: those with known criminal records and "men of color." Despite regulations, a few Afro-Americans crossed the color line and joined the army; several of these were later discharged "for having colored blood." More important, hundreds of blacks, free and slave, went through the Mexican campaigns as personal servants of officers. Junior officers were permitted one servant, majors and colonels two, brigadier generals could have three, and major generals four.[35]

During the Mexican War there was no military conscription or draft in the United States; all regular enlistees agreed to serve for five years, and terms for volunteers varied from six months to "the duration of the war." A recruit or private was paid seven dollars a month, but two dollars of this monthly pay was withheld until successful completion of the first enlistment term. A soldier who re-enlisted received three months' extra pay.[36] Of course, compensation also included army food, clothing, housing, and medical care. These conditions do not seem so oppressive that they would stimulate more than nine thousand men to "go over the hill."

There were a number of motives for Mexican War desertions—there may have been any one, or a combination of several, inducing soldiers to abandon their posts, and sometimes, country. These reasons will be examined in a later chapter. As the story of the organization of the Saint Patrick's Battalion is traced, some of the San Patricios tell why they defected.

CHAPTER 2

Organizing the San Patricios

THE MEXICAN GOVERNMENT's support of John Riley and other deserters—as well as its authorization of the Saint Patrick's companies—followed a long tradition held by that country of welcoming foreigners into its army. In the decade from 1810 to 1821, American, British, and French citizens fought in Mexico's war for independence from Spain. Some served with the patriot leader José María Morelos, and, in 1817, more than three hundred volunteers sailed from New Orleans to Tamaulipas with the Relief Army of the Republic of Mexico, headed by Francisco Javier Mina. In the 1830s four foreign-born generals—Gaona, Filisola, Tolsa, and Woll—served with the Mexican army in its Texas campaigns and in the brief war with France. By the time of the United States–Mexican War, there were sixteen foreign-born generals in the Mexican army; they came from Argentina, Cuba, France, Italy, the Philippine Islands, Spain, and Trinidad.[1] There were also resident aliens or foreign-born officers who held lower ranks.

During the Mexican War several outlanders held high positions in the regular Mexican military establishment. Doctor Pedro Vanderlinden, a Belgian by birth, was the surgeon-general of the Mexican army. James Humphrey, a Scottish surgeon who eventually joined the San Patricios, was one of his subordinates. Other prominent Mexican officers were Swedish-born Colonel Emilio Langberg, and German-born Johann (Juan) Holzinger, both of whom fought in several battles during the Mexican War.[2] Unlike the above-named soldiers of fortune, the San Patricios were primarily wartime defectors from the United States

Army. Although many famous generals throughout history—Augustus Caesar, George Washington, and Napoleon Bonaparte, for example—utilized foreign legions or alien mercenary corps in their armies, those foreign units were not composed of deserters from enemy forces. Thus, the Saint Patrick's Battalion of the Mexican army was unique.

John Riley was the key figure and organizer of the San Patricios. Very little biographical data is known about Riley, and existing facts are often conflicting. Although he said that he had been born in County Galway, Ireland, the exact date is not known, nor in which of the county's ninety-five parishes his baptism would have been recorded. One clue suggests that his home parish was Clifden. When he enlisted in the United States Army in 1845, he stated that he was then twenty-eight years old, which would have put the year of his birth at 1817. However, an American newspaper editor who saw him two years later estimated that Riley was thirty-five years old, which indicates a birth date of 1812, and a Mexican biographical dictionary states that he was born in 1795—a date that definitely is too early. All the records do agree that Riley was a tall, broad-shouldered, and muscular man; he stood six feet, one and three-fourths inches high, had dark hair, blue eyes, and a ruddy complexion. He was married in Ireland and had a son there, according to one of his letters, and he apparently returned to the "Old Sod" after his adventures in the New World.[3]

One of the confusing factors about John Riley, and a source of frustration to a historian, are variations of spelling of his surname. In some of his correspondence he signed himself Riley; at other times he used Riely, Reilly, or O'Riley. United States Army records show him enlisted as Riley, but court-martialed as Reilly, and Mexican army documents designate him variously as Juan Reyle, Reley, Reely, and Reiley.[4] Variation in patronymic spelling was common in Ireland, especially in County Galway, where the Gaelic language persisted. Neither John Riley (Seán

O'Raghailligh in Gaelic) nor many of his fellow soldiers spoke or wrote grammatically-correct English.

Circumstantial evidence and Riley's own testimony indicate that he had joined the British army, probably at a military post in Ireland sometime in the 1830s. In this first military career he was a non-commissioned officer, either a corporal or sergeant. He may have been in a Royal Artillery unit, for he later demonstrated that he knew how to service artillery pieces. Probably he was stationed in British North America—New Brunswick, Newfoundland, Quebec, or Canada—from whence he deserted and fled south to Michigan in about 1843. Later, after he enlisted as a private in the United States Army, he wrote that if God spared him, "I would again attain my former rank or die."[5] This statement implies previous military service at a rank higher than a private soldier.

An item published in two American newspapers in the fall of 1847 said that Riley, or Ryley, was a former sergeant in the Sixty-sixth Infantry Regiment of the British army, who deserted while stationed in Canada. Claiming that Riley then went to New York where he joined the United States Army, the article stated that he became a drill sergeant at the Military Academy at West Point and later a recruiting sergeant in New York City. Several articles about the St. Patrick's Battalion repeat these erroneous statements. A careful search of army muster rolls in Great Britain's Public Record Office failed to locate Riley in the Sixty-sixth Regiment, nor was that regiment stationed overseas between 1840–43. There were a number of Irish-born soldiers named John Riley (or Riely, Reilly, etc.), who served in British North America, and at least two of them deserted there in the 1830s, but none of these men was over six feet tall, nor had any been born in County Galway. Furthermore, John Riley testified that he had lived in the United States for only two years, during which time he was in Michigan.[6]

Between 1843 and 1845, Riley worked as a laborer in Mackinac County, Michigan, near the Canadian-United

States border. His employer was Charles M. O'Malley, a settler who had arrived seven years earlier from County Mayo, Ireland, and who eventually became a local magistrate, a member of the Michigan legislature, and unofficial leader of the numerous Irish immigrants who lived in the region. O'Malley later wrote, "The said Riley worked in my employ off and on for the space of two years, with whom I had more trouble than all the other men who worked for me, and more particularly as [I was] a Justice of the Peace, for he was always in variance with everyone he had any thing to do with."[7] Evidently Riley had a strong personality and was a true "fighting Irishman."

On September 4, 1845, Riley went to nearby Fort Mackinac, where he enlisted for a five-year term in the United States Army. Like other recruits of that era, he signed a printed enlistment certificate which stated: "I [name of enlistee] do solemnly swear, that I will bear true faith and allegiance to the United States of America, and that I will serve them honestly and faithfully against all their enemies or opposers whomsoever; and that I will observe and obey the orders of the President of the United States, and the orders of the officials appointed over me, according to the Rules and Articles of War." An examining surgeon then signed the enlistment form, attesting that he had "carefully examined the above named Recruit . . . and that in my opinion he is free from all bodily defects and mental infirmity, which would in any way, disqualify him from performing the duties of a soldier." The recruiting officer also signed and certified that he had "minutely inspected the Recruit previously to his enlistment, and that he was entirely sober when enlisted. . . ."[8] As a private in Company K of the Fifth Regiment of Infantry, Riley was under the orders of Captain Moses E. Merrill, a graduate of the Military Academy at West Point.

Only two days after Riley's enlistment, his regiment left for Texas; they journeyed most of the way by water, the last part from St. Louis down the Mississippi River to New Orleans, then by ship to Corpus Christi, Texas. There, in mid-October the Fifth Infantry joined General Zachary Taylor's Army of Occupation. That army of three brigades totaling almost four thousand men was the largest American military force that had been assembled since the War of 1812. At first the soldiers practiced military evolutions and marksmanship, but, with the onset of winter, drill ceased, illness became common, and the men grew disillusioned. Shivering in their leaky tents, they were unable to find adequate fuel for campfires or good drinking water. About the time the weather improved, the men were ordered to move farther south.

During the last three weeks of March, 1846, Riley, along with most of Taylor's army, marched about one-hundred-and-seventy miles across the uninhabited Texas prairie from the Nueces River to the Rio Grande, where they established a camp on the left bank of the river, opposite the Mexican town of Matamoros. At that base on Sunday, April 12, 1846, Riley obtained a pass from Captain Merrill to attend a Catholic mass, which he said a priest from Matamoros was holding on the Texas side of the river. But Riley "went south." He never returned to his outfit and was reported as a deserter.[9] This was two weeks before hostilities erupted on that frontier and a month before the American declaration of war.

Two and one half years later, when Riley was an American prisoner, he claimed that he had not deserted willingly. "I went to hear [a religious] service and was captured by the Mexicans, brought back as a prisoner to Matamoros to the presence of General Ampudia," he said.[10] Recounting that he was then interrogated for some days and finally given his choice of joining the Mexican army or being shot on the grounds that as an Irishman he was an alien to both Mexico and the United States, he chose the first option and was commissioned as a first lieutenant in the Mexican artillery. At that time he received his sword, the distinctive symbol and principal weapon carried by officers. It is worth noting that Riley had earned seven dollars per month as an American private, whereas his pay as a Mexi-

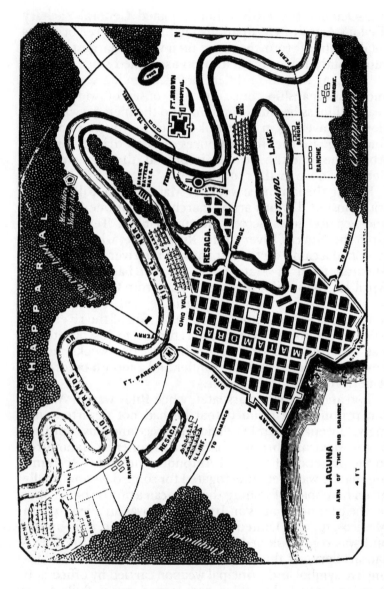

Matamoros and Fort Brown. Map by M. A. Haynes, Tennessee Regiment of Cavalry, 1847.

can lieutenant would be fifty-seven dollars monthly. Furthermore, Mexican generals promised that defectors to their side would receive generous land bonuses, as well as other rewards.

Desertions from Taylor's force increased after the army moved to the Rio Grande. When the Americans bivouacked opposite Matamoros, the soldiers were attracted to the other side by the excitement and bustle of a town, versus their life in a crude fortress. Because the river was only two hundred yards wide at that point, the men could see religious processions and hear the frequent ringing of church bells, which must have aroused yearnings in some of the foreign-born soldiers. Perhaps a few of them were lured by the sight of scantily-clad Mexican females swimming in the water, or gaily dressed sirens who lined the opposite bank of the river all day. These attractions were reinforced by two captured American dragoons who, after being repatriated, reported that deserters received handsome treatment in Mexico.[11]

When desertions escalated, American sentries were told to order any soldiers seen swimming across the river to return, and to fire on them if they did not obey the order. The first two victims of this policy were Privates Carl Gross and Henry Lamb, both foreign-born, who were killed by sharpshooting guards early in April, 1846. The penalty for desertion in peacetime did not call for capital punishment. As a result, Taylor's policy was criticized in Washington, to which the general caustically replied: "How far I should have been justified in seeing our ranks thinned daily . . . without resorting to the most efficient steps to stop it, I cheerfully leave to the decision of the War Department."[12] By the middle of April, the Matamoros *Gazette* claimed that forty-three Americans and six black slaves who belonged to American officers had sought refuge on the Mexican side.[13] Of course, not all of the deserters took up arms in Mexico, but some of them did.

Renegades who crossed the Rio Grande formed the nucleus of the unique San Patricio unit of the Mexican Army.

View of Matamoros. Courtesy The Bancroft Library

The Irish-born deserter, John Riley, later claimed credit for organizing the outfit. In a letter to the Mexican president he stated: "Since April 1846 when I separated from the North American forces . . . I have served constantly under the Mexican flag. In Matamoros I formed a company of forty-eight Irishmen. . . ."[14] By July of 1847, the number of San Patricios had increased to more than two hundred. Although the outfit was composed mostly of defectors from the United States Army—native-born Americans as well as European immigrant soldiers—members also included various foreign residents of Mexico and some Mexican citizens. Not all of the men who joined the unit became officers; their ranks ranged from private to lieutenant colonel.

Riley's second-in-command was Patrick Dalton, who had been born about 1824, in the barony of Tirawley, near Ballina, County Mayo, Ireland. When he enlisted in the United States Army on August 2, 1845, at Madison Barracks, New York, Dalton said that he was twenty-one years old and had been born in Quebec. That false birthplace undoubtedly was given to cover his recent tracks, probably as a British army deserter. George Ballentine, a Scottish veteran who enlisted in New York the same month and place as Dalton, said that American recruiters were ordered to turn down applicants who were known to be deserters from the British service because they "generally turned out [to be] bad soldiers."[15] Ballentine had to show his British "purchase discharge" before he was permitted to enlist. After fourteen months as a private in the United States Army, Patrick Dalton deserted from Company B, Second Regiment of Infantry, on October 23, 1846, when his unit was based at Camargo on the Rio Grande. He crossed over to the Mexican army, where he was commissioned as a first lieutenant; later he was promoted to captain in command of one of the Saint Patrick's companies.[16]

As can be seen by the roster in the Appendix, members of the San Patricio units came from many countries. The national origin of more than seventy men was verified by their statements at the time they enlisted in the United States Army; the birthplace of others was mentioned in correspondence or in periodical articles. Although records are incomplete, they show that Ireland produced the largest number of volunteers—about two-fifths of the men. Fourteen were born in some other part of Great Britain, twenty-two in the United States, fourteen in German states, two in Canada, and one each in France, Italy, Spanish Florida, and Poland.

The national origin or religious persuasion of every San Patricio is not known, but certainly all were not Irish, nor all Roman Catholic. The Irish-Catholic link had only a superficial meaning to the San Patricios—it gave them a distinctive symbol and provided cohesion for the group. That they were named for the Irish patron saint and fought under an emerald flag emblazoned with the Irish harp and shamrock was due to the whim of John Riley, not to the national origin or religious preference of the great majority of the members. Based on testimony of the San Patricios, there seemed to be no basis of fraternal feeling with Mexicans, nor sympathy for their being invaded

by a northern neighbor with a dominant Anglo-Saxon
and Protestant culture. Except for John Riley, the Irish-
Catholic connection was emphasized more by Mexicans
than by the San Patricios themselves. Mexicans still think
of the San Patricios as Irish Catholics, as will be seen in the
last chapter of this book.

Several British subjects who resided in Mexico joined
the Saint Patrick's Battalion. Prominent among these were
three Scots: John Sutherland, Henry Thompson, and
James Humphrey. The latter was a surgeon who had been
in the country since 1842. Irish-born civilian residents of
Mexico who joined the outfit included Richard Burke,
Thomas Donaley, John Hynes, Patrick Maloney, Peter
O'Brien, and Thomas O'Connor. An Englishman named
John Wilton had deserted from a British ship in Jamaica
before he came to Mexico, where he joined Patrick Dalton's company.[17] The "Irish Volunteers" also included a
few Mexican citizens. Three commandants of San Patricio
units were career officers in the regular Mexican army:
Lieutenant Colonel Francisco Schafino, Florida-born Major Francisco Rosendo Moreno, and Major José María Calderón. At least three other Mexicans were San Patricio
officers: Captain Ignacio Alvarez, Lieutenant Ramón Bachelor, and Lieutenant Camillo Manzano. The latter was
killed in the battle of Buena Vista.[18]

During the two years of war, Mexicans called this unique
outfit by various names; some designations were official,
others were coined by the people. Unofficially, the group
was called the Irish Volunteers, or the Colorados—or
Red Guards—so-named because of the many redheaded
and ruddy-complexioned men in it, or the San Patricio
Guards. Officially, the unit began as the San Patricio Company, an artillery outfit that was later expanded to two
companies. In mid-1847, the Mexican war department re-
assigned the men as infantrymen and merged the San Patricio companies into the newly-created Foreign Legion
(Legión extranjera), which some Britons and Americans
called the Legion of Strangers. And, in 1848, the Mexican

president expanded the companies and formed the Saint Patrick's Battalion.

When they joined the Mexican Army, American turncoats had to adjust to Mexican food and culture. The unique cuisine was based on native American products of *maíz* (maize) *frijoles* (beans), chiles, squash, and tomatoes, with some meat occasionally. Maize was the base; the ears could be roasted or boiled, or the kernels ground into flour for *atole* porridge, or for *pinole*, a spiced drink. Most often, however, the corn dough was patted out as *tortillas*, the thin unleavened cakes cooked on a slab over a charcoal fire, which are widely used as bread even today. Besides camp followers who accompanied the army and cooked for the soldiers, other women sold *tortillas*, *tacos*, *enchiladas*, and *tamales* in doorways and along the streets.

An American in Mexico in the 1840s described *tortillas*, which he called "buckskin colored victuals," and their variety of fillings in these words:

The hungry man squats down beside the seller—makes a breakfast or dinner table of his knees—holds out his tortilla spread flat on his hand for a ladle of chile and a lump of meat—then doubles up the edges of the cake sandwich fashion, and so on until his appetite is satisfied. He who is better off in the world, or indulges occasionally in a little extravagance, owns a clay platter. Into this he causes his frijoles, or chile and meat, to be thrown, and making a spoon of his tortilla, gradually gets possession of his food, and terminates his repast by eating the spoon itself![19]

The San Patricios soon became familiar with other aspects of Mexican culture, which, like the food, were a fusion of Iberian and American Indian elements. They saw Spanish architectural motifs such as arches, fountains, and red-tile roofs, incorporated with native adobe, or wattle and daub construction. Each block of cities and towns found adobe or stuccoed, flat-roofed houses joined to each other. The view from the street was thus only a long blank wall, pierced by an occasional massive door or window that was protected by a wrought-iron grille. Music from strumming guitars sometimes wafted through these barred windows. Most homes had one or more patios, generally visible and accessible only from inside the house. These courtyards were open to the sky and typically contained flower beds, trees, a fountain, and caged songbirds or a parrot. A pleasant feature of every town was the central public plaza, shaded by trees and graced with benches, often having a *kiosko* or bandstand in its center. Government offices and the principal church usually flanked this main square, with their imposing buildings often made of cut stone with impressive façades.

The San Patricios found that Mexico, like Ireland, was a land of shrines and churches, often coupled with exuberant amusements. Much Mexican social life revolved around Catholic church activities. Besides daily masses, there were baptisms, marriages, funerals, holy days, processions, meetings of various church guilds, and barbecues or church suppers. *Fiestas*, which occurred on the frequent religious holidays, began with a mass and ended with fireworks and a *fandango*. Bullfights were staged on Sundays and *fiesta* days. In their leisure time soldiers often could be found in the *cantinas*, bars, or *pulquerías* (taverns serving *pulque*, an alcoholic beverage made from maguey juice). People congregated almost every evening around the central plaza, some sitting on park benches or at tables in adjacent cafes, while young folks participated in the *serenata*— strolling around and around, flirting, and having a good time. These social activities continued despite the war.

The alien San Patricios also observed the caste and class system south of the Rio Grande. They may have seen more contrast in Mexico than anything they had previously encountered in "the Old Country" or in the United States. Simply by looking at the people in church, at bullfights, or anywhere, they could easily see a society that was sharply divided into three basic classes. This pyramidal structure was topped by a tiny, upper-class elite, most of whom were well-educated, considerable property-owners, and capable of boasting of their European ancestry. Below this elite there was a very small middle-class, composed mostly of *mestizos* (persons of mixed Spanish and Indian ancestry), who were shopkeepers, civil servants, professionals, or farm and ranch managers. The base of the social pyramid, which accounted for the great bulk of the population, was made up primarily of poor Indians who were peasants on *ranchos* and *haciendas*, or day laborers in towns and primitive industries. Ranking officers in the Mexican army were from the elite families; non-commissioned officers were generally *mestizos*; and the privates were typically *mestizos* or else acculturated and Spanish-speaking Indians from the bottom sector.

A Mexican's clothes revealed class and status. Elite men and women wore elegant garments made of silk, velvet, lace, and other fine cloth, often in the latest European fashion. In stark contrast, Indians dressed in their native garb—men in white cotton pants with a colorful *sarape* cloak, and the long-skirted women in the ubiquitous *rebozo*, or long, woven scarf, thrown over their head and crossed over the left shoulder, sometimes used as a sling for a child. Most Mexican visitors remarked on the peculiar, yet handsome, *charro* riding outfits worn by men. These consisted of a short jacket of deerskin or velveteen, often embroidered and trimmed with silver buttons and worn over a white shirt, with matching trousers that had silver buttons and a slit up the side of the leg, which showed a pair of white linen underpants. Worn with a red cummerbund around the waist and boots with enormous spurs and rowels, plus a broad-brimmed *sombrero* with a silver or gold cord, these were striking ensembles.

However, the San Patricios and other men probably paid particular attention to the appearance of Mexican *señoritas*, as revealed in the following excerpt from one young man's account:

The ladies wear no bonnet, but a scarf [rebozo] that they sometimes slip over their heads—skirts of different qualities, from cotton to satin—no waist to their dress—the chamise [*sic*] made so low in the neck as to leave the chest uncovered—sleeves short, and worked or embroidered—their skirts coming nearly to the ancles [sic]—their toes stuck into small slippers—the heel left loose—the dress of the women is principally white. . . . The people are very social, especially the women.[20]

Mexican military costumes were more colorful than Yankee uniforms. When the San Patricio defectors first joined the Mexican army, they exchanged their blue wool American garments for new military attire that was a darker shade of blue. Artillery officers and enlisted men wore Turkey-blue cloth coats, which had crimson collars, cuffs, and piping. Their stand-up collars were embroidered with a yellow exploding bomb, and two dozen brass buttons on the uniforms were stamped with the bomb design. Trousers were Turkey-blue with crimson piping along the outside seams. In summer, soldiers wore white canvas pants. The dress hat for all ranks was a black leather shako about eight inches tall, topped with a red pompon. In the field, the officers wore a blue kepi—a visored cap with a round flat top sloping toward the front. Enlisted men wore dark blue cloth barracks caps, piped in crimson, with a red tassel hanging in front.[21]

Because most turncoats received a higher rank under the red, white, and green flag of Mexico than under the Stars and Stripes, a comparison of the contemporary pay scales of the two armies is pertinent.

The San Patricios served under a distinctive military banner. John Riley said the emerald green ensign had an image of Saint Patrick emblazoned on one side, with a shamrock and the harp of Erin outlined on the other. In his wartime reminiscences, published under the title *My Confession*, Yankee soldier Sam Chamberlain commented on the San Patricios' standard: "A beautiful green silk banner waved over their heads; on it glittered a silver cross and a golden harp, embroidered by the hands of the fair nuns of San Luis Potosi."[22]

George Wilkins Kendall, a wartime newspaper corre-

TABLE 1.
Monthly Military Pay, 1847

	U.S. Army (dollars)	Mexican Army (*pesos* at $.96)
Colonel	81	200
Lt. Colonel	65	133
Major	54	100
Captain	44	67
1st Lieutenant	34	57
2d Lieutenant	29	45
1st Sergeant	16	20
Sergeant	13	16
Corporal	9	10
Musician	8	9
Private	7	8.5

SOURCES: Exley, *A Compendium of the Pay*, 9, 48, 50–51; Dublán and Lozana, *Legislación mexicana*, 5:323.

spondent from New Orleans who witnessed several battles, described the San Patricio flag captured at the battle of Churubusco:

The banner is of green silk, and on one side is a harp, surmounted by the Mexican coat of arms, with a scroll on which is painted, "*Libertad por la República Mexicana*" [Liberty for the Mexican Republic]. Underneath the harp is the motto "Erin go Bragh" [Ireland for Ever]. On the other side is a painting . . . made to represent St. Patrick, in his left hand a key and in his right a crook or staff resting upon a serpent. Underneath is painted "San Patricio."[23]

Exactly when the San Patricios' emerald flag was first unfurled is unknown; nor is the mobilization date and original table of organization for the outfit known.[24] Nevertheless, probably the earliest turncoats first served in regular Mexican army units, and were then later organized into their own outfit. John Riley said that he formed a company of soldiers in Matamoros. This would have occurred sometime between his defection in mid-April of 1846, and five weeks later, when all Mexican military forces abandoned the area. Riley and other San Patricios later fought in four major battles of the war. Their participation in those engagements is well documented, as will be seen in the following chapters.

CHAPTER 3

Fighting Under the
Shamrock Flag

LIEUTENANT JOHN RILEY and other American turncoats
gained their first Mexican War battle experience at the
town of Matamoros on the Rio Grande. Beginning at day-
light on May 3, 1846, they assisted Mexican artillerymen in
bombarding the American garrison across the river at Fort
Texas, which was renamed Fort Brown after Major Jacob
Brown was mortally wounded in the attack. The noise,
smoke, and smell of exploding gunpowder permeated the
gun emplacements and drifted over the town during the
cannonading and counter shelling that continued intermittently for a week. Riley later claimed participation in
that action, and General Taylor reported, "It is known that
some of our deserters were employed against us and actually served guns in the cannonade and bombardment of
Fort Brown."[1]

Meanwhile, Taylor had marched the bulk of his men toward the mouth of the river to reinforce Point Isabel and
to secure additional supplies. Seeing the American forces
split, General Arista crossed the Rio Grande about twelve
miles below Matamoros, where he hoped to cut the American supply line. As Taylor advanced across the level prairie
covered with shoulder-high grass, the two armies clashed
on May 8, near a water hole called Palo Alto. Arista had
3,700 men against Taylor's 2,290. During the fiercely-
contested battle, which lasted from 2:00 P.M. until dusk,
the effective and mobile American artillery was a major
factor causing Mexican withdrawal. When the Americans
continued their advance the next day, the Mexicans had
the advantage of a strong defensive position in an ancient
river bed called *Resaca de la Palma,* but they were unable to

Battlegrounds between the Rio Grande and Mexico City. Reproduced from Edward D. Mansfield, The Mexican War *(New York: A. S. Barnes, 1849), p. 8.*

stop the Yankee advance. Bested in battle, they retreated in disorder across the Rio Grande. As spoils the Americans retrieved almost five hundred muskets, eight pieces of artillery, the colors of the Tampico Battalion, and all of Arista's official correspondence. In these two battles Taylor's army sustained 177 casualties (killed, wounded, and missing) against an American claim of 800 inflicted on the larger enemy force. Whether any San Patricios or other American defectors fought with Arista in these two engagements is not known.²

Because of American victories on the lower Rio Grande, their blockade of the mouth of the river, and Taylor's announced plan to occupy Matamoros, General Arista and his staff decided to abandon the city. First, however, the Mexican officers parleyed with Taylor, proposing an armistice or a partial surrender of public property. When that delaying tactic failed, Mexico's Army of the North evacuated Matamoros on the afternoon of May 17th, just one day ahead of the town's peaceful occupation by American troops. Of the turncoats that marched out with Arista, we know the names of five: John Little, James Mills, John Murphy, John Riley, and Thomas Riley, all but Mills having been born in Ireland.³

The Mexican soldiers retreated upriver about ten miles, then they turned south toward the interior. Before leaving the Rio Grande, they jettisoned five cannon and much of their baggage, and they abandoned the sick and wounded. For the next ten days the army, with its train of nearly a thousand dependents and camp followers, straggled two hundred miles southwestward through a sparsely populated and harsh land covered with cactus and mesquite. Following dirt trails, which became quagmires after torrential rains, they finally reached the town of Linares at the end of May.⁴

In midsummer, the Mexican Army of the North marched about a hundred miles northwest from Linares across the rugged Sierra Madre Oriental to the city of Monterrey (sometimes spelled Monterey). Founded in the

late sixteenth century on the north bank of the Rio Santa
Catarina, this capital of the state of Nuevo León made a
favorable impression on the defectors. The new cathedral,
with its richly-carved baroque facade and graceful bell
tower, fronted the east side of the plaza. Many of the city's
thirteen thousand inhabitants passed daily between this
central area and the city market a few blocks away. Nestled
in a natural amphitheater with mountains on three sides.
Monterrey had a picturesque location. Two peaks with
distinctive shapes loomed over the place; on the east
was Cerro de la Silla (Saddle Mountain), and on the west,
Cerro de la Mitra, resembling the mitre of a bishop. Commenting on the mountains, an American said: "Some of
them are very pointed, and worn into various fantastic
shapes by the action of rains, and deeply furrowed on the
sides. They form a very singular and striking picture in the
scenery."[5]

In September of 1846, General Taylor led his American
troops toward Monterrey, following orders to take the important regional capital. Military planners in Washington
thought this tactic would force the Mexican government
to sue for peace. General Ampudia, who headed the city's
defense, met the American invaders with propaganda, as
well as with a large army. Besides issuing a series of patriotic proclamations, one of which threatened death to
any Mexican who traded with the Yankees, he authorized
the printing of English-language handbills, which were
scattered along the roads. Dated September 15, 1846, and
bearing Ampudia's name, the leaflets claimed that the war
carried on by the United States was "unjust, illegal and
anti-Christian, for which reason no one ought to contribute to it." The final paragraphs urged American soldiers
to defect:

Acting according with the dictates of honour and in compliance with what my country requires for me, in the name of
my Government I offer to all individuals that will lay down their
arms and separate themselves from the American Army, seeking

protection, they will be well received and treated in all the Plantations, Farms or Towns, where they will first arrive and asisted [*sic*] for their march to the Interior of the Republic by all the Authorities on the road, as has been done with all those that have passed over to us.

To all those that wish to serve in the Mexican Army, their offices will be conserved and guarranteed [*sic*].[6]

The battle of Monterrey began on September 21, 1846. Counting recently-arrived reinforcements, Ampudia's army totaled 7,300 versus Taylor's 6,200 men. The defenders had more than forty artillery pieces, some strategically located in the citadel at the northern approach, others on hills overlooking the city. Several historians have written that Riley and other defectors were employed in "refurbishing, emplanting, and servicing the cannons." A Mexican artillery officer in that campaign noted that General Taylor interrogated several captured Mexican officers, inquiring about the foreigners who serviced the Mexican batteries. In his two-volume history of the war, Justin Smith cited a detailed Mexican muster roll of the garrison at Monterrey and noted, "A party of deserters (mostly Irish) from the American army, which served at Monterey, was presumably included in the above return."[7]

Approaching from the north, Taylor's army split into two elements, one of which moved west to cut off the supply road to Saltillo, while the other attacked the city from the northeast. After three days of fighting, during which Taylor's men had captured the city's outer defenses, had penetrated toward the central plaza and clearly would triumph, the Mexican commander offered to capitulate under certain conditions. A joint commission agreed to the terms, which included an eight-week provisional armistice, surrender of the city, and retirement of all Mexican forces beyond Rinconada Pass, southwest of the city.[8]

Both sides had suffered heavy casualties during the battle for Monterrey. Taylor lost 120 men killed, 368 wounded, and 43 missing; Ampudia lost 367 men killed

ARMY OF THE NORTH.
GENERAL IN CHIEF. HEAD QUARTERS, MONTEREY SEPTEM-
BER 15 TH 1846.

It is well known that the war carried on to the Republic of Mexico
by the Government of the United States of America is unjust, illegal and anti-
Christian, for which reason no one ought to contribute to it.

The Federal Government having been happily re-established, a large number
of Batallions of the National Guard in the States of Coahuila, St. Louis Potosi,
Guanajuato, Zacatecas, Queretaro and others, are ready to be on the field
and fight for our independence.

Acting according with the dictates of honour and in compliance with
what my country requires from me, in the name of my Government I offer
to all individuals that will laydown their arms and separate themselves from
the American Army, seeking protection, they will be well received and treated in all the Plantations Farms or Towns, where they will first arrive and
asisted for their march to the Interior of the Republic by all the Authorities
on the road, as has been done with all those that have passed over to us.

To all those that wish to serve in the Mexican Army, their offices will be
conserved and guarranteed.

PEDRO DE AMPUDIA.

Ampudia's Leaflet Soliciting Desertion. Courtesy Yale University Library

and wounded.[9] There were also psychiatric casualties, as
well as those from gunshot, bayonet, and shrapnel wounds.
By our standards today, medical treatment of the wounded
was primitive. If a musket ball was imbedded close to the
surface, an incision was made and the lead sphere ex-
tracted with forceps. Amputation was the only major sur-
gery performed; after severing the arm or leg, the stump
was cauterized with hot tar. Because anesthesia was not yet
in general use, a soldier made the best of his pain by chew-

ing a lead bullet; this prevented him from crying out or biting his tongue. Mexican and American military forces treated their wounded and buried their dead during the first days of the armistice.

Under terms of the armistice, the retreating Mexicans were permitted to retain their personal weapons and one six-gun field battery. Between September 26 and 28, the American soldiers watched with dismay as the enemy troops marched out of Monterrey on the road to San Luis Potosí, their flags held high, giving the appearance of a victory parade. One Yankee eyewitness, a West Pointer, reported:

> Several of our deserters were recognized in the ranks of the enemy, the most conspicuous of whom was an Irishman by the name of Riley, who has been appointed a captain in the artillery of the enemy. He was recognized by his old mess-mates, and passed them amid hisses and a broadside of reproaches. The dastard's cheek blanched, and it was with difficulty he retained his position on his gun.[10]

During the subsequent six weeks, while Taylor's troops occupied Monterrey, desertion was a serious problem. Luther Giddings, a major in the First Regiment of Ohio Volunteers, said that more than fifty regular soldiers abandoned the service there: "These the enemy joyfully received and speedily enrolled in their ranks, where they served with a courage and fidelity they had never exhibited in ours. Doubtless the humblest soldier of the battalion of Saint Patrick, was honored with much consideration by the Mexicans. . . ."[11]

Major Giddings also told of a Mexican agent who made liberal and flattering offers of money and rank to potential defectors in his outfit. But the gallant soldiers turned the tables on the agent:

> They were all Irishmen and never did ferrets pursue a rat more indefatigably, than did their pretended friend. He was a wily rascal and scenting his danger, had, after many windings and

General Antonio López de Santa Anna, as painted by Juan Cordero.
Courtesy Enciclopedia de México

turnings esconced himself in a bake-oven in one of the back yards of the city, whence he was finally dragged by the heels and lodged in the guard-house.[12]

Captain William Henry reported another plot to seduce American soldiers in Monterrey. The men were promised sixty dollars, civilian clothes, a horse and guide to take them to the Mexican Army, and fifty cents to drink to the health of General Santa Anna. Pretending to go along with the scheme, the soldiers collected their money, then gave a signal that resulted in the capture of three Mexicans, one of whom was a son of the *alcalde* (mayor) of the city.[13] Yet, not all the plots failed, and a study of the muster rolls of the United States Army shows many desertions at Monterrey.

About the time the battle for Monterrey was taking place, General Antonio López de Santa Anna returned to Mexico from exile in Havana, Cuba. For three decades this ambitious man's career had been intertwined with the history of his country. As a young officer he had fought in Mexico's war for independence (1810–21); then he participated in various civil wars; he led troops against forces of Spain (1829), France (1838), and Texas (1835–36); and he served as president eight times in the turbulent years from 1833 through 1844. In the brief war with France a cannonball shattered Santa Anna's left leg, which had to be amputated below the knee; thereafter, his peg leg was a valuable symbol for this national hero. Santa Anna was a colorful military commander whose personal magnetism could attract a devoted following of soldiers or civilians. As a clever politician, he usually was able to shift his policies to match the currents of public opinion.

When the United States–Mexican War began, Santa Anna intrigued with American agents who facilitated his return from Cuba and passed him through the naval blockade at Veracruz. The Yankees hoped that he would live up to his promise "to negotiate a satisfactory peace treaty." After his arrival in the Mexican capital in August, Santa

Anna found the country's leaders so determined on war
that he could not carry out any peace plan, so he decided
to lead them in war. Assuming overall command of the
Mexican Army, the fifty-two year old general left Mexico
City on September 28, 1846, and headed north for San
Luis Potosí. There, he would join General Ampudia's
forces, which included the San Patricios, and organize the
Liberating Army of the North.[14]

San Luis Potosí, situated about three hundred miles
northwest of Mexico City, had been founded in the late
sixteenth century to service nearby silver mines of San
Pedro Mountain. The name "San Luis" came from the
Saint's day when the place was founded; "Potosí" was added
in hopes that the mines would rival the fabulously rich
Potosí mine in Upper Peru (Bolivia). Situated at an elevation of 6,300 feet and near good water and plentiful building stone, the city prospered, evidenced by its handsome
colonial churches, convents and monasteries, a theater,
and other buildings. One church that certainly must have
impressed the San Patricios was Our Lady of Carmen, located one block east of the main plaza; its interior was
richly decorated in the baroque manner with gold leaf,
and its domes were covered on the exterior with strikingly-
colored tiles of blue, green, yellow, and white. In 1846, the
population of the city was almost thirty thousand. Two San
Patricios, Patrick Dalton and Thomas O'Connor, later
mentioned that they had attended a bullfight while based
in that state capital.[15]

San Luis Potosí was the scene of a frenzied military
buildup during the last quarter of 1846. With funds from
national and state governments, ninety-eight silver bars
seized from the local mint, a two-million peso loan from
the Catholic Church, and part of his personal fortune,
Santa Anna created the Liberating Army of the North,
composed of more than twenty thousand men. Some payments made to the army were listed in the official newspaper, and one November item was for pay of "the artillery company organized from deserters of the invading

army." Of course, this was the San Patricio Company.[16] In December the Mexican Congress declared General Santa Anna to be *ad interim* president of Mexico; while he was at the military front, his vice-president, Valentín Gómez Farías, would manage the government in the capital. Late in January, of 1847, the editor of *El Republicano,* a Mexico City newspaper, published the following description of the San Patricios, whom he had seen in San Luis Potosí:

> We had the pleasure on Sunday last of seeing a company of American deserters, principally Irish, reviewed by His Excellency, the general in chief. They are perfectly armed and equipped, and are on the point of departure. . . . These brave men, who have abandoned one of the most unjust of causes for the purpose of defending the territory of their adopted country, will find in the Mexicans a frank and loyal heart, open and hospitable; and besides, a just and ample recompense for their merited services.[17]

Marching to the strains of a popular song titled "Adios," Santa Anna's army left San Luis Potosí on January 27, for a showdown with the Yankees, who were near the town of Saltillo, about two hundred miles north. The San Patricios were in the vanguard of Santa Anna's forces. Listed as a company of "Irish Volunteers" (Voluntarios irlandeses) that had been trained as artillerists, they were mentioned together with a battalion of engineers (*zapadores*) and three companies of foot artillery who were conducting fourteen pieces of artillery. Another Mexican source called them "the San Patricio Company, made up of deserters from the enemy army, almost all of them Irish."[18]

A few days later the San Patricios were sighted by a group of nineteen American prisoners who were being marched south by their Mexican captors. These unfortunate Kentucky cavalrymen had been surrounded and captured at the hacienda of Encarnación, which was south of Saltillo. One of the Kentuckians later recalled their encounter with Santa Anna's forces:

Between Metahuila [Matehuala] and San Luis [Potosí] we
met the great army of the "Napoleon of the South," twenty thousand strong, and marching in four divisions. First came his
splendid park of artillery of fifty guns; then a huge body of cavalry; then infantry and cavalry, together in large bodies; then
General Santa Anna in person, seated in a chariot of war drawn
by eight mules and surrounded by his staff elegantly and gor-
geously equipt; then fluttered on his rear a bevy of wanton
women; and lastly, covering his rear, his baggage train, in the
midst of which were five mules loaded with chicken cocks, from
the "best coops" of Mexico. These . . . were designed for his es-
pecial amusement. . . .

Among the mighty host we passed, was O'Reilly [Riley] and
his company of deserters bearing aloft in high disgrace the holy
banner of St. Patrick.[19]

Santa Anna's army quickly moved northward, hoping to
take advantage of Taylor's weakened position. Early in
January the Mexicans had intercepted an American message confirming that half of Taylor's troops—almost all the
regulars—were being transferred to the Gulf Coast to join
Major General Winfield Scott's expeditionary army, which
was destined to land in Veracruz. Because it was midwinter
in a semidesert, the San Patricios and the rest of the Liberating Army of the North suffered during the march toward their rendezvous with the Yankees. A contemporary
source reported:

The march was long and tedious. The army was scantily supplied with food, water and clothing; the weather was harsh and
inclement; and sickness and desertion fast thinned their numbers. Encouraged by the promise of their leader, that they would
soon be supplied from the well-filled storehouses of the American army at Saltillo and Monterrey, they continued to advance in
spite of the obstacles which were calculated to discourage them.[20]

Informed by scouts of the approaching Mexican legion,
the Americans chose to make a stand about twenty miles
south of Saltillo at La Angostura, which was near the ha-

cienda of Buena Vista. This narrow pass on the road connecting Saltillo and San Luis Potosí was squeezed between a network of impenetrable arroyos on the west and several spurs from an adjacent steep mountain range on the east. With about 4,700 officers and men, the United States forces were outnumbered three to one, but they had the advantage of being rested, well fed, and positioned in an advantageous site. When Santa Anna reviewed his troops on February 20, they totaled 14,048, not counting about 1,200 cavalrymen under Brigadier General José Vicente Miñón, who had separated earlier to bypass the Americans and cut off their retreat route.[21]

The battle of Buena Vista (called Angostura by Mexicans) began in the afternoon of February 22, 1847. Before launching his attack, Santa Anna sent an officer under a white flag to deliver a surrender request, which Taylor quickly refused. During the rest of the day there was light skirmishing while forward elements of both sides scaled adjacent ridges. General Ignacio Mora y Villamil, chief engineer of the Mexican Army, assisted by the head of artillery, General Antonio Carona, selected the location for the battery of three heavy guns: two twenty-four-pounders and a sixteen-pounder. (The measurement refers to the approximate weight of a solid iron cannonball that each gun could fire. The diameter of a twenty-four-pound iron ball was 5.5 inches; that of a sixteen-pound shot was 4.8 inches.) These three Mexican guns were manned by the San Patricio company of eighty men.[22]

The fieldpieces of the San Patricio battery were clumsy things made of cast iron—they weighed over a ton each. Heavy, wheeled carriages drawn by six horses were required to move these massive weapons. Other horse-drawn rigs pulled limbers or caissons loaded with ammunition chests. The guns fired iron balls, called "shot," or hollow balls filled with explosives, called "shell." Besides solid iron balls, other varieties of shot were grapeshot (a cluster of iron balls), and cannister (a container filled with musket balls). To fire the guns, the bore was first swabbed with a

wet sponge to make certain that no sparks were left from
the previous round. Then, a cloth bag of gunpowder and
the projectile had to be inserted into the muzzle and seated
with a ramrod, after which the charge was ignited by a
flash of priming powder through the vent hole. Useful artillery range was limited to the distance at which the effect
of the firing could be observed and corrections made, usually no more than one thousand yards. The effective range
for cannister shot, commonly used against people, was 350
to 500 yards.[23]

At dawn on February 23, both sides were poised for
what became the ultimate battle in northern Mexico. In his
memoirs, a Yankee dragoon recalled the scene:

I doubt if the "Sun of Austerlitz" shone on a more brilliant spectacle than the Mexican army displayed before us—twenty thousand men clad in new uniforms, belts as white as snow, brasses
and arms burnished until they glittered like gold.

Their Cavalry was magnificent—some six thousand cavaliers
richly caparisoned in uniforms of blue faced with red, with wav-
ing plumes and glittering weapons, advanced towards us as
if they would ride down our little band and finish the battle at
one blow.

They formed one long line with their massed bands in front,
and then a procession of ecclesiastical dignitaries with all the
gorgeous paraphernalia of the Catholic Church advanced along
the lines, preceded by the bands playing a solemn anthem. . . .
This ceremony offered a striking contrast to conditions in our
lines; there was not a Chaplain in our army![24]

When the early morning ceremony ended, Santa Anna
ordered a massive attack that soon flanked the American
left and threatened their supply depot at the hacienda.
After fierce and bloody fighting, United States forces re-
pelled the attack and regained most of the ground they
had lost. The San Patricios, like most of the soldiers on
both sides, were exhausted, stunned, and scared. They saw
men killed and wounded, heard the moans and screams of

others, and looked over a battlefield littered with muti-
lated bodies, dead horses, and miscellaneous debris.

Artillery units from both sides played a crucial role in
the series of actions on February 23. The San Patricio battery, situated on a ridge where it commanded the entire
plateau, fired cannister and shot that opened gaping holes
in American ranks. Above the defector's guns fluttered
their green flag with its silver cross and golden harp. General Taylor, worried about the San Patricio guns, ordered
the First Dragoons to "take that damned battery," but the
dragoon charge was unsuccessful. Furthermore, two six-
pounder cannon of the Fourth Artillery were captured by
the enemy at Buena Vista as a result of intense fire from
the San Patricio cannoneers, aided by support troops.[25] At
day's end both armies were badly battered and exhausted.

During the night, while Taylor's men anticipated a renewed attack, Santa Anna secretly struck camp and retreated southward. Subsequently both generals claimed
they had won the battle of Buena Vista/Angostura, and
both armies possessed enemy flags and other trophies to
bolster their claims of victory. However, a telling factor
was that Taylor possessed the battlefield, and Americans
remained in control of northern Mexico for the rest of the
war.[26]

The battle of Buena Vista caused an unusually high
number of casualties. American losses (272 killed, 387
wounded, 6 missing) totaled about 14 percent of the 4,594
men engaged, and the Mexican figure was almost 25 percent of their 14,048 participants (591 killed, 1,049
wounded, 1,854 missing). More than a third of the eighty
men in the Saint Patrick's Company were killed or wounded
at Buena Vista. Lieutenant Camillo Manzano, along with
two sergeants, two corporals, and seventeen privates all
lost their lives. The six wounded San Patricios included
their commander, Captain (Brevet Lieutenant Colonel)
Francisco Rosendo Moreno, one corporal, and four privates. In his post-action report of February 25, General

Angostura (Buena Vista) Cross of Honor. Courtesy Museo Nacional de Historia

Francisco Mejía, in whose brigade the deserter-gunners fought, cited the San Patricio company as "worthy of the most consummate praise because the men fought with daring bravery."[27]

Mexican commanders awarded military decorations to a number of San Patricios for their actions at Buena Vista/ Angostura. The following men were designated to receive a white-enameled Angostura Cross of Honor as soon as it could be fabricated: Ignacio Alvarez, Ramón Bachelor, Francisco Moreno, John Riley, and John Stephenson. After the battle, all except Alvarez were promoted to new permanent ranks. Moreno was made a colonel, Riley a captain, and the other two first lieutenants.[28]

Two days after the battle of Buena Vista, the Mexican commander-in-chief convened a junta with his subordinate generals, all of whom recommended a withdrawal to San Luis Potosí. The major reason for this decision was a lack of supplies, especially food—as they had no maize or beans, nor little hope of securing any where they were. Later, as the army moved south, the men were plagued by dysentery, typhus, and stomach disorders. The loss of about three thousand men, some of whom deserted, almost equaled casualties in the recent battle. Along the way a Mexican soldier wrote:

This is worse than three retreats from Matamoros put together. We move along leaving the road strewn with dead and dying, whom it is impossible to help or transport because we lack everything, and we ourselves are barely able to walk, being attacked by the same illnesses.[29]

Hurrying ahead of the army, Santa Anna reached San Luis Potosí on March 7, where he proclaimed his victory over the North Americans. However, that news was offset by two other disturbing developments: a seaborne American expeditionary army of 9,000 men under General Winfield Scott was about to land near Veracruz, and, in the Mexican capital, three battalions of National Guard troops

General Winfield Scott. Courtesy The Bancroft Library

had revolted against the government. Opposition to the radical program, such as confiscation of $15 million of church property, being pursued by Vice-president Gómez Farías, was a principal reason for the domestic turmoil. In his characteristic way, Santa Anna responded to this challenge by a proclamation. Dated at San Luis Potosí on March 14, 1847, his message said:

Dedicated totally to the country's service, I leave to take over the reigns of government, thereby making a most difficult sacrifice . . . but this step will end the civil war that is destroying our beautiful capital . . . and it will stimulate the just war which we wage against the perfidious invaders.[30]

In mid-March, before leaving for Mexico City with a small detachment, Santa Anna divided the remnants of his army into two forces. The first group was to remain in San Luis Potosí, where General Ignacio Mora y Villamil was charged with reorganizing the Army of the North. The other division, totaling 5,650 men, was ordered to march toward Veracruz to reinforce the Army of the East. This relief army, which left San Luis on March 15, and traveled almost to Mexico City before turning east, was composed of two infantry brigades commanded by General Pedro de Ampudia and General Ciriaco Vásquez, a cavalry brigade under General Julián Juvera, and two artillery batteries. At San Juan de Teotihuacán they were joined by a brigade under General Joaquín Rangel. John Riley and the San Patricio artillerists accompanied this force, which arrived in Jalapa on April 5, and saw action on the eastern front two weeks later.[31]

Only two weeks after the battle of Buena Vista in northern Mexico the main focus of the war shifted to the Gulf Coast. There, just south of the major port of Veracruz, Major General Winfield Scott's American invasion force of almost nine thousand men stepped ashore unopposed on March 9, 1847. This combined army-navy maneuver was the first major amphibious landing in United States history. Once ashore, the commander's decision to take the port of Veracruz by siege rather than by direct assault prolonged the campaign, but it undoubtedly saved many American lives—fewer than twenty of his men were killed in the action. After surrounding the city and cutting its supply line, Scott called for the surrender of the garrison. When that was refused, he resorted to bombarding the city from land and sea for four days. Finally, after about two hundred civilians and soldiers had been killed and much property damaged, the Mexican commander capitulated on March 27. Scott permitted the port defenders to leave the city after he paroled them under their promise "not to take up arms again in the present war."[32]

In character and training, Winfield Scott was quite different from the backwoodsman, Zachary Taylor. Born into an aristocratic family of Virginia, Scott had a good education at the College of William and Mary, and he studied law for a few years before being commissioned in 1808 as a captain in the United States Army. During the War of 1812, he was promoted to general, was badly wounded in battle, and became a hero for his stand against the British near Niagara Falls. At the end of that war he wrote the first set of American infantry drill instructions, which he later revised, enlarged, and published under the title of *Infantry Tactics*. He participated in several Indian wars, visited Europe twice to study military developments there, and held duty in Washington, where in 1841 he was made general-in-chief of the army. Scott had a magnificent presence—he was six feet, four inches tall and heavily built, had the social graces of a southern gentleman, and he dressed elegantly. His nickname was "Old Fuss and Feathers."[33] After conquering Veracruz, this well-experienced man made plans to march inland toward healthier highlands.

Meanwhile, General Santa Anna had returned to Mexico City from San Luis Potosí on March 21. Temporarily taking over the presidency, he ended the National Guard rebellion by revoking the decree that confiscated $15 million of church property in exchange for a $2 million loan from the church. He also sent military reinforcements to the Gulf Coast. When he announced his intention of going to the eastern front, himself, Congress abolished the office of vice-president and named General Pedro Anaya as substitute president to govern in the interim. Before leaving,

Santa Anna had the official newspaper publish a short statement to his Mexican compatriots, which said:

My duty is to dedicate myself [to oppose the invaders], and I shall know how to fulfill this obligation. Perhaps the American hordes may tread haughtily on the capital of the Aztec empire, but I shall not have to witness such infamy, for I am determined to die fighting before that.[34]

Meanwhile, the commander of Mexico's Army of the East, Major General Valentín Canalizo, who planned to stop the Yankee advance at the pass of Cerro Gordo, was about sixty miles inland, near the town of Jalapa. Santa Anna hastened there, and on April 7, he inspected the site whose topography he knew well because it was located between two of his haciendas. Taking supreme command of the Army of the East, he made the final disposition of men and guns in what was considered an impregnable site. The position seemed ideal. On three hills he placed artillery batteries overlooking a steep ravine through which ran the National Road. Santa Anna believed this was strategically advantageous because he thought the Americans could advance with their artillery only along the highway. After April 12, when the three brigades and the San Patricio artillery company arrived from San Luis Potosí, the Mexican commander reported to the minister of war that his forces totaled 6,000 infantry, 2,000 cavalry, and an unspecified number of artillerymen with thirty-four large guns. To deter desertion, Santa Anna issued a circular that contained this warning: "Every deserter from the Army of the East—permanent corps, regular, or National Guard—who might be apprehended, will be executed without remission, in accordance with regulations."[35]

The first division of Scott's invading army left Veracruz on April 8, and other units soon followed it up the National Road to the higher elevations. Camping at Plan del Rio, a small village only five miles downstream from Cerro Gordo, the Yankees spent several days reconnoitering

Mexican positions. A frontal assault seemed foolhardy because the enemy's guns commanded the highway, but two of Scott's wily engineers, Captain Robert E. Lee and Lieutenant Pierre G. Beauregard, found that a difficult passage for men and cannon could be made through the chasms and brush along the far right flank. If successful, a division using this route could reach the Jalapa road behind Santa Anna, trap him, and cut off his retreat.

Scott decided on two-pronged attack. Part of his army of 8,500 men would secretly traverse the rough path blazed by engineers, while another brigade would mount diversionary attacks designed to convince Santa Anna that the main thrust of the invaders was against his central fortifications. Shortly after noon on April 17, American forces moving along the makeshift road were discovered and fired upon by Mexican infantrymen. This led to a series of skirmishes during the afternoon, but it did not betray the American plan. That night several teams of five hundred soldiers used ropes to drag three twenty-four-pounder cannon up the steep slopes of a hill overlooking a principal Mexican position.[36]

The next morning, while Yankees attacked from the hill and others created the diversion, a third force made its way toward the Mexican rear. After three hours of battle, the Mexicans retreated in total disorder along the road to Jalapa. George Wilkins Kendall, a correspondent of the New Orleans *Picayune* who accompanied the American Army, wrote:

Santa Anna himself, cutting the saddle mule from his travelling coach, fled through the chaparral and escaped. The victory in this quarter of the field was complete. All the artillery of the Mexicans, an immense amount of ammunition, military stores and provisions, fell into the hands of the Americans, with several wagon loads of specie. Even Santa Anna's tent, private papers and all his camp equipage were among the spoils.[37]

Casualties in the two-day battle of Cerro Gordo were high. Mexican army losses were not published in the official newspaper; they have been estimated at 1,000 to 1,200 killed and wounded. American losses totaled 417, of whom 64 were killed. After the battle the Americans paroled about 3,000 Mexican prisoners, spiked forty captured artillery pieces, and destroyed 4,000 stand of arms.[38]

Mexican army records for the battle of Cerro Gordo and its immediate aftermath are scarce—many papers were lost or destroyed in the rout. General Santa Anna and a few followers rode overland about sixty miles southwest to the city of Orizaba, where he set up his headquarters on April 23. It appears that the San Patricio company retreated from Cerro Gordo back to Jalapa, then moved to Puebla, and finally, to Mexico City. An army commissary report dated May 1, 1847, shows the San Patricio company still attached to the Army of the East; later in the month the group was in Mexico City. Although "twenty-nine Irishmen" served in a hospital corps at Cerro Gordo, aiding the Mexican wounded, these sons of Erin were not part of the San Patricios; whether they were deserters from the American military forces is not known.[39]

As Scott's army marched from Cerro Gordo to Jalapa, and then on to Puebla, bands of irregular Mexican forces harrassed his supply trains and reinforcements that traveled along the National Road. These guerrilla fighters killed stragglers, ambushed small groups, and plundered mule trains. They were excellent horsemen, knew the terrain, and had the support of peasants and villagers. Furthermore, their unconventional warfare continued during the entire time the United States Army remained in Mexico. Padre Celedonio Jarauta, a clever and hard-riding priest, headed the most active group that hampered the American advance; his success was reported from time to time by the Mexican correspondent of the London *Times:*

Considerable delay has been occasioned by the attacks of the guerrilla parties on an American convoy of money and ammunition between Vera Cruz and Jalapa. A Spanish priest, named Jarauta, has given unexpected energy to these bands, and distin-

HEAD QUARTERS.

KNOW ALL MEN:

That Antonio Lopez de Santa-Anna, President of the United States of Mexico and Commander in chief of the mexican armies has been duly authorized to make the following concessions to all and every one of the persons now in the American army who will present themselves before me or any of the commanding officers of the mexican forces, viz:

1.st Every soldier in the American army who appears before me or any of the commanding officers of the Mexican armies is to receive immediately *ten dollars* cash, if coming without arms, and a larger amount if he is armed, in order to cover the cost of the arms he may bring.

2.nd Every person who deserts the American army followed by 100 men is entitled to receive as soon as he presents himself with his men, $500 cash, besides the $10 to which every one of the soldiers is entitled, as well as the extra allowance in case they be armed.

3.rd He who deserts with 200 men has right to claim and shall be paid immediately $1000 cash, and so on at the rate of $500, for every hundred men; or the proportional amount if the number be under one hundred; without including the $10 allowed to every soldier, nor the cost of arms and ammunitions, all of which will invariably be paid besides.

4.th All and every one of the soldiers in the American army who will desert and appear before me or any af the Commanding officers of the Mexican forces, as aforesaid, besides the abovementioned gratifications in cash, are hereby entitled to claim and will immediately receive from me or any of the Commanding officers a document or bond by which the propriety of a grant of land consisting of 200 square acres will be ensured to them as well as to their families or heirs. The division of such grants will be made as soon as the present war is over.

5.th The Officers in the American army are not only entitled to the aforesaid document or bond but the number of acres in addition to the 200 allowed to the soldiers, will be computed in proportion to the respective grades they hold.

6.th Those who desert the American army and enter the Mexican service are to continue in it during the present campaign, and those of the same nation are to remain together if they choose and under the immediate command of their own officers, who will continue in the same grades they held in the American army.

7.th All those persons who come over to the Mexican armies shall be considered, rewarded and promoted in the same way as the Mexicans and according to their services in the present campaign.

The preceding articles shall be duly published in order that the Mexican Authorities may act in conformity thereto.

Head Quarters, Orizava the   April 1847.

Antonio Lopez de Santa-Anna.

Santa Anna's Handbill Urging Desertion. Courtesy Yale University Library guished himself personally on various occasions. The clerical and military characters do not seem to be considered incompatible either in Spain or here.[40]

General Scott not only had to oppose the Mexican Army of the East and combat the guerrilla forces, but he also had to deal with secret agents who solicited deserters from his army. One intriguer was Martin Tritschler, an immigrant watchmaker from Germany who had become a naturalized Mexican citizen and a captain in the National Guard of Puebla. After his military unit was devastated by the Americans in the battle of Cerro Gordo, Tritschler agreed to foment trouble among the invading soldiers. Dressed in civilian clothes, he distributed handbills printed in the German language and addressed to German-born soldiers, urging them to desert with their horses and arms. American soldiers captured Tritschler and in June, 1847, tried him before a special American Council of War, which found him guilty of being an enemy agent and sentenced him to be shot. General Scott, however, was deluged with pleas by Puebla citizens to spare the man's life, and he remitted the sentence on the grounds that the agent had become partially insane during his imprisonment. Upon his release Tritschler became miraculously cured and later was considered to be a Mexican war hero.[41]

The American Council of War also heard cases of a Belgian and a Mexican who were instigating desertion. Some details about the proceedings and outcome can be gleaned from the published letters of Captain Robert Anderson, an American artillery officer who sat on this special tribunal. He wrote: "The Mexican was acquitted. The Belgian is to be imprisoned in the Castle of Perote, during the continuance of the war between the United States and Mexico, to pay the treasury of the United States $300, not being released till this fine be paid."[42]

In the spring of 1847, Manuel Baranda, the Mexican minister of foreign affairs, concocted a plan to entice Irish-born soldiers to desert from the American army and join the San Patricios. Baranda engaged several writers including Luis Martínez de Castro and Guillermo Prieto to prepare handbills in English for distribution among the American troops. A political ally, José Fernando Ramírez, was delegated to inform General Santa Anna about the recruiting scheme and to arrange the guarantees. The plan culminated at the end of April, 1847, when Santa Anna issued a printed circular from his headquarters in Orizaba. In this English-language flyer, he listed seven concessions that would be made to any American soldier who came to the Mexican side. Each deserter was promised $10 in cash, payment for his musket, $5 for every comrade brought along, a minimum of 200 acres of land at the end of the war, and other bonuses.[43]

A supplement to Santa Anna's call for desertion was entitled, "Mexicans to Catholic Irishmen." It read, in part, as follows:

Sons of Ireland! Have you forgotten that in any Spanish country it is sufficient to claim Ireland as your home to meet with a friendly reception from authorities as well as citizens?

Why, then, do you rank among our wicked enemies?

Is it because you wish to have a grant of land that you may call your own?

. . . .

By conquest you can take cities, and towns, but never possess two feet of ground unmolested as long as there is a Mexican. The last of Mexicans is determined to fight without release for his country and his God.

But our hospitality and good will towards you tenders you what by force you can never possess or enjoy—as much property in land as you may require, and this under the pledge of our honor and our holy religion. . . .

Our sincere offers have already been realized with many of your countrymen, who are living as our own brothers among us.[44]

As part of their plan to recruit deserters and weaken the invading forces, the Mexican foreign minister and his cohorts conferred with leaders in the city of Puebla, which seemed to be the next destination of the Americans. By design, United States troops would be permitted to occupy Puebla with little or no opposition. Then the town's priests and leading citizens would encourage the foreign Catholic soldiers to defect. When this goal was achieved, by a prearranged signal the eighty thousand residents of Puebla would rise up against the Yankees, being aided by the timely arrival of Santa Anna's army.[45]

Although the Americans occupied Puebla in mid-May, the planned uprising never occurred. This inaction may have been a result of the strong anti-Santa Anna sentiment in that city, especially on the part of the clergy, who resented the general's earlier demand for $60,000, only $10,000 of which he received. This passiveness could, however, have stemmed from Scott's promise of protection for all civilians who would remain neutral, coupled with his threat of retribution against those who caused trouble. While the Americans were in Puebla, thirty-three soldiers deserted and joined the San Patricios, but this was a far cry from the three thousand defectors anticipated by the Mexican foreign minister.[46]

The American forces rested at Puebla, Mexico's second largest city, for three months, treating their injured and ill, awaiting reinforcements, and hoping for a negotiated end to the war. For off-duty soldiers there was a plethora of entertainment: theatrical performances in Spanish and English, bullfights, a circus, and no shortage of *cantinas* and gambling dens. When Mexican government officials rejected peace offers, General Scott determined that his army would have to march the last hundred miles to the Halls of Montezuma.

CHAPTER 4

The Place of the War God

DURING THE LATE SPRING and early summer of 1847, many aspects of life in Mexico City continued as usual, even though ten thousand Yankee soldiers were in Puebla poised for an attack on the capital. The San Patricios joined the metropolitan residents in enjoying the amenities of that grand city which then had a population of about 150,000. Its monumental architecture included the national palace, which covered an entire city block; the municipal palace, or city hall; the San Carlos Art Academy; the College of Mines; and dozens of convents, monasteries, and churches. The impressive Metropolitan Church on the north side of the main plaza was the largest and most distinguished cathedral in all of Latin America. An American who visited it in 1847 noted the following in his journal:

The interior of the cathedral is gorgeous beyond description— chapel succeeds chapel—the roofs groined and gilded with massive church ornaments and wondrously ornamented altars, which together with the richly set paintings presents a melange of barbaric splendor, and sometimes of tasteful arrangement, which fills the beholder with curiosity and astonishment. . . .

Fewer of the higher classes are seen to worship here, but crowds of lepers in gaudy and ragged scraps with matted hair and naked limbs; wretches in the foulest rags; mendicants and humble, half naked Indians kneel and creep on the floor. . . . Look at the building, you think of Heaven. Look at the inmates, you think of Hell.[1]

For public entertainment there were museums, parks, a bullring, and several theaters, one of which, the Teatro Nacional de Santa Anna, held 7,500 patrons. Soldiers also

THE PLACE OF THE WAR GOD

frequented the numerous cafes, *cantinas*, gambling dens, cockpits, and brothels. One young man summarized his activities in Mexico City as follows:

I visited the great cathedral, the museum and state house [national palace]. Saw the equestrian statue in bronze, 25 feet high, of Charles the [IV] . . . of Spain, the iron armor of Cortez and feather armor of Montezuma, the celebrated calendar and sacrificial stones and many interesting relics of the Aztecs and Spanish conquerors; walked through the Bazaar and Alameda [park], had my pocket picked and got a general insight into everything around.[2]

In spite of the imminent danger threatening the capital, Mexican civilian *políticos* seemed not to be terribly concerned. The resident correspondent of the London *Times* reported, "Notwithstanding the dislike which Mexicans entertain towards all foreigners, and the tenacity with which every offer of peace from the Americans has been rejected, there is little show of warlike enthusiasm here."[3] He also noted: "A party, too, exists who desire the subjugation of the country, not from any love to a foreign yoke, but from disgust at their own internal dissensions, and a conviction of the impossibility of their establishing a permanent government among themselves."

In his dispatch of June 29, the *Times* correspondent indicated that politics in the Mexican capital was at an impasse. He reported the following:

The reflecting portion of both factions (Puros and Moderados) is, doubtless, aware of the necessity of negotiating for peace with the United States; but neither dare to propose it, from an apprehension of the bare suggestion giving an advantage to their opponents. . . . Santa Anna has made some exertions (real or pretended) to get the Congress together; but that body, from mutual jealousies, carried to an inconceivable height, will neither meet in sufficient numbers to transact business, nor consent to be declared in recess, and leave the Executive unfettered. It is difficult to discover the clue to Mexican politics, which seem to be a compound of Spanish intrigue and Indian cunning.[4]

Although the Mexican Congress seemed incapable of action, other officials, such as the chief executive and the military governor of the Federal District, took certain measures to defend the capital from the American invaders. They declared martial law in the Federal District and adjacent states; released political prisoners from jail; ordered all able-bodied Mexican males aged fifteen to sixty to enlist in some military unit; organized volunteer National Guard companies; authorized guerrilla forces; commissioned privateers; conscripted a civilian work force to build fortifications; required all Mexicans who owned guns or swords to turn them in; requisitioned surplus horses; and ordered American civilians to leave the capital.[5]

General Santa Anna, who had resigned as interim president on May 28, withdrew his resignation five days later and became, in effect, a dictator. He raised a war chest through forced contributions, as detailed by the London *Times* correspondent:

. . . he remains in possession of nearly absolute power, which he has, as usual, abused to the prejudice of the foreign residents. Forced loans, nominally on all the inhabitants, but really confined chiefly to foreigners, were an old expedient of his for raising money. . . . Santa Anna now plays a bolder game. For a forced loan he has substituted a forced contribution of 1,000,000 dollars, the *maximum* to be paid by each person being 2,000 dollars, and the *minimum* 25 dollars. The Governor is the sole judge of who is to pay, and how much; and the penalty for nonpayment within three days . . . is the duplication of the contribution.[6]

By presidential decree early in June of 1847, Santa Anna created a Foreign Legion (*Legión extranjera*) as part of the Mexican army. Various foreign residents of the capital soon enlisted in the Legion, and, on July 1, the San Patricios were transferred from the artillery branch to the infantry and merged into the Foreign Legion. A decree, of July 1, contained regulations for the new organization:

Article 1. Two infantry companies of territorial militia will be formed with personnel of the specified Foreign Legion. They will be called the First and Second Militia Infantry Companies of San Patricio.

Article 2. Each company will consist of a captain, one first lieutenant, two second lieutenants, one first sergeant, four sergeants second class, nine corporals, four buglers, and eighty privates.

Article 3. The uniform which they will use will be that designated for the Active Infantry.[7]

Except for the distinctive insignia and a lighter color of trousers, the Mexican infantry uniform was similar to that prescribed for the artillery. Infantry officers and men wore sky-blue trousers with scarlet piping. Their dark-blue coats had scarlet collars, cuffs, and piping on the lapels and tri-pointed pocket flaps. (The First Active Regiment had yellow lapels and piping.) The regimental number was embroidered in gold on the collar, and the two dozen brass buttons were stamped with the unit designation. Campaign hats for officers were blue kepis trimmed in red; the enlisted men wore blue cloth barracks caps with red piping and tassel.[8]

Mexican infantry officers carried swords as their principal weapon and to give visual commands to their men; enlisted infantrymen were armed with muskets. The commonest firearm was the old "Brown Bess," a big English flintlock musket of .75 calibre. It weighed twelve pounds, had a smooth barrel, fired a round ball three-fourths of an inch in diameter, and had a powerful kick. Another shoulder arm in service was a smoothbore flintlock of .69 calibre that fired lead balls weighing one ounce. It is known that the San Patricios were issued muskets that used cartridges of 19 *adarmes*, the size of the "Brown Bess."[9]

The muskets used by the San Patricios were muzzle-loading weapons with a flintlock mechanism to ignite the charge. Usually the gunpowder charge came pre-measured and wrapped in paper with the ball; this was called a cartridge. In action, an infantryman stood the gun on its

stock, tore open the cartridge with his teeth, poured the
powder down the barrel, dropped in the ball, using the
cartridge paper as a wad, and then seated the ball with a
long ramrod. The musket at this point had to be primed
by pouring a pinch of fine gunpowder into the pan. After
the gun was cocked and the trigger pulled, the flint struck
a steel plate, causing a spark that fired the priming powder, whereupon the flash passed through a tiny hole into
the breech of the barrel, setting off the main charge. But
sometimes only the primer would go off, producing a
mere "flash in the pan."[10]

Infantry tactics of that era called for soldiers to fire while
standing upright and in formation. Because the effective
range of smoothbore weapons was only around sixty yards,
attackers advanced close to the enemy before opening fire.
The weapons were so inaccurate that the men generally
did not aim at a specific target; instead, they tried to deliver a concentrated barrage of fire at the enemy. Trained
troops could fire three rounds a minute; thus, a company
of one hundred men could get off about three hundred
rounds a minute, but only for a very limited time. Sometimes, after an exchange of fire one side would close in on
the other and initiate hand-to-hand fighting with the bayonet.[11] Such was what the San Patricios could look forward
to in their role as Mexican soldiers.

On July 1, 1847, when the San Patricio volunteers were
incorporated as infantrymen into the Foreign Legion, they
were obliged to sign the following contract that specified
what they would receive in return for their military service:

FOREIGN LEGION—SAN PATRICIO COMPANIES

We, the undersigned foreigners, voluntarily contract ourselves to serve in the said Legion for the term of six months,
counted from this date, legally serving the Mexican Republic
under the following conditions:

1. The Mexican government will give us lands to cultivate at
the conclusion of the war.

2. Those who do not wish to remain in this country will be

embarked for Europe at the expense of the supreme government, which will also give them a gratification in money.

3. The Mexican government agrees to give to [members of] the Legion, during the time of their service, quarters, clothing, shoes, etc.

4. First sergeants will receive five *reales* daily, second class sergeants four *reales*, corporals three, and privates two and a half *reales* per day. [There were eight *reales* in a peso, and a peso equaled one United States dollar.]

5. We acknowledge Colonel Francisco R. Moreno as commander of the Legion, in conformity with the order of the supreme government. All the orders which the said chief may give will be obeyed by the Legion; and if not, the punishment prescribed by the regulations of the Mexican Army will be applied to us.

6. The Legion will be subject in every respect to the said regulations of the Army.[12]

During July and August of 1847, the *Diario del Gobierno* (the only Mexico City newspaper permitted to publish between July 11 and September 13), often listed payments transferred from the treasury secretariat to the Foreign Legion, sometimes calling the unit "The Foreign Legion of San Patricio." As mentioned above, the overall commander of the Legion was Colonel Francisco Moreno. He had two company commanders: Captain John Riley, with a brevet rank as major, headed the first company, and Captain Santiago (sometimes called Saturnino) O'Leary, also a brevet major, was in charge of the second. Other officers included Lieutenants Ramón B. Bachelor, Patrick Dalton, Matthew Doyle, Agustín Mestard, and Auguste Morstadt. An American soldier later reported that Major O'Leary was an American deserter whose real name was Reid, and although originally from New York, he had deserted from a Louisiana volunteer unit.[13]

In the summer of 1847, Captain John Riley, principal organizer of the San Patricios, tried to recruit additional members for his outfit. Upon visiting captured Yankee soldiers, who were imprisoned by the Mexicans in the former monastery of Santiago Tlatelolco, he cajoled them with blarney, urging them to switch to the Mexican uniform. Colonel Francisco Moreno, commander of the Foreign Legion, was more direct; he frequently used physical force on men to get them to enlist, according to some defectors. Marquis Frantius claimed that his collarbone was broken when the colonel smashed a rifle butt against it while coercing him to join the Legion.[14]

Besides prisoners of war, there were other Americans in Mexico City who were persuaded to join the San Patricio units. Most of these men were army deserters who had not joined the Mexican army, but had straggled south to the Mexican capital. A few of them had been serving as civilian volunteers in the Lancer Escort Company, a group that accompanied Mexican citizens on journeys to and from the capital. As lancers they had received twenty-five *centavos* a day; but when they joined the Foreign Legion, they received more pay, barracks lodging, and uniforms. Hezekiah Akles and John Bowers, both deserters from Company H of the United States Third Artillery Regiment, were among the lancers who joined the San Patricio contingent of the Legion.[15] Other San Patricio recruits included a number of British-born deserters from the American army. On arrival in Mexico City, at least two dozen of these men appealed to consular agents of the United Kingdom, asking for financial assistance, passports, or letters of identity, and help in obtaining transportation to, and employment in, such places as the English-owned Real del Monte silver mine near Pachuca, or the British colony of Honduras.

In their letters the men sounded desperate. The following excerpts are from a letter dated June 23, 1847, signed by eighteen Anglo-American deserters:

The undersigned humbly state that they are subjects of Great Britain or its dependencies who, having enlisted in the service of the United States and on their arrival in Mexico not wishing to carry arms against a country at peace with Great Britain and in which our Fatherland has a peculiar interest, deserted the army at various periods, and after many privations and dangers have arrived at the City of Mexico where they are hourly subject to insults and in danger of assassination . . . added to which is the probable arrival of the American Army, in which case we must inevitably share the fate of deserters—that of death. At the same time . . . we are continually subject to the importunities of certain persons who are desirous of enlisting us in the service of Mexico, and who have placed two of our companions in confinement in consequence of their refusal to join said service. . . . We pray that you will grant us information as to . . . whether you intend to place us in a situation where we may live secure from the above dangers, or not. . . .[16]

When the deserters received little sympathy from the British Consul-General, some of them, including Matthew Doyle, Francis O'Conner, and Henry Hudson, joined the San Patricios.

In the summer of 1847, British diplomats shuttled between Mexico City and Puebla trying to arrange a peace treaty between the United States and Mexico. Nicholas P. Trist, chief clerk of the State Department, who had arrived in May with a draft treaty, also possessed power to arrange a suspension of hostilities, which infuriated General Scott, who considered it an infringement of his command and who refused to cooperate. Bypassing Scott, Trist talked with the secretary of the British legation and with an English friend of Santa Anna, who hinted that secret expenditure of money in the capital, a bribe, might produce results. By mid-July, Trist and Scott were working together, and the latter advanced $10,000 to a particular individual in the Mexican government, with a promise of $1 million on the conclusion of a treaty. The negotiations ended, however, when key Mexican officials judged their actions inexpedient to circumvent a law that declared it high treason for anyone to treat with the invading army.[17]

The restrictive law, passed by the Mexican Congress on

April 20, just after the battle of Cerro Gordo, contained
the following points:

1. The chief executive is not authorized to make peace with
   the United States, enter into negotiations with foreign
   powers, nor alienate in whole or part any territory of the
   Republic.
2. All arrangements or treaties made between the government of the United States and any authority delegated by
   the supreme powers of Mexico will be null and void.
3. Any person who, as a private individual or public official,
   enters into a treaty with the government of the United
   States will be declared to be a traitor.[18]

In this diplomatic impasse, General Scott decided to advance on the Mexican capital.

Before leaving Puebla, the Americans recruited their
own "foreign legion," a spy company of a hundred men
composed entirely of Mexican citizens. The majority—if
not all of these men—had been bandits who preyed on
travelers along the Mexico City–Veracruz highway—indeed, twelve of the robbers were released from a jail in
Puebla to join the group. Operating under orders from
Colonel Ethan Allen Hitchcock, inspector-general of the
invading force, they were to act as couriers, guides, and in-
telligence scouts, as well as counter-guerrillas on the Veracruz supply route. First outfitted with riding trousers
and gray jackets, the men were later issued parrot-green
coatees with red collars and cuffs. Their distinctive broad-
brimmed and flat-crowned black felt hats were encircled
with a red band. These Mexican scouts, whose uniforms
bore the insignia of the United States Army, were paid $20
per month (U.S. Army sergeants received $16). Leader
of the spy company was Manuel Domínguez, who as-
sumed the rank of colonel and was paid more than the rest.
Hitchcock described him as "a very extraordinary person—a Mexican, rather portly for one of his profes-
sion. . . . He has been a very celebrated captain of robbers
and knows the band and the whole country."[19]

Accompanied by members of the spy company, the vanguard of 10,000 American soldiers left Puebla on August 7, headed for the Valley of Mexico. Five days later they reached Ayotla, twenty-five miles east of the capital. Waiting for them was General Santa Anna, who deployed his 20,000 defenders in several positions guarding major approaches to Mexico City. Anticipating a direct attack from the east, Santa Anna established his headquarters at a fortified hill known as El Peñón, about ten miles southeast of the city. Here, he commanded 7,000 men, including those in the two San Patricio companies.[20]

From the Peñón fort, on August 15, Santa Anna disseminated a new batch of English-language handbills designed to entice American soldiers to defect. Part of the text of the leaflets follows:

The circumstances of war have brought you to the beautiful valley of Mexico; in the midst of wealthy and fertile country. The American governement [sic] engaged you to fight against a country from which you have received no harm. . . .

In the name of the Nation I represent, and whose authority I exercise, I offer you a reward if, deserting the American standard, you present yourselves like friends to a nation that offers you rich fields and large tracts of land, which being cultivated by your industry, shall crown you with happiness and convenience.

The Mexican nation only look upon you as some deceived foreigners and hereby stretches out to you a friendly hand, offer you the felicity and fertility of their territory.[21]

About the same time, another Mexican broadside aimed at American soldiers was being prepared, undoubtedly with the cooperation of newly-promoted Major John Riley, whose name was signed to the circular. A comparison with letters written by Riley obviously shows that he did not pen this plea, at least in its final form—the formal, archaic language smacks of being translated from Spanish. Because of the rapid progress of military events, this appeal was never printed, but the draft copy, found later in a Mexico City printing office, merits extensive quotation here. It was

The President of the Mexican Republic to the troops engaged in the Army of the United States of America.

The circumstances of war have brought you to the beautiful valley of Mexico; in the midst of a wealthy and fertile country. The American Governement engaged you to fight against a country from which you have received no harm; your companions have after the battle received and shall only receive the contempt of the United States and the scorn of the nations of civilized Europe that, quite surprized, see that that governement seek engagements for their battles in the same manner as they look for beasts to draw their carriages.

In the name of the Nation I represent, and whose authority I exercise, I offer you a reward, if deserting the American standard you present yourselves like friends to a nation that offer you rich fields and large tracts of land, which being cultivated by your industry, shall crown you with happiness and convenience.

The Mexican Nation only look upon you as some deceived foreigners and hereby stretch out to you a friendly hand, offer you the felicity and fertility of their territory. Here there is no distinction of races; here indeed there is liberty and no slavery; nature here plentifully sheds its favors and it is in your power to enjoy them. Rely upon what I offer you in the name of a nation; present yourselves like friends and you shall have country, home, lands; the happiness, which is enjoyed in a country of mild and humane customs; civilization, humanity and not fear address you through me.

General Quarters in the Peñon August the 15th 1847.

Antonio Lopez de Santa-Anna.

Santa Anna's Second Appeal for Deserters. Courtesy The Bancroft Library headed "To My Friends and Countrymen in the Army of the United States of America", and excerpts follow:

> Actuated by nought but the purest motives, I venture to address you on a subject of vital importance. . . . The President of this Republic, in hope of giving every advantage to the foreigners in the American army, through a feeling worthy of his high station both military and civil, and through motives of the purest friendship towards the misguided inhabitants of other countries than the United States who have foolishly embarked in this impolitic and unholy war, once more offers to you his hand & invites you, in the name of the religion you profess, the various countries in which you first drew the breath of existence, of honor and of patriotism, to withhold your hands from the slaughter of a nation whose thoughts or deeds never injured you or yours.
>
> My countrymen, Irishmen! I call upon you for I know your feelings on this subject well, for the sake of that chivalry for which you are celebrated, for that love of liberty for which our common country is so long contending, for the sake of that holy religion which we have for ages professed, I conjure you to abandon a slavish hireling's life with a nation who in even the moment of victory treats you with contumely & disgrace. For whom are you contending? For a people who, in the face of a whole world, trampled upon the holy altars of our religion, set the firebrand upon a sanctuary devoted to the blessed Virgin, and boasting of civil and religious liberty, trampled in contemptuous indifference all appertaining to the dearest feelings of our country. . . .
>
> My Countrymen, I have experienced the hospitality of the citizens of this Republic; from the moment I extended to them the hand of friendship, I was received with kindness; though poor, I was relieved; though undeserving, I was respected, and I pledge you my oath, that the same feelings extended towards me awaits you also. . . .[22]

The momentum of the American army and the physical separation of the opposing forces nullified Santa Anna's and John Riley's appeal for deserters.

One factor helping Mexican defenders was the topography of the Valley of Mexico. There were not only several

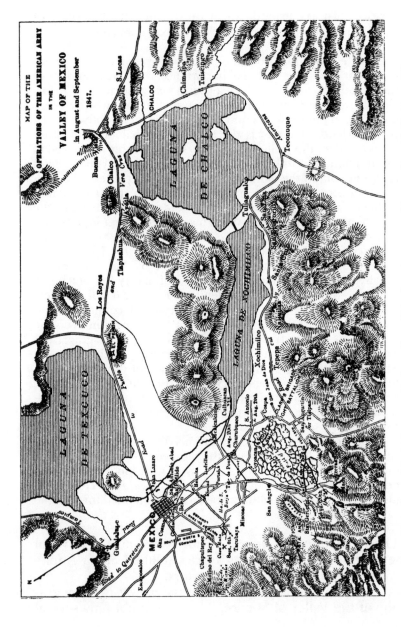

Map of the operations of the U.S. Army in the valley of Mexico, August and September, 1847. From The Eagle: The Autobiography of Santa Anna, ed. Ann Fears Crawford (Austin, Texas: Pemberton Press, 1967), p. 175.

lakes in the basin, but extensive marshes and low-lying fields, which could be traversed by an army in the summer rainy season only on raised highways or causeways. After American engineers reconnoitered possible attack routes, General Scott decided to bypass the Peñón fort and approach the capital from the south. By August 17, the Americans had skirted Lakes Chalco and Xochimilco and were at the village of San Agustín, about nine miles south of Mexico City. Top civilian officials in the capital appealed to all able-bodied citizens to oppose the invaders. The acting president issued the following decree to governors of the states of Puebla, Mexico, and the Federal District:

The president commands you to order the local authorities of all places, large and small, which are located within a radius of thirty leagues [78 miles] of any point where the enemy is found, to raise up the people en masse so that with the weapons that each individual has, large or small, firearm or shield and sword, with sticks and stones when they have no other arms, to make war on the enemy in whatever way they can. . . . And when the robust citizens have a gun to their shoulder facing the enemy, those who have remained in the city will defend it to the last ditch, for which you will command them to take stones and other projectiles to the rooftops.[23]

About the same time, the archbishop of Mexico held extraordinary public masses, and he circulated a lengthy published exhortation addressed to "Pious Mexicans," whom he admonished to pray for a Mexican victory. Otherwise, he predicted the following:

With foreign domination, if such an abominable misfortune occurs, you will see altars erected against altars, and sects and dissident communions formed, which secretly and openly will make cruel and incessant war on our sacred, uniquely true religion. . . .
If the invaders triumph and subjugate us, ultimately they will try to eradicate us and carry off to their country, as an object of

our credulity and fanaticism, or of speculation, our image of
Our Lady of Guadalupe. The result: they will have robbed from
us that precious gift from Heaven, that lodestone of Mexican
hearts, that precious object of our worship and hope.[24]

Meanwhile, to meet the American military threat from
the south, Santa Anna transferred the majority of his men
to positions in that quarter. Most of the troops were deployed at the villages of San Angel, Coyoacán, and San Antonio, north and west of the American camp at San Agustín.
Quartered at *la Ciudadela* (the Citadel) in Mexico City for
two days, the San Patricios were marched on the nineteenth
about five miles south to Churubusco, which was near
Coyoacán and only five miles north of the Yankee base.[25]

Major General Gabriel Valencia disobeyed Santa Anna's
orders when he failed to pull back his Army of the North,
comprising upwards of four thousand men, who were
positioned at an extreme forward site on the Padierna
ranch near the village of Contreras, west of the American
camp. Between the opposing forces was the Pedregal, an
"impenetrable" lava field. Nevertheless, during a stormy
night, Captain Robert E. Lee and other American engineers pioneered pathways through the boulder-strewn
terrain, and at dawn, on August 20, various American
units surprised and utterly defeated Valencia's men in a
seventeen-minute battle. Mexican losses at Contreras were
700 men killed, 843 captured, including 4 generals, and
the rest were scattered. American casualties totaled 68.
Among the American prizes were twenty-two pieces of artillery including the two six-pounder guns that had been
lost six months earlier at Buena Vista due to intense fire of
the San Patricio battery there.[26]

On August 20, 1847, the retreating, holding, and ad-
vancing forces seemed to converge at the tiny village of
Churubusco, on the highway about halfway between San
Agustín and the capital. Here, the chief landmark was the
stone-walled former monastery (*convento,* in Spanish) of
Santa María de los Angeles, established by Franciscans in

The Battle of Churubusco. Courtesy The Bancroft Library

the sixteenth century, and its adjacent church of San Diego (originally called San Mateo). The entire complex was generally known as the convent of Churubusco, the place's name being derived from an Aztec word meaning "place of the war god."[27] That was fitting, because this became the site of one of the bloodiest battles of the Mexican War, an engagement that also marked the military zenith of the San Patricios and their last battle in the war as a unit.

Major General Manuel Rincón commanded about fourteen hundred Mexican soldiers in defense of the fortress-convent of Churubusco. Besides the Independencia and Bravo battalions, there were two San Patricio companies totaling just over two hundred men, most of whom functioned as infantrymen but some of whom serviced three of the garrison's seven cannons. During the battle about two hundred pickets from the Tlapa, Chilpancingo, and Galeana battalions arrived as reinforcements, along with a wagonload of ammunition, which proved to be the wrong caliber for all the muskets, except those carried by the San Patricios.[28]

In a letter to the *New York Courier,* an American soldier described the formidable fortifications at the Churubusco convent, which he likened to an hacienda:

They consisted of a fortified hacienda which was surrounded by a [twelve foot] high and thick wall on all sides, forming a large square. Inside the wall was a stone building [monastery], the roof of which was flat and higher than the walls. Above all this was a stone church, still higher than the rest, and having a large steeple [dome]. The wall was pierced with loopholes, and so arranged that there were two tiers of men firing at the same time. They had thus four different ranges of men firing at once, and four ranks were formed on each range and placed at such a height that they could not only overlook all the surrounding country, but at the same time they had a plunging fire on us.

Outside the hacienda, and completely commanding the avenues of approach, was a field-work extending around two sides of the fort, and protected by a deep wet ditch, and armed with seven large pieces [four eight-pounders, one six-pounder, and two four-pounders] of cannon.[29]

Three hundred yards to the northeast, on the south bank of the Churubusco River, there was a fortified *tête de pont,* or bridgehead, which controlled movement along the principal causeway or highway between San Agustín and Mexico City. There were three artillery pieces at the bridgehead, and the site was defended by a separate infantry regiment, while two other regiments guarded the river bank. Mexican cavalry and additional infantry units formed a reserve along the highway north of the river.[30]

Although some authors of books and articles about the Mexican War have maintained that one company of San Patricios was stationed at the bridgehead while the other was at the convent, official Mexican military records show both companies were at the convent the afternoon of that fateful day. General Santa Anna's report to the Minister of War notes that early on the morning of the twentieth, the

San Patricios were first at the *tête de pont* before he sent them as reinforcements to the convent garrison. The post-battle report of the convent commander, General Rincón, substantiates this deployment:

It was ordered that the Independencia battalion would cover the heights of the convent and the right flank. . . . The Bravos battalion and the San Patricio companies occupied the parapets and screens of the front and left, fortified with breastworks. In this position we were vigorously attacked by the enemy divisions with a force of more than 6,000 men. . . .[31]

A combined American offensive against the bridgehead and fortified convent at Churubusco began shortly before midday on August 20, 1847. Advancing northward along the road from San Antonio, Brigadier General William Worth's First Division pursued the retreating Mexican forces, who soon clogged the bridgehead. When the Yankees were within striking distance, they charged the bridge but had to retire twice due to heavy Mexican fire; nor could they use artillery because the ground was too muddy and soft to bring up the big guns. The adjacent cornfields, marshes, and dikes made enveloping moves difficult, but some Americans did outflank the Mexican position. Finally, the center forces crossed the twenty-foot-wide ditch, climbed the parapet, and took the bridgehead in hand-to-hand fighting. Almost two hundred Mexican prisoners were captured, along with three cannons and an ammunition park.[32] The captured guns were then turned on the convent.

Meanwhile, a division under Brigadier General David Twiggs assaulted the convent from the southwest, approaching the position through tall, uncut stands of maize. The Mexican defenders withheld fire until the Americans were within musket range, then General Rincón ordered a fusillade that devastated the attackers and forced them back. To repel subsequent advances, the Mexican gunners, many of them San Patricios, directed a withering fire

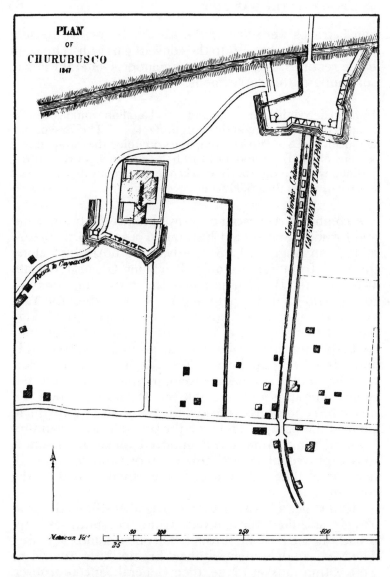

Plan of Churubusco, 1847. From Ramón Alcaraz et al., eds., The Other Side; or Notes for the History of the War Between Mexico and the United States, *trans. Albert C. Ramsey (New York: J. Wiley, 1850), following p. 282.*

against the Americans. For more than three hours a savage battle raged. One participant later wrote: "The flower of both armies were now engaged in terrible combat. The rattling of the musketry, the clash of arms, and the deafening roar of the cannon and the groans of the dying, made the scene truly awful!"[33]

By midafternoon the American bombardment of the Churubusco convent, coupled with infantry sharpshooting from all directions, began to weaken the Mexican resistance, and their gunfire slackened. When some artillery powder caught fire, it seriously burned General Pedro Anaya, along with San Patricio Captain Santiago O'Leary, and three other artillery men. According to General Rincón, his men ran out of flints and musket ammunition of the proper caliber, three of their artillery pieces were inoperable, and there remained only a few cannon shots because the park had been exhausted. At that point the defenders retreated into the interior of the convent to make a final stand.[34]

As blue-coated Yankees encircled the building complex, other American infantrymen scaled the garden walls and pressed forward. George Kendall of the New Orleans *Picayune*, the first newspaper correspondent to accompany an American army in battle, told what happened next:

A lodgement being thus effected inside San Pablo [San Diego], the entire garrison, with the exception of a few who attempted successfully to escape in the early part of the strife, surrendered. The boldest in holding out were the deserters of the San Patricio battalion, who fought with desperation to the last, tearing down, with their own hands, several of the white flags hoisted by the Mexicans in token of surrender. Many attempted to escape towards the main road when they found further resistance unavailing; but headed off either by the victorious troops of Worth or Shields, they were taken or driven back. . . .[35]

Finally, Captain James M. Smith of the Third United States Infantry Regiment put an end to the fighting when he, himself, raised a white handkerchief over the fort. An American general's report said, "To the 14th Infantry belongs the honor of capturing a San Patricio flag on this fort, and taking a large number of prisoners in the fort, among whom was the body of deserters." Kendall commented, "It was with much difficulty that the American soldiers could be prevented from bayonetting these miscreants on the spot, so deep was their indignation against them."[36]

Among those who triumphantly entered the convent at this time were Manuel Domínguez and his squad of former bandits, now members of the spy company. General Anaya, horrified to see these Mexicans dressed in American uniforms, castigated them as traitors. A Mexican history of the war said that ". . . while Anaya was apostrophizing the 'cabecilla' [ringleader] in, no doubt, the most refined Castilian, Twiggs and Worth were ventilating their vocabulary of Saxon expletives, not very 'courtesly,' on Riley and his beautiful disciples of St. Patrick."[37] The meeting of two opposing turncoat units—the spy company and the San Patricios—was certainly an unusual coincidence, one arousing deep resentment on both sides.

For the Americans, their victory at the Churubusco convent was a momentous and dramatic event. Besides its strategic and psychological importance, the battle yielded 1,259 prisoners including 104 officers, one of whom, Anaya, was a former president, and another, Colonel Manuel Gorostiza, was an erstwhile cabinet member and former minister to the United States. Of special importance were the captured San Patricios, among them Brevet Major John Riley. "Their capture proved a greater source of gratification to our entire army than any other single event of that memorable day's victories," wrote Captain George T. Davis.[38] After Churubusco, some American units pursued the enemy almost to the city gates. Then there was a respite while both sides gathered their wounded and buried the dead.

San Patricio casualties at Churubusco were devastating. When the battle began, the two companies were apparently at full strength of 102 men each. Three hours later 60 percent of the men were either dead or had been captured by the enemy. Killed in action were 2 lieutenants, 4 sergeants, 6 corporals, and 23 privates. Captains John Riley and Captain Santiago O'Leary were wounded in the battle, as was Francis O'Conner, an enlisted soldier. Eighty-five San Patricios, including those who had been wounded, were taken prisoner. Seventy-two of them were accused of having deserted from the United States Army.[39] The remaining 84 men (or perhaps as many as 90) had escaped, but they were scattered.

A Prussian-born San Patricio named Othon de Groote, who evaded capture at Churubusco, later wrote a letter describing his ordeal and hinting at his fear of being captured by the Americans:

. . . almost by a miracle the writer escaped, managing to hide in a maize field, where, unsheltered for three days, he withstood thirst and hunger, nourished only by ears of corn. Eventually, security was found in a Mexico City house, which provided asylum against the searches and persecutions of the enemy. I remained there for five months. . . .[40]

However, the bulk of the apprehended San Patricios either surrendered or were captured at the Churubusco convent, while others fled to the bridgehead where they were taken by Americans under General Worth. He reported:

Of prisoners we paused to make but few; although receiving the surrender of many, to disarm and pass them was deemed sufficient. Among them, however, are secured twenty-seven deserters from our own army, arrayed in the most tawdry Mexican uniforms. These wretches served the guns—the use of which they had been taught in our own service—and with fatal effect, upon the persons of their former comrades![41]

Although the San Patricios were defeated at Churubusco, their proficiency and bravery elicited praise from various Mexicans. Santa Anna said that if he had commanded a few hundred more men like them, he would have won the battle. A Mexican history of the war lauded the men who fought under the shamrock flag:

Their deportment deserves the greatest eulogies, since all the time the attack lasted they sustained the fire with extraordinary courage. A great number of them fell in the action; while those who survived, more unfortunate than their companions, suffered soon after a cruel death or horrible torments, improper in a civilized age, and from a people who aspire to the title of illustrious and humane.[42]

August 20, 1847, was a memorable date for both sides in the Mexican–American War. On that single day more than a third of Santa Anna's 20,000 soldiers were killed, wounded, or captured; eight of his generals were among the prisoners; most of his artillery pieces and vast quantities of ammunition were lost. Scott reported as American casualties that out of 9,000 men, 16 officers and 139 men were killed and 876 were wounded, with about forty men missing.[43]

On the morning of August 21, military officials of both sides met to arrange a short armistice during which negotiations for peace would be pursued. Scott believed that Mexican commissioners would agree to a favorable peace rather than permit the invaders to occupy their capital. In the interim Mexicans used the cessation of hostilities to revitalize their army and fortify defensive bulwarks, and Santa Anna wrote to Domínguez of the spy company, offering a pardon to any of the *Poblanos* (men from Puebla), should they "abjure their criminal error and abandon the flag of the enemy." During the two-week truce virtually no progress was made toward peace. The Mexicans rejected Nicholas Trist's draft treaty and they insisted on the Nueces

River boundary for Texas, along with other unrealistic demands. They also discussed the imprisoned San Patricios and demanded "freedom for the captured Irishmen."[44] Instead, however, the San Patricio prisoners appeared before American military courts that determined their fate.

CHAPTER 5

Trials and Punishment

FOLLOWING AMERICAN VICTORIES at Contreras and Churubusco on August 20, 1847, General Scott had to deal with
the approximately three thousand prisoners captured that
day. Most Mexican officers were soon released under a parole arrangement whereby they agreed not to bear arms
for the duration of the war. Many enlisted soldiers, including the wounded, were set free; others were treated as prisoners of war and confined in various secure locations for
the next few months. Those prisoners, though, who were
accused of having deserted from the United States Army
and subsequently joining the Mexican forces were speedily
brought to trial. This last group numbered seventy-two
men, seventy of whom proved to be members of the San
Patricio companies.

During the fortnight after August 23, which coincided
with the armistice arranged by Generals Scott and Santa
Anna, two courts-martial met in the outskirts of Mexico
City to try the San Patricio prisoners. Based at Tacubaya,
the first court of thirteen officers was presided over by
Brevet Colonel John Garland, who ordered the board to
"sit without regard to hours, as the cases to be tried require
immediate example." Captain W. Chapman, Fifth Infantry, served as judge advocate, a peculiar military office that
embraced being both prosecutor as well as counsel for the
accused. In two weeks the board judged forty-three cases.
A few miles away in the village of San Angel, Colonel
Bennet Riley convened the second court with a similar
board composed of two colonels, two majors, eight captains, and one lieutenant. Captain S. C. Ridgely as judge
advocate prosecuted twenty-nine prisoners.[1] Colonel Riley

was an American-born officer who was Catholic and of Irish descent, but he was not related to either of the two Irish-born defendants with the same surname: John Riley and Thomas Riley.

The original court-martial records, now located in the National Archives in Washington, show that procedures for each individual trial were similar at Tacubaya and San Angel. After convening the court, the judge advocate ordered a prisoner to be brought in and asked whether he had any objections to the members who served on the board. Patrick Dalton was the only defendant who objected to a specific officer; he complained that when the San Patricios were marched into San Angel, Captain Alexander had "used violent language towards them." That judge withdrew from the case.[2] An interpreter assisted four German-speaking prisoners: John Benedick, Frederick Fogel, John Klager, and Henry Ockter. The charges were then read to the prisoner: each man was charged with desertion, and the specifications included "serving in the Mexican ranks," or a similar phrase. Sixty prisoners pleaded "Not guilty," eleven pleaded "Guilty," and one man, Edward Ellis, refused to enter a plea, because, he said, he had never been sworn in as a soldier in the United States Army.[3] With the exception of Sergeant Abraham Fitzpatrick, all the defendants had been privates or recruits in the American army at the time of their disappearance.

Testimony in the San Patricio trials followed a pattern. First, a prosecution witness, either a noncommissioned or a commissioned officer of the United States army, stated that he knew the accused man, who had served under him in the same outfit until he had deserted on a specified date. In a few cases, evidence was also presented that the deserter had a poor military record. Then, in virtually every case, another witness swore that the prisoner had been in the Mexican service and had fought at Churubusco. Because of this evidence, coupled with the fact that they were still in their Mexican uniforms, the prisoners could hardly deny that they had served under the Mexican flag. Seemingly no difference was made to the court whether the prisoners had deserted voluntarily or had been captured by Mexicans, as many claimed. Nor did it matter how they came to be wearing a Mexican uniform, willingly or forced. Questions surrounding their Mexican enlistment seemed to be considered as unimportant, once the fact of its occurrence had been established.

Two foreign witnesses helped the Americans build their case against the defectors. Both men were British subjects who had served in the San Patricio companies until their capture; neither had ever served in the United States forces. John Wilton was a former English sailor who had jumped ship at Jamaica before proceeding to Mexico, where he eventually joined the San Patricios as a sergeant. The other star witness was an Irish muleteer, Thomas O'Connor, who had lived in Mexico City for nine years before he became a member of the Foreign Legion. During the trials of the captured San Patricios, these two men often provided the damning testimony: "The prisoner was in the Legion with me; he fought against the Americans at Churubusco, and he was taken prisoner there with me." Wilton testified in twenty-six cases and O'Connor in twenty-two. The records do not indicate why the two men testified; perhaps they hoped it might lead to their own early release from prison. O'Connor was freed in September, 1847, but Wilton was confined until the following June.[4]

In their own defense, the San Patricio prisoners were given the opportunity of presenting testimony. In some cases the men asked for witnesses to attest to their good character while in the American service. Although the prisoners could not deny their affiliation with the Mexican military establishment, many offered excuses to justify the situation. None of the defendants claimed a religious or ideological reason for their action, nor did anyone mention the land grants, cash bonuses, or military rank promotions promised by Mexican authorities. Instead, two-fifths of the defendants blamed liquor, saying that they had been drunk when they were seized by Mexicans. Private John McDonald's testimony was typical: he "got on a frolic" in Puebla about a month before the battle of Churubusco, and was grabbed by Mexicans who carried him to a town about sixteen miles away where he was kept for fourteen days. Then, with ten other American prisoners, he was taken to Mexico City, and on his arrival there was forced to take up arms. Private Martin Lydon's story was similar. "I did not desert but was taken by Mexican rancheros. I was on a spree at Monterrey at the time."[5]

The case of Private Henry Longenheimer was particularly wrenching, especially if his story were true. He was accused of having deserted from his unit in Puebla on August 6, only two weeks before the battle of Churubusco. Longenheimer's sergeant testified that he had given the private a pass to attend the theater, and had not seen him since until the trial. In his defense the prisoner said that he got drunk in the theater and was taken from there by Mexicans to the City of Mexico. He was in the capital "only two hours when he was compelled by Colonel Moreno to put on the Mexican uniform, and marched out to the field of battle at San Mateo [Churubusco convent] on the 20th." The prisoner then claimed that he never fired his Mexican gun, and that he gave himself up to the first Americans that he saw near him on that day.[6] Many of the defendants testified that after they were seized by the enemy, they found themselves to be aliens in a hostile country, with no means of support. Patrick Dalton, commander of one of the San Patricio companies, told of his experiences following his capture by two Mexican ranchers on horseback

These horsemen brought me to the town [Montemorelos] & gave me up to the Alcalde. He set me at liberty when he heard the circumstances. I then inquired if there was anybody who spoke English in the town. I next met a German who spoke English. He advised me not to attempt to go back & not to go forward without a passport. The next day I got a passport & set off for the interior of the country. I then arrived at San Luis [Potosí] & was brought before General Santa Anna, who asked me whether I would join the artillery or not. I told him how I had been taken and that I did not come there to be a soldier in the Mexican Army. He said he would not compel me to soldier, but at the same time told me I was in danger of my life if I proceeded further, and having no means to live, I concluded that it was better to join the army until I could get an opportunity to leave it.[7]

A few San Patricios claimed that they had been forced to don the enemy uniform. John Bartley said that he and four other deserters had been so severely beaten by Mexican civilians that they were hospitalized for six weeks. He added, "When I left the hospital, I had no clothes and I went into the Legion rather than go naked through the streets." Another legionnaire, John Bowers, graphically described his induction into the Mexican Army:

Riley, Batchelor, and Dalton . . . got all they could to join the Legion. After they did that they went to Santa Anna and got authority to take all foreigners in the employment of the government & put them in the Legion. They came to me & asked me if I was willing to go. I said no. They then came with a guard & took me, took off the clothes I had on, sent them back, and put the uniform on me. They told me I would never be brought to fight against the Americans at all.[8]

However, other witnesses for the prosecution denied that prisoners of war were forced to join the Mexican army. Several San Patricios admitted that there had been pressure, but no absolute coercion, to take up arms. When the first case was tried in Tacubaya, the judge advocate asked a witness for the defense, "Was there any other threat or compulsion made use of against the prisoner except that of keeping him in confinement, if he would not take arms?" The answer was, "No! Everyone who joined and took arms received $2.00 and a suit of clothes, and then was allowed to go about the city."[9]

Similar questions were posed by the judge advocate in San Angel. In one case he asked witness John Wilton, "Do

you know of any Americans who would not enlist in the
Mexican service and what was done with them?" Wilton replied, "I know some who would not enlist at all and they
were sent prisoners to Santiago [Mexican military prison].
A party of the Legion, by order of Major O'Leary under
the command of Lieutenant Mestard, escorted them."[10]
There was also testimony by two American deserters who
had declined to bear arms for Mexico. James Doyne, a witness for the prosecution, said that he had been captured
by Mexicans near Veracruz at the same time as John Bartley and four other soldiers, but unlike them, he did not
join the San Patricios. He said the deserters were taken to
Mexico City where the following events occurred:

We were sent up to the Commanding General, who asked us if
we would join the [San Patricio] Company or take passports to
go anywhere through the country. He did not mean to keep us
prisoners, and he could not support us if we did not join the
Company the Mexicans were raising, that we must take care of
ourselves. When he told us that he would not support us, we
went to the British consul, who gave us a dollar apiece and told
us that he would see that we were supported and that they had
no right to make us enter the Company, no right to compel us to
soldier.[11]

A number of San Patricios on trial presented interesting
pleas to offset the serious charges against them. John Bowers claimed that he and other deserters had wanted to rejoin their American outfits, but they had been marched to
battle "with Mexicans before us and behind." Thus, they
could not escape. Bowers also said that at Churubusco he
purposely broke the flint screw off his musket so that it
would not function. More than half the defendants swore
they had not fired a shot at the Americans attacking Churubusco, but that claim was impossible to prove, one way
or the other. Henry Ockter [Oetker in enlistment file] said
that he could not fire a gun because of a broken collarbone
sustained months before on the Rio Grande. He said, "The
reason why I ran away was because I could not do duty and

they made me do it." The trial was adjourned while a surgeon examined the prisoner's arm and shoulder, confirming that his collarbone had been broken and that the bones
did not unite for some time. Another deserter, Thomas
Millett, told how he took the first opportunity to surrender
himself and the flag of the Legion "in retaliation for having been forced into their service."[12]

The trial of John Riley (spelled Reilly in court-martial
records) received special attention. He was widely believed
to be the organizer of the San Patricios, who also had ac-
tively solicited many defectors from American ranks. In his
defense, Riley submitted a six-page account telling of his
alleged capture and how he was forced by circumstances to
join the Mexican army. He said that he was imprisoned in
Matamoros, where General Ampudia interrogated him
about the size and composition of Zachary Taylor's army
and then later tried to entice him to accept a lieutenant's
commission in the Mexican Army. Riley continued:

The answer that I made him, that in case that I took arms
against the United States, that I was taking them against my
brothers and countrymen. He has told me, that as being an alien
to the United States and Mexico both, I should suffer death;
brought me out on the plaza, with my hands tied behind my
back as a prisoner and sentenced me to be shot in 25 minutes
from the time, to which General Arista rode up on horseback
and said to Ampudia, that no such business should take place
while he was in command of the Army.[13]

According to Riley's testimony, General Arista then had
the prisoner marched to his camp, where he asked him details about the troops under Taylor's command:

I made him an answer, that that was something I did not know,
or no other private soldier in the ranks. . . . He told me that he
would give me four days for to consider whether I should take
arms in the defence of the Republic of Mexico or not. If not, that
I should suffer . . . I made him an answer that . . . if I was sentenced to death as a British subject, that I would sooner serve as

a commissioned officer and fight against my brothers and countrymen than to receive death. No consul belonging to Great Britain being in that part of the country at the time, I thought fit to
accept of the commission for fear of being immediately shot. I
accepted of it.[14]

At his court-martial Riley also presented four character
witnesses. One was his former company commander, Captain Moses E. Merrill, who testified, "His character was
very fair. I don't recollect ever having to punish him in any
way." (Eleven days later Captain Merrill was killed in the
battle of Molino del Rey.) Attempting to show that he had
aided American deserters and drifters in Mexico, Riley
posed questions to H. R. Parker, an English-speaking resident of Mexico City. Parker said that Riley "came to my
room, showed me an order in Spanish, by which he was
empowered to take up all the Americans who remained in
the city, but said that he would not trouble me, and that he
did not want to trouble the Americans."[15] Unimpressed by
Riley's defense, the judges ruled against him, as they did
each man brought to trial.

With the exception of two prisoners, Ellis and Pieper,
the military courts at Tacubaya and San Angel found all of
the defendants guilty of desertion, and they sentenced the
men to death. The case against Edward Ellis was dismissed
when his company officers could not prove that he had
been officially sworn into the United States Army, nor
could they find any records that he had ever been paid.
During the trial of Lewis Pieper (spelled Prefier in court-
martial records), who was not a San Patricio and had not
joined the Mexican army, it was apparent that he was insane, "a perfect simpleton." Found guilty of being "absent
without leave from August 10 to 26," he was discharged on
the spot, forfeiting all pay due him. Sixty-eight of the remaining seventy prisoners were sentenced "to be hanged
by the neck until dead," a punishment reserved for traitors. Recommending favor for the last two, Martin Miles
and Abraham Fitzpatrick, the court sentenced them to a

more honorable punishment: "to be shot to death by a firing squad."[16]

While these sentences were being reviewed by the commander-in-chief, dozens of individuals begged American
authorities to spare the lives of the San Patricios. Besides
Mexican officials—civil and military—the appellants included the Archbishop of Mexico and other residents of
the capital. Answering an appeal from clergymen of San
Angel, Brigadier General David Twiggs told them "that to
Ampudia, Arista and Santa Anna did these men owe their
deaths, for they stooped to the low business of soliciting
desertion from our ranks and had succeeded in seducing
from duty and allegiance the poor wretches who had to
pay so dearly for their crimes."[17]

George Kendall, correspondent for the New Orleans
Picayune, wrote from Tacubaya: "all the Mexican ladies
from this town, La Señora Cayetano Rubio among the
number, have signed a warm petition in their favor, which
has been sent to Gen. Scott. The lady whose name I have
given is the wife of the rich Rubio, who has a country
house here in Tacubaya. The English, and perhaps some
of the other foreign ministers have also interested themselves in behalf of the scoundrels."[18] One letter, signed by
twenty "Citizens of the United States and Foreigners of
different Nations in the City of Mexico," requested clemency for John Riley:

We . . . Humbly pray that His Excellency the General in Chief
of the American forces may be graciously pleased to extend a
pardon to Captain John O'Reilly of the Legion of St. Patrick, and
generally speaking to all deserters from the American service.
We speak to your Excellency particularly of O'Reilly, as we
understand his life to be in most danger, his misconduct might
be pardoned by your Excellency in consideration of the protection he extended in this city to the persecuted and banished
American citizens whilst in concealment, by notifying an order
he held to apprehend them and not acting on it. We believe him
to have a generous heart admitting all his errors.
Your petitioners therefore repeat that their humble prayer

may be granted by your Excellency, and as in duty bound will every pray.[19]

Several men who signed the letter had a special interest in the Foreign Legion. Two were Scots who were acquainted with John Riley and who eventually joined the San Patricio units. One of these men was John Sutherland, a resident of Mexico since 1841; the other man, James Humphrey, had served as a surgeon in the Mexican army since 1842. An Irishman named Peter Tracy also signed the appeal. He, along with another Irishman, merchant-tailor John O'Sullivan, an Englishman named Field, and Noah Smith, an American horse trader and resident of Mexico City, had provided food, clothing, and shelter for a number of American prisoners of war in central Mexico.[20] This letter and the other appeals were taken into consideration by the American commander-in-chief.

General Scott, who had practiced law briefly before beginning his long army career, carefully reviewed the findings of the courts-martial. His decision was somewhat of a surprise. One of his assistants said that "Old Fuss and Feathers" sat up nights trying to find excuses for not executing the seventy prisoners sentenced to death.[21] In his General Orders 281 and 283, issued the second week of September, 1847, Scott confirmed the capital punishment verdict for fifty San Patricios, but he pardoned five men and reduced the sentences of fifteen others.

Scott based his modification of the sentences on humanitarian grounds as well as on the Articles of War. Two prisoners, John Brooke and David McElroy, were pardoned because they were "mere youths" who had enlisted without parental consent; at the time of their trial Brooke was sixteen and McElroy was only fifteen years old. Henry Neuer (spelled Newer in court-martial records), a German-born soldier, had his sentence remitted on verification that after he was captured by the Mexicans, who forced him into a San Patricio company, he had refused to fight. Neuer rejoined his artillery company and served throughout the rest of the war. Cancellation of the death sentence for Sergeant Abraham Fitzpatrick, who had deserted, but had not joined the Mexican army, was based on his prior good conduct and for having voluntarily surrendered himself to an American officer. Demoted to the rank of private, he rejoined his outfit. A sixty-year-old soldier named Edward McHeran (McHerron in court-martial records) was freed from the gallows and returned to service because of his long military record and in consideration of his son who served in the same company and "in the hour of greatest temptation was loyal and true to his colors." Captain George Davis said that when he told McHeran the reason for his reprieve, the overwrought deserter exclaimed, "This is worse than death! I would rather have died!"[22]

Finally, General Scott set aside the death penalty for fifteen other prisoners. John Riley and five companions were reprieved from death because they had deserted before the American Congress declared war; thus, having deserted in peacetime, they could not receive the maximum penalty. Besides Riley, the others were James Kelley, John Little, James Mills, John Murphy, and Thomas Reiley (Riley on court-martial records)—all but Mills having been born in Ireland. Mitigating circumstances surrounding their capture and impressment by Mexicans saved nine others from the gallows: Privates Hezekiah Akles, John Bartley, John Bowers, Thomas Cassady, John Daly, Roger Duhan, Alexander McKee, Martin Miles, and Samuel Thomas.[23]

Instead of being hanged, John Riley and the fourteen other reprieved San Patricios were to be given fifty lashes, "well laid on their bare back," and to be hot-iron branded with a two-inch letter "D" for deserter. Twelve were branded on the right cheek, the others on the right hip. (Flogging was abolished by the army in 1861; branding of culprits was eliminated in 1872.) In addition, the fifteen reprieved men were to be imprisoned in Mexico as long as the army remained there, then have their heads shaved and be drummed out of the service. The three who were branded on the hip also had to wear an eight-pound iron collar with three prongs, each a foot long. The iron yokes seem to have been removed after six weeks.[24]

American servicemen in Mexico complained bitterly when they heard that the death sentences of fifteen deserters had been commuted to flogging, branding, and imprisonment. They were especially angered that John Riley, who was believed to have been the principal instigator of defection, would not be hanged. Sergeant Thomas Nugent wrote to his brother, "Riley was the greatest artillerist of the day, and we had suffered greatly on his account."[25] Some officers advised General Scott that sparing the life of Riley would be attributed by the enemy to American fear and weakness; thus, it would bolster Mexican resolve to resist the Americans. But, according to an aide-de-camp, the general-in-chief declared that "he would rather with his whole army be put to the sword in the assault he was about to make upon the gates of the City of Mexico," than to take the life of Riley, who had been tried according to the Articles of War and laws of the United States.[26]

The armistice ended on September 7, 1847, and during the next week, while battles raged in the outskirts of Mexico's capital, the convicted San Patricios met their fate. A military detachment punished the first batch of turncoats at the village of San Angel on the morning of September 10. "I shall never forget the punishment meted out to these deserters," wrote a young Yankee private who stood close to the scene, where he saw the blood and smelled the burning flesh. Captain George Davis, who was also nearby, noted that all the American generals with their staffs were required to be present, "but for which order nothing on earth could have influenced my witnessing what I did." He described the scene:

The fourteen that were to be whipped and branded were tied up to the trees in front of the Catholic church on the plaza, their backs naked to the waistband of the pantaloons, and an experienced Mexican muleteer inflicted the fifty lashes with all the se-

verity he could upon each culprit. Why those thus punished did
not die under such punishment was a marvel to me. Their backs
had the appearance of a pounded piece of raw beef, the blood
oozing from every stripe as given. Each in his turn was then
branded. . . .[27]

Editors of the *American Star,* a newspaper serving the invading force, commented on the drama at San Angel:
"Riley, the chief of the San Patricio crowd, came in for a
share of the whipping and branding, and right well was
the former laid on by a Mexican muleteer, Gen. Twiggs
deeming it too much honor to the Major to be flogged by
an American soldier. He did not stand the operation with
that stoicism we expected." Riley was the only prisoner
that was branded twice. Perhaps out of spite, or following
orders, the brander put the first *D* upside down on his
face; thus, it had to be redone correctly on the other cheek.
In an extra supplement, distributed the evening after Riley's flogging and branding, the official Mexican newspaper falsely reported that the Irishman had been "executed and decapitated, his head speared on a pike and put
on display in Churubusco." A month later the important
American newspaper, *Niles National Register,* printed a
translation of this gruesome falsehood.[28]

After the flogging and branding, the drama heightened
when the Americans hanged sixteen other San Patricio
traitors. A scaffold of heavy timbers, forty-feet long and
fourteen-feet high, had been erected. Under it were eight
mule-drawn wagons, alternating in directions, with two
prisoners standing at the end of each wagon, directly under the suspended nooses. Still dressed in their Mexican
uniforms, the San Patricios had white caps drawn over
their heads. Captain Davis, who called the scene "revolt-
ing," gave more details:

The drivers were mounted upon the saddle-mule of each team,
ready to make an instantaneous start at the tap of a drum as a
signal. In the front of the prisoners were arranged five Catholic

priests in their canonicals, with a crucifix in one hand, engaged in appropriate devotional services, from the time the prisoners were stationed at the tail end of the wagons until they were swung off. . . . They all, but one died without a struggle; the exception, who was named Dalton, was literally choked to death.[29]

The bodies of the hanged San Patricios were buried nearby. Ordered to do it, John Riley and the other branded prisoners dug graves directly under the gallows for nine of their companions. The other seven, who before their execution had declared that they were practicing Catholics, were interred by priests in the nearby cemetery of Tlaquepaque (called Tlacopac, today). Captain Patrick Dalton was one of those who confessed to a priest and asked to be buried in sanctified ground. The next day, September 11, four additional convicted San Patricios were hanged and buried in the village of Mixcoac, about two miles north of San Angel.[30]

The sixteen San Patricios who were hanged in San Angel dangled from a wooden gallows erected for that purpose, but two American writers claimed that the culprits were hanged "from the limbs of a large tree," and a history of San Angel said that "twenty soldiers were hanged from a bell support." That same Mexican historian also reported the following stories without suggesting that they were myths:

There is the general belief that some of the men were buried before they had died, when they were merely unconscious from suffocation. Yankee doings! . . . In order to forget those savage outrages, the people petitioned for the removal of the large ash trees to which the defenders of the country had been tied for whipping. When the city council did not act promptly, the people rose up, tore the trees down, cut them into firewood, and burned them on the spot.[31]

Three days after the San Angel hangings, Colonel William Selby Harney executed with unwarranted cruelty the remaining thirty convicted San Patricios. Was he detailed for

Hanging of Four San Patricios. Courtesy San Jacinto Museum of History Association

the duty through random choice, or was he chosen because he had a reputation as a sadist who had a penchant
for morbid activities? Harney, who had been in the army
for twenty-nine years, had served in the Seminole and
Blackhawk Indian wars. In the Florida campaign he was
accused of indiscriminately hanging Indians without the
semblance of a trial, and a soldier said he "had ravished
young Indian girls at night, and then strung them up to
the limb of a live oak in the morning." In St. Louis, in
1834, he was indicted for beating a female slave named
Hannah, who died the next day from the effects of the
blows. One of his officers said, "For this diabolical murder
he would then and there have been hung by the outraged
citizens, but for his precipitate flight from the city." Harney was later acquitted of the murder. Some years later he
was charged with forcing enlisted soldiers to work on his
private farm. Testimony in the War Department correspondence said, "his character, particularly in the army, is
anything but enviable, being notorious for profanity, bru-

tality, incompetency, peculation, recklessness, insubordination, tyranny and mendacity."[32]

Harney—whose obituary in the *Journal of the United States Cavalry Association* noted that he was "a right hard hater always; somewhat ferocious, too, in the award of punishment,"—arranged a dramatic finale for the doomed San Patricios. He selected a high rise of ground near Mixcoac where he supervised the erection of a gallows almost twice as long as the one used at San Angel. At daybreak on, September 13, when the escorted prisoners arrived at the site, the colonel was furious because there were only twenty-nine; the other man, Francis O'Conner, had been wounded at Churubusco, and was in the field hospital. Harney rode over to the medical tent where a surgeon told him that O'Conner had lost both legs and would soon die. Nevertheless, the colonel ordered the dying man to be transported to the gallows where he was propped up alongside his companions.[33]

Colonel Harney showed a theatrical streak as well as his malevolent nature when he decided to coordinate the executions with the American assault on Chapultepec Castle. The battle for this Mexican fortress and military college, atop a hill clearly visible two miles away, had already begun, evidenced by the sound of gunfire and puffs of smoke dotted the hillside. Placing the hapless San Patricios under the gallows and with nooses around their necks, Harney announced that they would stay there until the American flag was raised over Chapultepec, at which time the trap would be sprung. Seated on boards laid across the ends of wagons, their arms and legs tied, the prisoners waited. Finally, shortly before 9:30 A.M., when the Stars and Stripes replaced the Mexican tricolor over the castle, the colonel gave the signal by a wave of his sword. An artilleryman recalled the moment:

As soon as the flag was seen floating in the breeze they were launched into eternity by him with as much sang-froid as a mili-

Hanging of Thirty San Patricios. Courtesy West Point Museum Collections, United States Military Academy, and LIFE Picture Service

tary martinet could put on. What must have been the feelings of those men when they saw that flag—for they knew their time had come! But on the other hand, a cheer came from them which made the valley ring.[34]

Most of the American servicemen in Mexico approved of the executions as just punishment for wartime treason and as a deterrent to further desertions. This viewpoint was well expressed by a naval lieutenant who was in the Valley of Mexico on special assignment as an aide to General Worth:

These executions, which would have been proper at any time, were particularly so now, as we were in the midst of the enemy's country, with a desperate struggle before us, and with greatly inferior forces; there were many foreigners in our ranks; some of them not even naturalized citizens, and the enemy was making every effort still, to entice them away. The salvation of the army might depend upon an example being made of these dishonored and dishonorable men, and General Scott had the firmness to make it. The brave Irish, who remained faithful to us, and who were always among the foremost, and most devoted of our troops, were more rejoiced at this event than the native-born Americans even, as they had felt keenly the stigma which this conduct of their countrymen had cast upon them.[35]

William Tobey, editor and publisher of the *North American* in Mexico City, was hostile not only to the San Patricios, but also to those American soldiers who continued to desert after "the terrible example from Mixcoac." One of his editorials was especially vehement:

We can paint no man, however cursed by conscience and despised by all, so perfectly unmanned, so infamously degraded, as the deserter. To his country a traitor—the mark of Arnold upon his forehead; to his God a perjurer; and the guilt stamp burned deep into his soul; in the world a wanderer and an outcast, without the poor self-excuse that the authors of other crimes hug— lost now and eternally—damned of his own hands! . . .
There is no punishment too severe for the traitor; no infamy too blackening for his name. There is no word in the language that implies so much shame as that of deserter. With Americans it expresses more than all the epithets of the language; for if all crimes were bundled together and stewed down into one, they could not convey the strength of the blackest of all—DESERTER![36]

When news of the executions reached the United States, various writers penned essays approving the action. One historian said, "It was a terrible spectacle, and only to be justified by the enormity of the crime, which had, however, been provoked throughout the whole war, by the allurements with which the Mexican generals basely tempted them." Several concurred that "treason must be punished with death." The editor of the *New York True Sun* wrote:

We feel but one sentiment in the court-martial, and that is the
justice of their doom. By all the laws of war, by all considerations
of safety to an army, the deserter merits death. He goes into the
ranks knowing his fate if he turns recreant, and all order and
security depends upon meting out to him, wherever he is found,
the severest punishment. But this "Foreign Legion" were more
than deserters . . . they joined the enemy against whom they had
enlisted, and in solid column turned their weapons of death
against their brothers and their country. . . . No good citizen or
man of country will mourn their death, though every one may
exclaim, "God have mercy on their souls!"[37]

Edward Mansfield, whose book was entitled *The Mexican
War* (first published in 1848), sustained the courts-martial
judgments. Admitting that the lesson given by the executions
was a severe one, he noted that it was a concomitant of war
and was necessary for maintaining army discipline. He
elaborated:

Desertion in the face of an enemy, and during the existence of
actual war, has been, among all nations and in all time, punished
with death. It is treason—disloyalty—in its worst, least excus-
able, and most dangerous form. Of this crime were "the companies of St. Patrick" palpably and undeniably guilty. They had
fought in the ranks of the Mexican army, at the batteries of
Churubusco; they had fought longest and hardest against those
colors which they had sworn to defend. . . .[38]

In Mexico the reaction to the whippings and hangings
was quite different. Many Mexicans viewed the Americans
as barbarians who took cruel vengeance on the unhappy
soldiers who, for apparently good reasons, had changed
their allegiance. Writing to a friend, Senator José Fernando Ramírez said, "I was frightened and horrified by
news of the terrible slaughter of our luckless Irish soldiers
who fell into the enemy's hands. I call this an atrocious
act. . . ." Another congressman, Guillermo Prieto, wrote in
a similar vein, "The punishment of the Irish prisoners of
San Patricio has left a very deep impression on me. As you

know, these men belonged to the American Army and were in great part seduced by the religious influence. . . ." In the city of Toluca an uproar occurred when residents demanded retribution against the hapless American prisoners of war who were confined there. Luckily Mexican officials prevented any retaliation.[39]

Ignoring the fact that his newspaper had recently published General Santa Anna's decree that deserters from the Mexican Army would be executed, the editor of *Diario del Gobierno* issued a special supplement regarding the fate of the San Patricios. He also took the occasion to castigate the Americans and incite his countrymen to fight harder against them:

> Mexicans: Among the European volunteers whom the American army has hired to kill us, there are many unfortunate men who are convinced of the injustice of this war, who profess the same Roman Catholic religion as we do. . . . Some of these men, renouncing their error and following the noble impulse of their heart, have passed over to our army to defend our just cause. From them the president formed the Foreign Legion, known under the name of the San Patricio Company. At Angostura [Buena Vista] and Churubusco they fought with utmost bravery, and after the enemy took this last place, they were made prisoners. . . .

> Well, then, will you believe it my countrymen? This day, in cold blood, these [American] Caribs, from an impulse of superstition, and after the manner of savages and as practised in the days of Homer, have hanged these men as a holocaust. . . .

> Mexicans: The supreme government entreats us for the honor of our race, in the name of our dignity as men and of God himself, that we should all unite in one unanimous and continuous effort to revenge those great outrages, never yielding to dismay, and to wage this war without truce and without relenting.[40]

Although the San Patricio companies were decimated by the hanging and imprisonment of those captured by the

Americans, as well as by battle losses, the foreign unit survived those reverses. Indeed, a number of San Patricios
fought in the last engagements around Mexico City, and in
the ensuing months they welcomed additional recruits
who deserted from the United States army.

CHAPTER 6

In and Out of Prison

THE OPPOSING MEXICAN and American armies resumed hostilities in the outskirts of Mexico City on September 7, 1847, after General Scott terminated the armistice. He said the two-week truce had produced no concessions and that the Mexicans had reinforced the defenses of the capital and stopped the sale of provisions to his forces, both of which violated terms of the truce. Responding to the changed situation, General Santa Anna alerted his forces in the Valley of Mexico and sent a message to the Mexican people. Part of his address, which was published in the official newspaper, follows:

Countrymen. The enemy, availing himself of idle pretexts, has determined to commence hostilities upon your beautiful city. Presuming us to be disheartened and humiliated by the reverses of fortune, he expected that I should subscribe a treaty by which the territory of the republic would have been considerably reduced and the republic covered with shame and ignominy. Mexicans do not deserve such a disgraceful fate, and, having been called upon spontaneously to direct their destinies, I have felt it my duty to respond with all loyalty to their noted mark of confidence. . . .

Mexicans! You will find me, as ever, leading in your defense, striving to free you from a heavy yoke, and to preserve your altars from infamous violation, and your daughters and your wives from the extremity of insult. The enemy lifts the sword to strike your front ranks; we will raise it also to punish the rancorous pride of the invader.[1]

The first renewed attack occurred on the morning of September 8, when the Yankees fought at an old stone flour mill called the Molino del Rey. This battle was the bloodiest single encounter of the war; the American casualties of 799 out of 3,447 engaged amounted to 23 percent, and the Mexican losses were perhaps 2,000 killed and wounded, 700 prisoners, and an indefinite number dispersed. It was a pyrrhic victory because the Americans thought the place housed a foundry for cannon, but when they occupied it, they found no arms factory. A Mexican account of the battle, published soon after the war ended, concluded: "It was the greatest decisive victory ever gained in Mexico or on the American continent, but it is a picture too blood-stained for any portion of the American army or people yet to look upon except in grief and sorrow."[2]

Five days later the Americans assaulted Chapultepec Castle, which was on the narrow crest of a hill dominating several approaches to Mexico City. Formerly a palace for viceroys, this stone building had been converted in 1837 to a military college. In addition to two mobile Mexican brigades that guarded the base of the hill, about nine hundred soldiers and forty-seven cadets of the military college located there defended the castle. Following an early morning artillery barrage, the attackers stormed the fort, using scaling ladders and pickaxes to ascend the rocky cliff and breach the walls. The approaches had been mined, but an American soldier found and cut the powder train to the mines. By mid-morning, after fierce hand-to-hand combat with bayonets, the Stars and Stripes replaced the Mexican flag over this heavily fortified position. American casualties were 862; Mexican losses were estimated at three times that, including 823 men taken prisoner. Four of the teen-aged cadets were wounded in the battle, thirty-seven were taken prisoner, and six died, one of them reputedly having wrapped himself in the national flag and hurled himself over the wall rather than surrender. These *Niños Héroes* (boy heroes) were later commemorated by a large monument erected by the Mexican government at the base of the hill.[3]

After the loss of Chapultepec, a delegation of Mexico

City's leaders begged Santa Anna to abandon the capital
rather than have it destroyed by battle. According to his
Autobiography, he convoked a council of war at the Citadel
beginning at eight o'clock on the night of September 13:

> Tired, hungry, and with my uniform tattered by the enemy's
> bullets, I discussed the grave situation with the junta of generals
> for three hours. During the entire session I was bowed down
> with pain. Each of the generals took the floor in turn. Each gen-
> eral bitterly deplored the lack of enthusiasm the people showed
> toward the war.
> The generals felt that it was useless to continue to defend the
> city without the people's support. They also felt that the people
> would be spared useless sacrifices if we surrendered. For these
> reasons and other insignificant ones, the junta unanimously
> agreed to withdraw from the capital. They felt that the national
> honor had been upheld by our defense and that it was impos-
> sible to defend the capital. . . .[4]

Vowing that the Mexican army would continue the war
from other bases, Santa Anna also concurred with the plan
that civilian government leaders should set up a provisional headquarters at Querétaro, about 170 miles to the
northwest. Very early on the morning of September 14,
the Mexican military forces of about five thousand infantry and four thousand cavalry abandoned Mexico City and
retreated to the village of Guadalupe Hidalgo. Later that
day Scott made a triumphal entry into the Halls of Montezuma where the American flag was unfurled on the National Palace. Although the war would not be over for more
than eight months, and guerrilla hostilities and military
buildup continued in the interim, no more large battles
were fought. Military government, rather than fighting,
became the principal concern of the occupation army,
which also took over other important cities such as Toluca
and Cuernavaca.

Less than a week after Scott's entry, the Mexican capital's
first English-language newspaper, the *American Star,* made
its debut there. The paper was established by John H.

Peoples and John R. Barnard, newspapermen from New
Orleans, who earlier in the year had founded the Veracruz *Eagle* and preliminary versions of the *American Star*
published in Jalapa and Puebla, Mexico. First a triweekly,
then issued twice a week, and, after October 12, a daily,
this Mexico City newspaper published proclamations and
orders of American military commanders as well as news
items from Mexico and abroad. Some articles were addressed directly to the Mexicans in the section printed
in Spanish. The first issue, dated September 20, 1847,
summarized the punishment inflicted on the San Patricio
deserters.[5]

The second issue of the *American Star* printed Scott's
General Order 296, dated September 22, 1847, in which
the commander-in-chief admonished his troops to beware
of hostile Mexican agents. He said that some agents had
formed a conspiracy to surprise and murder American
soldiers; others were fomenting desertion. The general
cautioned that there were Mexicans dressed in disguise,
aided by thieves and "several false priests who dishonor
the holy religion which they only profess for the special occasion." Then he mentioned continued efforts to entice
"our gallant Roman Catholic soldiers, who have done so
much honor to our colors, to desert, under a promise of
lands in California." Finally, he warned the troops:

Let all our soldiers, Protestant and Catholic, remember the fate
of the deserters taken at Churubusco. These deluded wretches
were also promised money and land; but the Mexican government, by every sort of ill usage, drove them to take up arms
against the country and flag they had voluntarily sworn to support, and next placed them in front of the battle—in positions
from which they could not possibly escape the conquering valor
of our glorious ranks.[6]

Two American writers, G. T. Hopkins and Edward S.
Wallace, later distorted Scott's words, thereby casting as-
persions on Catholic soldiers by intimating that they were

the only ones who deserted. Instead of correctly citing Scott's warning, "Let all our soldiers, Protestant and Catholic, remember the fate of the deserters . . .," these writers misquoted him as saying, "Let all our Catholic soldiers remember the fate. . . ."[7] In spite of the general's admonition and the recent example of the punished San Patricios, deserters continued to leave the American ranks, some to join the Mexican army.

After Santa Anna abandoned the capital, he resigned from the presidency and split his army into two sections. He led cavalry units east, where they joined guerrilla warriors led by General Joaquín Rea, and the combined forces then harassed and laid siege to the American garrison and hospital at Puebla. The siege, unsuccessful in its primary goal, lasted for a month. Meanwhile, General José Joaquín de Herrera took the infantry and artillery units, including about eighty San Patricio survivors, northwest to the city of Querétaro. There a fugitive government was established, the Mexican Congress was convoked, and Manuel de la Peña y Peña, senior justice of the supreme court, became acting president until November 12, when he was replaced for two months by General Pedro María Anaya, who styled himself "Interim President of Mexico."[8]

Querétaro, capital of the small state of the same name, was a very old city with an estimated population of 36,000 in 1847. In addition to its handsome residences, some with noble escutcheons over the massive *zaguán* doorways, there were a dozen distinguished colonial churches. The church and convent of Santa Clara, which once sheltered upward of 8,000 nuns, was one of the outstanding landmarks. Glazed tiles in blue, yellow, white, and light green covered the dome and towers, reconstructed in part by Eduardo Tresguerras, an outstanding architect-artist-sculptor, who had been born nearby in the city of Celaya.

Henry Wise visited Querétaro during the Mexican War and was impressed with the city's monuments and its de-

lightful climate. He also mentioned, "A noble aqueduct of
two miles in length, with arches ninety feet high—span-
ning a plain of meadow-land—joins a tunnel from the opposite hills, and leads an abundance of excellent water,
from ten miles beyond, to the city." Commenting that the
city had grown because it was the temporary seat of government, he said, "not a tenantless house or spare nook
was to be found. Crowds were thronging the wide, well-
paved streets, and mounted troops and foot-soldiers, with
ear-aching music of cornets, trumpets and drums, were
moving in all directions about the city as we entered."[9]

While Mexican government officials in Querétaro were
preoccupied with measures to continue the war, various
residents of Mexico City visited the San Patricios imprisoned in the capital. Twenty-one of the "Irish Volunteers,"
including six who had not been in the American service,
were quartered on the second floor of the former Acordada prison on Patoni Street (later renamed Avenida Juárez) near the southwest corner of the Alameda park. More
than five hundred other Mexican prisoners of war were
housed on the main floor of this colonial building. The
Mexican *Ayuntamiento* (city council) appointed a committee
that visited the Acordada prison regularly. It reported that
each prisoner was given a new shirt, a pair of shoes, a blan-
ket, and a sleeping mat; the daily food received by each
man consisted of half a loaf of bread, *atole* (porridge made
from maize meal) in the morning, rice and a pound of
meat at midday, and rice and beans at six in the evening.
The report also noted that the chapel of the building had
been converted into an infirmary, staffed by male nurses.[10]

William C. Tobey, editor of the *North American*, the second English-language newspaper established in Mexico
City, commented on the imprisoned San Patricios, noting
that several *señoritas* and priests regularly brought them
food and other gifts such as shirts, mattresses, and fine bed
linens. "The guard over these prisoners is importuned
daily by persons apparently occupying a respectable position in society, who drive to the place in their carriages,

Acordada Prison. Courtesy The Bancroft Library

and carry to them all sorts of luxuries, while their own countrymen, prisoners also, the sick and wounded officers and privates, are utterly neglected. The greater portion of these ostentatiously benevolent people are women. . . ."[11]

Responding to Mexican complaints about the treatment of the San Patricios, editor Tobey visited the prison and printed an account in his newspaper. He said the apartments were clean and comfortable and that the prisoners, who were "dressed as well as most soldiers," had adequate mattresses or mats and blankets. Tobey saw John Riley, whom he described as about thirty-five years old. His account continued:

He is six feet one or two inches high, broad shouldered and muscular, and, we should suppose, a man of great strength and capable of enduring fatigue or hardship with indifference. He is not a good looking man, in our estimation of good looks. The letter "D" branded on his cheek has been picked out, leaving a scar that has the appearance of a severe burn. Thus all external evidence of his disgrace is gone. When we saw him he was in his

shirt-sleeves and wore good shoes, pants and vest, and his shirt
was fine and clean. He complained that a shirt made for him by a
woman of the city had been kept from him, but did not appear
to be in need of it. He had a camp bedstead and comfortable bed
clothing, which was also clean.[12]

From this same prison on October 27, 1847, Riley wrote
a letter to Charles O'Malley, his old employer in Michigan.
Besides sending his greetings to more than a dozen Irish-
surnamed acquaintances in Mackinac, Riley summarized
some of his wartime experiences:

I have had the honour of fighting in all the battles that Mexico
has had with the United States and by my good conduct and
hard fighting, I have attained the rank of Major a rank which no
other foriner who has fought for the Mexican government has
ever attained. I suppose from the account you have seen in the
United States papers that you have formed a very poor opinion
of Mexico and its government, but be not deceived by the prejudice of a nation which is at war with Mexico, for a more hospi-
table or friendly people than the better or upper class of Mexicans there exists not on the face of the earth. That is to a foriner
and espetially to an Irishman and a catholick. It grieves me to
have to inform you of the death of fifty-one of my best and brav-
est men who has been hung by the Americans for no other reason than fighting manfully against them. . . .
    You may possibly have thought strang at my not writing to you
before but there being no communication allowed between Mexico and the United States, it was impossible for me to address
you before now, but as I am at present a prisoner of war by the
Americans it is imposable for me to state facts as they are but in
my next letter I will give you a full and true account of the war as
it has progressed. . . . N.B. Direct you[r letters] for Major John
Riley, Major of the Legion of St. Patrick to his Excellency the
President of the republic of Mexico.[13]

One of Riley's fellow prisoners, a twenty-two-year-old
Irish-born San Patricio named Roger Duhan (Deehan on
enlistment roll), escaped from the Acordada prison at the
end of November, 1847. A few days later Lieutenant J. N.

Whistler, who was the American officer in charge of the guard at that time, was summoned to a general court-martial, charged with "Neglect of duty." At his trial he offered the following explanation:

All the American prisoners were put in a room at night & were not permitted to leave it & a guard of one Cpl. & three men put over the door. In the morning they were let out, as usual, & the Cpl. informed me that the absent man was among the others at that time. About 7 o'clock the Cpl. of the Guard came & in-formed me that one of the American prisoners could not be found. I immediately sent for the Sergt. I had the whole prison searched but could not find him. I then questioned the Sergt. I found that two women had passed out about half an hour before. One of them he recognized as a woman calling herself the wife of one of the deserters. I then found out that the man she called her husband was the one that was absent & the woman that was with her must have been the prisoner as he was a very small man & could easily be disguised in woman's clothing. I have to state that the women were allowed to pass in and out. . . .[14]

Lieutenant Whistler was acquitted of the charge, and a few weeks later Roger Duhan was reincorporated into the Mexican infantry and promoted to the rank of lieutenant. Duhan's American enlistment record gave his height as five feet three; thus he easily could have donned a Mexican woman's dress. Incidentally, neither of the two American newspapers published in Mexico City reported the escape; it seems to have been hushed up by the army. It is curious that Lieutenant Whistler's court-martial record does not mention the name of the escaped San Patricio; that was ascertained from a Mexican newspaper account of Duhan's rejoining the Mexican army.[15]

During the last months of 1847, a number of Mexicans tried to secure the release, exchange, or parole of the San Patricios. On October 2 "some of the principal ladies of Mexico City" called on General Scott with a petition soliciting parole for the "Irish volunteers," but he refused to meet with them and instructed his aide-de-camp to inform them that he would not grant their request. Commenting on this petition, John Peoples, editor of the *American Star* said, "There are many Mexicans, prisoners of war, in our hands, who were taken on the field of battle fighting for their contry's cause. Such men we honor and respect in their misfortune; but for the apostatized and toad-spotted traitors who were taken in arms *against* their country, feelings of loathing and disgust take possession of us whenever we think of them."[16]

Several times Mexican Archbishop Manuel Posada y Garduño appealed to Scott, requesting him to parole all the Mexican prisoners. At a meeting early in November the general pointed out that the men captured at Veracruz and Cerro Gordo had been released under their word of honor, but subsequently many of them rejoined their army. Later, Scott proposed additional prisoner releases if the archbishop would refuse absolution to those men who violated the pledge, or if the archbishop would give the oath of the church that the men would not take up arms again. Finally, three days before Christmas the Americans released more than five hundred Mexican prisoners held in Mexico City—not including the San Patricios. Each man was given a paper signed by the archbishop and the president of the *Ayuntamiento* certifying that they were bound by an oath not to soldier again in the present war.[17]

At the end of December, 1847, John Riley and the other San Patricio prisoners were transferred to the military fortress of Chapultepec, on the western edge of Mexico City. From that stone castle Riley wrote a letter to the British minister in Mexico, asking for his help in getting released so that he could return to Ireland. Here, in his colloquial English, is the text of the letter:

Your Excellency with opportunity of riting to you hoping that your honour will take compassion on me as a brittish subject as I am unfortunate to be hier in prison, I rite hoping that you will do your utmost with general Scott the commander of the American forces in the sitty of Mexico on the condisions that I do not

take up arms against them on no consideration what ever here
after and that I shall go to my home that is to the old contery as
soon as I get some little business settled in this sitty. I hope you
will excuse me for making so free with your honour but nesses-
sity compells me to call up on you in my behalf. No more at
present from your humble servant.[18]

In his reply to Riley, Percy Doyle, *chargé d'affaires* of the
British embassy, said, "I would not fail to speak to the General in your behalf, were there any chance of my being of
service to you, but I see none at the present moment." This
cool response was in line with previous instructions received from the Foreign Minister in London, who said that
former British subjects who had become Mexican citizens,
"have no right . . . to resume their original national character, and to cast off Mexican citizenship, without the consent of the Mexican government."[19] While Riley and the
other San Patricio prisoners languished in prison in the
Valley of Mexico, their companions who had escaped from
Churubusco and additional deserters were reformed into
a fighting unit at Querétaro, northwest of Mexico City.

Because of heavy losses of men and material, plus the
continuing war and the occupation of parts of the country
by American forces, the Mexican army was completely reorganized in the autumn of 1847. In early November the
men under arms totaled 8,109. More than a third of the
soldiers were in Querétaro; the others were at military
posts scattered throughout the country. In addition there
were several bands of government-supported guerrillas
who operated along the American supply route between
Veracruz and Puebla, in Baja California, and in other
places. Under the new plan decreed by the acting president, nine states in central Mexico were assigned quo-
tas totaling 16,000 new soldiers for the permanent army.
There were to be twenty battalions of infantry, twelve cavalry corps, four battalions of artillery, plus one battalion
each of sappers, engineers, and staff. The published decree specified the number of companies in each battalion,

Mexican Medal for Churubusco. Courtesy Museo Nacional de Historia

the table of organization for companies, the number of horses and mules authorized, and a pay and grade scale.[20] While deciding on army matters, the government at Querétaro created military decorations to honor those men who had fought so bravely in the Valley of Mexico. The medal for Churubusco was described as follows: "In the center, a red iron cross encircled by a white enameled band with the legend: *Defensor de la independencia en Churubusco* [Defender of independence at Churubusco]. Officers will wear the cross suspended around their neck by a one-inch ribbon of the same colors as the national flag. Enlisted men will fasten it to a buttonhole on the left side of their dress coat."[21]

In the reorganization of the Mexican army there was no mention of the defunct Foreign Legion, but the San Patricio company of infantrymen was recognized, sanctioned, and paid. Indeed, the secretary of war ordered: "The San Patricio Company will remain as presently established, and in the future all persons who present themselves will be incorporated." That last phrase referred to any stragglers or new defectors. By the following March, the San Patricios had grown to two companies of 114 men each, bolstered by additional deserters from the United States Army.[22]

The continued desertion of American soldiers prompted the United States military authorities to court-martial those who were apprehended, and to search out Mexican agents suspected of complicity. In January, 1848, a Council of War in Mexico City heard the cases of four civilians—Ramón Rebero, Tiburcio Rodríguez, Manuel Sanzeda, and José de la Luz Vega—charged with "enticing, persuading and endeavoring to induce enlisted soldiers of the American army to desert the American service and join the Mexican army." Rebero, who provided a disguise for the defectors, was sentenced to hard labor for the duration of the war. Because the testimony against him was contradictory, Rodríguez was acquitted. Sanzeda received a sentence of one month at hard labor. Specifically charged with soliciting the desertion of Private J. Boone, Señor

Vega was sentenced to be shot to death, but ten days later
General Scott pardoned him because of "a doubt as to the
sufficiency of the evidence."[23]

While the American army was busy with occupation duties and Mexican military forces were being reorganized,
civilians on both sides worked for a peace settlement. At
the end of 1847, one or more anonymous Mexican liberals
drafted a long tract examining causes and progress of the
war. This published essay painted a grim picture for the
future and even suggested the possibility of a United
States protectorate over Mexico. Its prediction included
the following assessment:

Exhausted and without the means to fight, with an invading
army that has already seized its ports, its principal sources of in-
come, and even the capital itself, and with a refugee government
that lacks resources, prestige, and is unable to take measures
necessary to uphold the rights and honor of the nation, it is easy
to predict that the final act of this tragic drama will be highly
damaging and shameful for Mexico, and that we will lose a large
part of our territory to indemnify the victorious enemy for the
war he has had the grace to bring us.[24]

At the same time, President Polk and his advisors in the
United States were growing dissatisfied with the lack of
progress toward a peace treaty. Mexico's intransigence and
the growing toll of war casualties prompted the American
officials to demand even more territory as an indemnity. A
movement to "annex all Mexico" developed in the United
States. Dissatisfied with peace commissioner Trist's performance, Polk ordered him to return to Washington. However, General Scott, British diplomats, and Mexican peace
advocates persuaded Trist to remain, and, early in 1848,
he met with a new set of Mexican commissioners who finally signed a draft treaty at the village of Guadalupe Hidalgo on February 2, 1848.[25] The treaty would have to be
ratified by legislatures of both countries.

By terms of the Treaty of Guadalupe Hidalgo, Mexico
would give up all claims to Texas and agree to a new fron-

tier with the United States. This new line ran from the mouth of the Rio Grande to the southern boundary of New Mexico, then generally west to a point just south of San Diego, California. For the ceded land north of that line (529,000 square miles), the United States agreed to pay $15 million and to assume previous monetary claims. Article IV of the treaty specified that "All prisoners of war taken on either side, on land or on sea, shall be restored as soon as practicable after the exchange of ratifications of this treaty."[26]

Ratification of the Treaty of Guadalupe Hidalgo took almost four months because the agreement was debated and modified by the Senate in Washington and by both houses of Congress in Querétaro. Mexican leaders disagreed; some wanted to continue the war, but others pointed out the futility because the enemy occupied more than half the states and controlled all of the significant ports. General Pedro María Anaya, the minister of war, favored peace because of the lack of manpower and munitions. Reporting, on May 8, that the total strength of the army was only 926 officers and 6,487 enlisted men, he added, "Here is the true status of the army, which not only is incapable of carrying out the purpose for which it was organized, but also it is so reduced in numbers that it is not even sufficient for keeping domestic order." He also noted that the army was trying to subdue Indian revolts in five different states. Another report said that there were some three to five hundred American deserters in Querétaro who took a strong stand for peace, because they were likely to be captured and shot if the war continued.[27]

Meanwhile, in February opposing military commanders agreed to a suspension of hostilities, pending ratification of the treaty. This same month, Major General William Butler replaced Winfield Scott as commander-in-chief, and General Santa Anna made plans to leave for exile. Both Scott and Santa Anna had been censured by their respective governments, and official inquiries about their conduct were underway. During this cessation of active

warfare some prisoners were exchanged—in one case a
Mexican general bartered sixteen American prisoners of
war for General Santiago Blanco. An American officer
who visited Querétaro in May said that before the North
American peace commissioners arrived there, "The battalion of traitors, under the banner of San Patricio, who
amounted to some hundreds, had very judiciously been
withdrawn from the city."[28]

In Mexico City during the last month of the war, the San
Patricio prisoners were quartered in the Citadel (*la Ciudadela*), several blocks south of the Alameda park. The editor
of the *American Star* reported that the *Ayuntamiento* had
sent fifty dollars to these deserters, and he called on other
Mexicans to contribute to their support. At the end of May
when the Treaty of Guadalupe Hidalgo was ratified and
signed, an announcement declared that the jailed San Patricios would be taken to New Orleans, where they would
be dishonorably discharged from the United States Army.[29]

Several Mexicans petitioned the American commanding
general to release the San Patricios in Mexico City. The
editor of a leading Mexican newspaper printed an open
letter to General Butler:

We would humbly beg the commander in chief to show his clemency by pardoning these unfortuante men and remitting the rest
of their term of punishment, setting them at liberty and allowing
them to remain among us. Nothing would, in our opinion, be a
more appropriate act in celebration of peace, or more conducive
to forgetfulness of the past, than the exercise of the act of pardon towards these unfortunates, who would not have suffered
had the war not taken place. . . . Should His Excellency read
these lines, we hope he will be persuaded that they represent the
sentiment of every Mexican heart.[30]

In accordance with a provision of the Treaty of Guadalupe Hidalgo, modified perhaps by Mexican appeals, Major General Butler issued General Orders 116, dated June
1, 1848, which freed all persons confined by the American
army. The last paragraph of the orders read, "The pris-

La Ciudadela *(The Citadel). Courtesy The Bancroft Library*

oners in confinement at the Citadel, known as the San Patricio prisoners, will be immediately discharged." At the
Citadel (*la Ciudadela*) the officer of the guard read General
Butler's orders to the San Patricios; then their heads were
shaved, the buttons stripped from their uniforms, and they
were ushered out of the fortress while fifers and drummers
played the "Rogue's March." Words to that tune were:
"Poor old soldier, poor old soldier / He'll be tarred and
feathered and sent to Hell / Because he wouldn't soldier
well." The names of the sixteen discharged San Patricios
were listed in the orders, Hezekiah Akles, John Bartley,
Thomas Casaday (Cassaday), John Chambers, John Daily
(Daly), James Kelly, Alexander McKee, Martin Miles, James
Miller, James Mills, Peter O'Brien, John Riley, Samuel
Thomas, Edward Ward, Charles Williams, and John Wilton.[31]
     Coincident with the end of the war and release of pris-
oners, Mexican government officials moved back to their
ancient capital, and American troops evacuated Mexico
City as the first stage of their journey back to the United

States. After escorting General Butler and his staff to Veracruz, all members of the Mexican spy company, except
Colonel Domínguez, were paid and discharged. Domínguez, who said that he "would be killed like a dog" if he
remained in Mexico, was transported with his family to
New Orleans. Six months later he was still living there in
poverty with his family of nine. Meanwhile, other members of his band moved north to the Rio Grande frontier
to escape persecution as traitors.[32] As far as the United
States Army was concerned, the end of the Mexican War
terminated its connection with the San Patricios. However,
the story of "the Irish Volunteers" continued in Mexico.

CHAPTER 7

The Postwar Battalion

WHEN THE WAR with the United States ended, Mexico
found its territory diminished by two-fifths (one-half counting the loss of Texas), its economy in a shambles, and its
demoralized people subject to another period of turmoil.
Troubles during the summer of 1848 included a serious
Indian rebellion in the mountains of San Luis Potosí, a
continuing caste war between Maya Indians and whites in
Yucatan, roving bandits who menaced major highways,
military revolts in three states, and an attempted coup
d'etat in the capital. Surprisingly, San Patricios were impli-
cated in the last two of these disorderly events.

At the beginning of June, 1848, there were two distinct
groups of San Patricios in Mexico. By far the largest contingent was in Querétaro, where the Irish Volunteers composed two infantry companies totaling some two hundred
and thirty men. The others were veterans located in or
near Mexico City; they included John Riley and the fifteen
former prisoners who had been released by the Yankees,
plus about a dozen stragglers who surfaced after the American Army departed. Because those San Patricios in the
capital had no means of support, a few were reported to be
begging in the streets. On June 6 the editor of *El Siglo Diez
y Nueve* started a subscription to aid the former prisoners,
and on subsequent days the newspaper reported the names
of contributors with amounts pledged. Two weeks later
the newspaper published a letter from John Riley, who
acknowledged the receipt of 232 pesos (dollars) which
he had distributed among the following "companions at
arms": William H. Akles, John Bartley, Thomas Cassady,

Fandango at a pulquería (tavern). Courtesy The Bancroft Library

John Hamilton, James Kelley, John Little, John McCor-
nick, Alexander McKee, James Miller, John Murphy, Peter
O'Brien, Samuel Thomas, Edward Ward, Charles Williams, and John Wilton. Riley, who signed his letter with
the rank of captain, ended it with the following statement:
"All the individuals, and I also, give the most affectionate
thanks to the persons who have honored us with a show of
consideration."[1]

During the first half of June, Riley and ten of his companions were living in the village of Tlalnepantla, just
north of the capital, where town authorities provided them
with food and shelter. The San Patricios spent their few
pesos on drink at a local *pulquería*, which was enlivened
with a nightly fandango. Reporting on their situation, a
newspaperman commented: "The excessive use of liquor
has made them intolerable there because of the frequent
and serious disorders they provoke. Yet we congratulate

the said authorities for the fine sentiments of humanitarianism and public gratitude shown in favor of the valiant defenders of Mexico."[2]

In a letter to the treasury minister, a local judge described the arrangement and asked for additional funds to support the former soldiers:

> As much as the small total of my resources has permitted, I have aided the Irish defenders of Churubusco, giving food and lodging in my house to eight or ten of them and to their worthy captain, Don Juan Reilly. But because this gentleman urgently needs money for the daily pay of his seasoned soldiers and the new ones that frequently arrive—and they are among the best troops of General Worth—he has asked me to furnish it.
>
> In spite of the intense efforts I have taken to obtain the funds, it has not been possible, because this town is very poor. That forces me to bother you, distracting you from your many concerns, requesting that, if it is possible, you give appropriate orders so that the necessary sum of money be given to the aforementioned Señor Reilly.[3]

A subsequent letter indicated that the minister of war had forwarded fifty pesos to support the unemployed San Patricios.[4]

Shortly after the middle of June, 1848, John Riley and his companions found employment—they were reincorporated into the Mexican army. Joined by renegade San Patricios who had been in hiding, and by recent deserters from the United States Army, they were organized into two infantry companies. One unit was assigned to sentry duty in the capital; the other was stationed at the suburb of Guadalupe Hidalgo. As commander of both companies, Riley's brevet rank was lieutenant colonel (with a permanent rank and the pay of major); his adjutant was Major José María Calderón.[5] The two new companies, along with the San Patricio companies based at Querétaro, comprised the newly-created San Patricio Battalion.

On June 18, two weeks after he took over as the new

president of Mexico, General José Joaquín Herrera issued
the following decree setting up the San Patricio Battalion.

Considering the benefits which will accrue to the service of
the Republic by organizing a force of individuals, who by their
antecedents have given proof of loyalty and constancy to the
defense of national interests, I have been pleased to decree the
following:

Article 1. The existing San Patricio companies and those that
will be newly organized will form a battalion under that same
name. It will be subject to the regulations which the decree of
December 1 of last year established for permanent battalions.

Article 2. All the individuals who serve in this corps will be
obliged to agree to the following conditions:

1. The term of enlistment will be for one year, at the end of
   which they may obtain a discharge.
2. If they wish to reenlist, and their conduct in the service of
   the nation has been good, they will receive a ten-peso
   bonus each time they sign up.
3. The San Patricio soldiers will receive pay of thirty pesos
   each month plus an outfit composed of the articles of
   clothing specified in regulations.

Article 3. Irishmen, Germans, Spaniards, and Frenchmen will
be admitted to serve in the San Patricio Battalion.

Article 4. The commanders and officers will be chosen by the
supreme government, and the sergeants and corporals will be
named by the officers. The officers will receive the same pay as
Mexican officers.

Article 5. The nation will grant 170 acres of land to each individual who serves in the San Patricio Battalion, provided that he
completes five years of satisfactory service to the republic. Those
who desert during the time of their enlistment, and those who
commit crimes for which the punishment is imprisonment or
greater, will lose the right to this concession.

Article 6. The nation will concede a double portion of land
to the commanders and officers according to their merit and
conduct; if their service is distinguished by their fidelity and
good conduct in campaigns, the concession of land will be qua-
drupled.

Article 7. The commanders and officers will serve for a definite period which will be noted on their commission, and if by

their conduct they are deserving of the consideration of the government, they can continue in the service, in which case they will be given new commissions. In any case, the nation is not obliged to give any recompense other than what is stipulated in the previous article.

Article 8. If any individuals of the San Patricio Battalion become disabled by wounds or mutilation in the service and defense of the nation, they will be granted the retirement and pension which Mexican military personnel enjoy, and this will not preclude their receipt of property in the concession of lands indicated in Article 5 and 6 of this decree.

Article 9. All the individuals in the category of commanders, officers, and troops to which the previous articles refer are required to maneuver in conformity with the military tactics of the Mexican Army, and in all cases they are subject to the same civil and criminal laws as the national army.[6]

Soon after announcement of the presidential decree forming the San Patricio units into a battalion, the treasury allocated money for military pay, and the following items of clothing and equipment were issued to the men: 200 cloth jackets; 200 cloth barracks caps; 200 pair trousers; 200 pair of shoes; 400 linen shirts; 200 blankets; and 200 stocks (neckware).[7]

Meanwhile, early in June, one of the San Patricio companies that was stationed in Querétaro was ordered to march northwest toward Lagos de Moreno, where a military rebellion was underway. This insurrection was headed by General Mariano Paredes y Arrillaga, a career officer who had overthrown the government three years earlier and served briefly as president until he had been ousted and exiled. Shortly before the end of the war with the United States, Paredes returned to Mexico, but he was not permitted to enter active service. Angered by this treatment and bitterly opposed to the peace treaty, he conspired with military officers based in the city of Aguascalientes, where he launched his revolt in May, of 1848. Paredes also had the help of a noted guerrilla leader who had been active during the recent war, the Spanish-born

priest Celedonio Domeco de Jarauta. With fifty men Jarauta was sent to Lagos de Moreno, and on the first of
June he won over the military garrison of that city.[8]

From Lagos and other cities the rebels issued manifestos
announcing their rebellion and denouncing those Mexican leaders who had signed the peace treaty with the United
States. Stating that "government officials had sacrificed the
honor and territory of the Republic for the convenience of
some money," their printed plan asked Mexicans to dis-
avow the central government, and it called on the states
to "resume their sovereignty" and to decide on ways to
replace the federal government. By mid-June the rebellion had spread from Aguascalientes and Lagos to the important city of Guanajuato, where Paredes won over the
troops and replaced an uncooperative governor with one
who pledged that "Mexicans would witness the recovery of
national honor and revocation of the peace of defeat."[9]
Supporters of Paredes also staged a military revolt and occupied the seaport of Mazatlán on the Pacific coast. At almost the same time, and perhaps encouraged by Paredes
or his supporters, hundreds of Indians of the Sierra Gorda
in the state of San Luis Potosí went on the warpath. Pro-
claiming their independence from Mexico, they abolished
all taxes or contributions to the central government and
announced the expropriation and reassignment of lands
in their area. The Indian rebellion raged intermittently
for more than a year until it was finally settled by the combination of a decisive battle and a peace treaty.[10]

Crushing the Paredes revolt took less time. After seven
weeks of marches and skirmishes, military forces loyal to
the Herrera administration put down the military insurrection at the end of July, 1848. Father Jarauta was captured near Guanajuato on July 19, and shot as a traitor
three hours later. General Paredes, who managed to elude
his pursuers, took refuge in a Mexico City convent where
he remained in hiding until his death the following year.
During the campaign one San Patricio company marched

almost a hundred miles from Querétaro to Silao, where it was based for a month.[11]

Captain James Humphrey, one of the San Patricios in Querétaro, seems to have conspired with Paredes, in whose name he offered promotions and money to any of his comrades who would defect to the rebels. Humphrey was later arrested and imprisoned. At his trial he was accused of attempting to seduce Captain O'Leary; Lieutenants Peel, Maloney, and Thompson; and Sergeants Donaley, Burke, Winitt, and Mauray.[12] Before the Paredes revolt had been subdued, John Riley and other San Patricios in Mexico City were accused of plotting to overthrow the supreme government. According to a newspaper account, the coup was planned for the evening of July 23, when the conspirators would enter the Government Palace through the guardhouse, then overpower the president along with any cabinet ministers who might be with him. "The attack for that part would be by the San Patricio company, under the orders of its commander Lt. Colonel Reily," according to *El Siglo Diez y Nueve*. At the same time revolutionaries based at the nearby monastery of Santo Domingo would open fire on government troops at the customhouse, while other collaborators would ring the cathedral bells calling the people to arms.[13] This plot seems to have been connected to the Paredes revolt; perhaps the conspirators in the capital wanted to pave the way for Paredes to return to power.

Forewarned, the government arranged for an agent in disguise to follow Riley and arrest him when he met with his associates. In the evening of July 23 when Riley entered a house at 11 Medinas Street, "a place known as a hangout for conspirators," he and fourteen other suspects, including two military officers and a printer, were taken into custody and placed incommunicado.[14] The next day members of the San Patricio company stationed at Guadalupe Hidalgo heard rumors that Riley was to be executed, other officers would be arrested, and the unit disbanded.

This led to a new rebellion, which some reports said was tied to the Paredes revolt. A Yankee businessman in Mexico City recorded the following in his journal under the date of July 25, 1848:

The San Patricio troops, which for security were sent to Guadalupe yesterday, have made a pronunciamiento, having been joined, it is said, by some of the disaffected Mexican officers from the City. The government has sent a force of two or three hundred men of the national guard, with three pieces of artillery, against them, but doubts are entertained of their being able to subdue them. On the contrary, it is feared that they may be beaten and lose their cannon, which would give much additional strength to the revolt. All must remain this night in suspense and anxiety.[15]

Major José María Calderón, commander of the Saint Patrick's company at Guadalupe Hidalgo, gave a Mexico City newspaper the best account of what happened in the mutiny:

About four in the afternoon Second Lieutenants Peel and Maloney came to the barracks shouting, "Riley was to be shot, many San Patricios had been assassinated, all the foreign officers were to be put on a prison ship, and the battalion would be disarmed within half an hour." On hearing this, the frenzied soldiers grabbed their arms and headed for the plaza, but I and a sergeant blocked the doorway until they wounded the sergeant and swarmed into the plaza. There, I assured the troops that Lieutenants Peel and Maloney lied. Only the good sergeant Milord listened and joined me; many unruly men surrounded me and pointed their weapons my way. At that moment Peel ordered the men to march, and they obeyed; I also marched with them because I believed that the troops would soon understand their error and return to order.

About a league from Guadalupe I talked with the Polish Sergeant Vinet and to others, asking them to tell the Irishmen that nothing the officers had said to them was certain. . . . That night fifty men returned to Guadalupe.

Peel marched in the midst of his soldiers, promising them to sack the town of Cuautilán . . . I separated from them in order to notify the authorities. . . .[16]

Later that night twenty-five of Peel's followers were arrested near Tlalnepantla, and the other twenty-five or thirty soldiers separated into small units and scatttered in the countryside. Some of the errant soldiers proceeded toward the area where Paredes was defying the government; others seem to have headed toward the Gulf Coast. Nine months later James McFarland wrote a letter to the British minister relating what had happened to him and his Irishborn companion John Hynes:

We were members of the Legion of St. Patrick at the time of its disgraceful desertion from the city of Guadalupe. . . . On the night of the third day myself, John Hynes, and six others left the Legion and took our route for Querétaro. Within two days of that place we surrendered our arms to the Alcalde of the town and were given a passport for there, but learning on the following day that there were orders ahead of us for the imprisonment of those belonging to the Legion, we concluded to scatter two by two and make for Tampico. Hynes and myself . . . on the fourth [of August] entered Sanegia where on the morning of the 5th we were made prisoners with some 20 others whom they termed Serranos [those of the Sierra Gorda] and taken with them to San Luis de la Paz where they charged us with having been with the rebel Indians for 5 or 6 months. . . . We have now been prisoners nearly nine months . . . and God only knows how much longer we may remain here unless your Honour deigns to speak in our favour to the President of this "so termed" Republic. . . .[17]

McFarland and Hynes eventually were released from prison, but the recalcitrant, if not treasonous, activities of their companions-at-arms led Mexico's military president to terminate the San Patricio Battalion soon after the mutiny at Guadalupe. The last commissary report for the unit was for the month of August, 1848.[18]

When the San Patricio Battalion was disbanded, most of

the soldiers were discharged from the army. However, fifty of them, "men in whom the Supreme Government has confidence," remained in the military service—at least for a while. Three of these men were British subjects named August Geary, Henry Fitz-Henry, and Michael O'Sullivan.[19] As will be seen later, John Riley also continued in the Mexican military service. In mid-August a Mexico City newspaper reported that some of the unemployed former San Patricios were back on the streets "begging and insulting women who were not generous enough with their gifts." The editor advocated that the government should take action—either expel the men or give them something to do. At the end of that month twenty "Irishmen" were in Veracruz where they appealed to Governor Juan Soto for money to help them return home. The governor wrote to the Minister of Foreign Relations, who, after conferring with President Herrera, replied that federal funds had been released in Veracruz for "the embarcation of the discharged soldiers of the San Patricios and the rest of the Americans who have remain loitering in that place."[20]

After eight months in the guardhouse, two former San Patricio officers were deported. For his role in supporting the Paredes revolt, Captain James Humphrey was expelled; before leaving, he appealed to the British minister, who helped him secure $3,045 in back pay. Humphrey also took his two children aboard the brig *Providence,* which left Veracruz on April 26, 1849.[21] John Sutherland seems to have received no back pay; a letter from the Mexican minister of war explained the reason for his deportation:

In the conspiracy formed last year by Riley, in which the persons who compose the cabinet were to have been victims, Sutherland was one of the principal agents and promoters, being interpreter for the foreigners who were in the service of the Republic, whom he tried to win over, being also commissioned to distribute the money that the leaders of the revolt would receive. . . . The President received many secret warnings that

Santiago Tlatelolco Prison. Courtesy The Bancroft Library

Sutherland intended to assassinate the undersigned [Major General Mariano Arista].[22]

Although the Irishman John Riley was not deported, he was confined for a month and a half in the military prison at Santiago Tlatelolco. From that prison on August 20, 1848, the first anniversary of the battle of Churubusco, he sent the following letter in Spanish to Ewen Macintosh, the British consul general in Mexico:

As consul of my native country, I hope that you will please present to the Supreme Government [of Mexico] the enclosed request for my military discharge. I don't consider myself a traitor to the Mexican Government, and in view of the suffering endured for the Mexicans, which is well-known by everyone, I can scarcely bear to be treated in a manner which I do not deserve. They don't treat me according to the laws of the country, concerning which I call to your attention so that you might claim the protection which is owed me. If I were guilty, I would want to be punished; similarly, being innocent, I ask for my freedom.

At the same time, I must entrust you to collect in my name five hundred and thirty-three pesos given by me to the San Patricio Company, which debt the Government knows very well is legal and just.

With that in mind, I repeat that I am your attentive and trust-worthy servant.[23]

Riley, or someone writing for him, penned in Spanish on official sealed paper his two-page request for a discharge. He addressed it to *"Excelente Señor,"* by which he meant the president of the republic, who at that time was General José Joaquín de Herrera. In the letter Riley listed his services for Mexico:

In the month of April 1846, listening only to the advice of my conscience for the liberty of a people which had had war brought on them by the most unjust aggression, I separated myself from the North American forces. Since then I have served constantly under the Mexican flag. I participated in the action at Matamoros, where I formed a company of 48 Irishmen; in Monterrey I did the same with another company of Mexicans; I was in [the battle of] la Angostura [Buena Vista] with 89 Irishmen; with them I was at Cerro Gordo; at Churubusco I presented myself with 142, all gathered by me. Here I was injured and taken prisoner, and my treatment by the American government is well-known and notorious, having received 59 whip lashes and two brand marks on my face, which will always remind me of what I have suffered for the Mexicans.

Considering the suffering, and for the merit incurred on behalf of a nation to which I had resolved to give my life, I want only one concession. That favor is that I be given a discharge in order to retire from a career in which I will always be regarded with the mistrust which inspires all men of arms in a country torn apart by factions and civil wars, where individual guarantees promised in the constitution are scarcely observed in the courts, and where, although I have been charged as a supposed conspirator, I have not seen the conclusion [of the proceedings] after twenty-six days of intense suffering and delays beyond what the law provides. . . .[24]

Finally, on September 5, 1848, a military judge released John Riley from prison and ordered him to rejoin the Mexican Infantry. During the next four months he was stationed at Veracruz, then, early in 1849, he was transferred "on account of health" to Puebla de los Angeles, about a hundred miles east of Mexico City. John Perry, a New Englander who passed through Puebla at the end of February 1849, reported, "I saw several Americans here that probably deserted from the army. Here also I saw the famous Riley, who was cropped and branded by order of General Scott, at the time time fifty Irish deserters were hung at Mexico. . . . He wore his hair long, to hide the marks on his cheek and ear. He stands over six feet in height, is quite social, but a miserable, dissipated fellow."[25]

Major (brevet Colonel) John Riley served his last eighteen months in the Mexican army while based at Puebla. Situated in a fertile plateau at an elevation of 7,000 feet, the place had a mild climate and striking views in all directions because of the four imposing, snow-capped volcanoes—Orizaba, Popocatépetl, Iztaccihuatl, and Malinche—that overlooked the city. With a population of about 70,000 inhabitants in the mid-nineteenth century, Puebla was Mexico's second-largest city. Renowned for its stunning religious architecture, and sometimes called "the Rome of Mexico," the city boasted more than sixty churches and convents, some ornately decorated with colorful *azulejos* (glazed tiles) inside and on the exterior. The stately Cathedral of the Immaculate Conception, completed by the Spaniards two hundred years earlier, faced the central plaza where many of the city's residents gathered for the evening *serenata* (promenade) or to have refreshments under the arcades.[26] The military garrisons were at forts Guadalupe and Loreto, which were less than two miles from the plaza.

Brantz Mayer, an American diplomat who was in Mexico in the 1840s, called Puebla a "really beautiful city" and put some of his impressions in his journal, from which the following is excerpted:

There is an air of neatness and tidiness observable everywhere. The streets are broad, well paved with flat stones, and have a washed and cleanly look. The crowd of people is far less than in

TABLE 2.

Riley's Mexican Army Pay Record, April, 1846, through June, 1849
(in *pesos*, *reales*, at 8 per *peso*, and *granos*, at 12 per *real*)

	Jan.	Feb.	March	April	May	June	July	Aug.	Sept.	Oct.	Nov.	Dec.
1846												
Received				25.0	0	57.0	12.0	50.0	14.4	20.0	57.0	28.4
Due				32.0	57.0	0	45.0	7.0	42.6	37.0	0	28.4
1847												
Received	28.4	57.0	14.2	28.4	12.0	28.4	32.4[a]	24.0	81.0	0	0	0
Due	28.4	0	42.6	28.4	45.0	28.4	32.4	41.6	41.6	65.6	65.6	65.6
1848												
Received	0	0	0	0	0	65.6	122.3.9[b]	61.1.6	81.0	122.3	122.3	81.0
Due	65.6	65.6	65.6	65.6	65.6	0	0	61.1.6	41.6	0	0	41.6
1849												
Received	122.3	122.3	122.3	122.3	81.0	122.3						
Due	0	0	0	0	41.6	0						

Total Pay Received	$1919.2.3
Total Pay Earned	$3194.1.9
Balance Due	$1274.7.6

NOTE: The figures here are those sent by Riley to the British consul in Mexico City, July 14, 1849, GB/PRO FO 203, 94: 110–15. Discrepancies are due to that record.
[a] Riley became a captain in May, 1847.
[b] Riley became a major in July, 1848.

the Capital, and they are not so ragged and miserable. . . . Near the centre of the city is the great square. It is surrounded on two sides by edifices erected on arches through which the population circulates. . . . On the northern side is the Palace of the Governor . . . and directly in front of this is the Cathedral, equal perhaps in size to that of Mexico. . . .

This church is, in all its details and arrangements the most magnificent in the Republic. . . . The material is blue basalt; the stones are squared by the chisel; the joints neatly pointed; and the whole has the appearance of great solidity, being supported by massive buttresses, and terminated at the west by lofty towers filled with bells of sweet and varied tones. Between the towers is the main entrance, over which there is a mass of sculpture of Scripture history in stone and moulded work. . . .[27]

Although Puebla was obviously a pleasant duty station and Riley was a field-grade officer in the Mexican army, he seems not to have received adequate pay or subsistence. In July, 1849, he appealed to the Puebla office of a British firm for financial assistance. With the assurance that he had a valid claim against the Mexican government, the British merchants advanced forty dollars to "Colonel Riley of the Corps of San Patricio in the service of the Mexican Government, having represented himself to us as suffering the greatest want in consequence of the nonpayment to him of certain amounts due him by the Government."[28]

The Puebla merchants then forwarded a letter from Riley to the British consul in Mexico City, in which the Irishman said, "I have been starving on the streets of Puebla." With the letter, Riley sent two enclosures: one was a communique from the Minister of War denying him a leave of fifteen days so that he could go to Mexico City to present his financial claim for back pay. The other was an important and revealing (especially for this book) account of his pay record in the Mexican army from April 12, 1846, to July 14, 1849. As indicated in table 2, these ledger pages show how much pay he received and how much was due him for each of his thirty-nine months of service to July, 1848.[29]

In his covering letter, Riley asked the British consul to present his account to the Mexican government. According to his own reckoning, Riley's back pay totaled 1,275 pesos (U.S. $1,224). In a note at the bottom of the account, he said that the government also owed him 456 pesos for personally securing the enlistments of 152 men in the San Patricio companies—the agreement called for 3 pesos a head. Furthermore, he requested his discharge from military service, along with nine leagues of land in Sonora or Jalisco, as such a land bonus had been promised him.[30]

Apparently Riley did not receive his back pay, for a few weeks later he again wrote to the British consul for financial assistance. His letter follows:

Sir. Nessaty compls me to call on you once more for to do me the favour to lend me four hundred dollars to send to my son as I received a letter from him yesterday and tells me he is in a state of poverty and likewise his friends owing to the poor condation of Irland at the present time. Sir if you will remit me this money I pay you 50 dollars per month with interst to your satesfaction. I will give you the prommeseary [note] here or in Mexico [City] as my secuerity to pay you that sum with the interest if you will lend me the money. . . . Sir as you are awair of my claims against the Government I hope you will not refuse me this requist. And I shall ever remain your humbel servant.[31]

Riley's financial condition did not improve—indeed, it became worse according to his letter of November 9, 1849, addressed to "His Britannic Majesty's Minister to Mexico":

Your E[xcellent] Sir, nesicetty compels me to call upon you for protection as a British subject being the first time that I have troubled you E. sir since I have been in this country. The cause is this, on the night of the 6 inst my house was robbed of goods and money to the amount of $825. The robbers I detected and brought them before the Magistrate and he denied my justice without giveing me a hearing.

Pardon me sir, for thus molesting your E. But I have no other redress than to call upon the laws of my country for justice.

I will await the answer of your E. hopeing you will please to take notice of this as the robbers may leave this city. I retire with all respect & due submission.

Riley's claim to be a British subject when he had been an officer in the Mexican army for more than three years may seem strange. At the end of his letter, Riley added that he was a "Native of the County of Galway, Ireland, G.B." The minister's notation on the envelope was that Riley should send him details of the case.[32] No further records about Riley were found in the British diplomatic and consular correspondence.

The last record found for John Riley in Mexico was a notice of his discharge from the Mexican army in the summer of 1850. In mid-August the official government newspaper published a list of promotions and retirements for the months of June and July 1850. Among them was the following: "Retirement to Veracruz, with full pay for service disability, to permanent Major D[on] Juan Reley."[33] The disability may have been based on his wounds received in the battle of Churubusco; or was he later incapacitated? Note that he was to receive his full back pay, which must have been about eight hundred dollars. Why was he discharged to Veracruz, Mexico's principal port? This was doubtless so that he could board a ship that would take him to Havana, Jamaica, or some port where he could catch a transatlantic vessel and eventually return to Ireland. Although Veracruz newspapers for the summer of 1850 printed names of ships that arrived and departed, they failed to list names of passengers. Nor do the United States or British consular dispatches from that port in the summer of 1850 mention John Riley.

Many members of the Saint Patrick's Batallion left Mexico within two years after the war ended, but a few of the "Irish Volunteers" remained in their adopted land. Records about those who stayed are meager; indeed some are only legends or suggestive hints. James Kelley, originally from County Cork, seems to have settled in Taxco, where he, and later his son and grandson, worked as a silversmith. The grandson, who never married, died in the 1960s. In the 1950s there was a "Kelley's Silver Shop" in Taxco, but it is no longer there. Another veteran, Michael Bachiller, operated the "Farmacia San Patricio" in Pachuca or one of the mining towns north of Mexico City. In the late nineteenth century, it was said that the walls of the pharmacy were decorated with memorabilia relating to the San Patricios.[34]

A few of the San Patricio veterans who settled in Mexico tried to cover their tracks. One of these, a man who called himself "Baldwin," was interviewed thirty years after the Mexican War by a *Chicago Tribune* newspaper reporter who was passing through the small village of Tasquillo, about ninety miles north of the capital. Primed with tequila, Baldwin, who by then was "a shabby old man—an habitual drunkard," related how he had deserted from the American army in August, 1847, lured by thought of strong drink and "a good time with the pleasant *señoritas*" in nearby Mexico City. He said that after a few days of dissipation, he was then forced into the Mexican ranks and fought in a couple of the battles in the outskirts of Mexico City. After the war ended he found little favor in the metropolis, where the words "deserter and traitor" were often applied to him. He continued his story:

I soon left the capital, and now for more than thirty years I have been, more or less like Cain, a vagabond and a wanderer upon the earth. I am, in truth, a man who has no country, and I freely confess that I deserve to be in that condition. I was married many years ago, but my wife, a pretty Mexican woman to whom I was much attached, died long ago, leaving no children. I am now all alone in the cold world, without wife, child, or friend. My native country is closed against me forever. I'd be taken and executed if I dared to return there, because, even changed as I am, some old comrade would be sure to run across and recognize me. In spite of my long residence in Mexico, I never could warm up to it as a home. I banish care by drinking, when I have the money to pay for liquor, and by moving constantly from one place to another. Nobody knows my real name, and nobody shall—it will die with me.[35]

Baldwin said that he found little favor in Mexico because he was a Yankee and a heretic. "If I had been foreign born and a Catholic, I would have been better treated, perhaps, because some Irish and German Catholics who deserted from Taylor's division afterward settled down, married, and grew rich in this country."[36] Baldwin may have been right about those who settled in Mexico, but they have left few, if any, records.

CHAPTER 8

Why They Defected

DURING THE MEXICAN WAR newspaper editors and government officials in the United States questioned why so many
soldiers deserted from the army in Mexico and why so
many of them defected to the enemy. The answers were
not forthcoming then; nor have they been in the hundred
and forty years since. Because virtually none of the men
left written records—letters, diaries, journals—it is hard
to establish or verify their reasons for desertion. John Riley
did write some letters, which have been preserved, but in
none of them does he mention why he deserted. Sworn
testimony in their courts-martial trials by captured turncoats is about the only firsthand evidence, yet for various
reasons the prisoners may not have told the truth. Moreover, an individual's reasons for deserting probably cannot
be known with certainty because men may not fully understand what motivates them, and sometimes may deceive
themselves or others about their motives. Also, there may
not have been one reason but a combination of several that
stimulated some men to "go over the hill."

There were many possible reasons for desertion. Contemporary sources indicate that the following were principal ones: brutal military discipline, which seemed unjust
to some soldiers; hatred of military life or unsuitability for
it; sickness and disease, which may have disoriented some
men; harassment or discrimination against foreign-born
soldiers by their native-born officers; religious sentiments
and ideological beliefs; the lure of women; drunkenness,
which sometimes led to their capture by the enemy; and
enticements of cash prizes, rank promotions, and land
bonuses offered by Mexican military officers.

Of those deserters who left any records concerning their abandonment of the flag, only one or two hinted that it was because of their love for a woman. Certainly, a number of Yankee soldiers had romantic affairs with Mexican *señoritas,* and when their military units moved on or returned home, saying goodbye was difficult. In his memoirs of the war, Samuel Chamberlain told about a Mexican woman who begged him to leave his post, marry one of her attractive daughters, and settle on their ranch in Durango. Although Chamberlain, who was enamoured of the young damsel, did not consent to this arrangement, his army buddy did desert and departed with the elder daughter of the family.[1]

Dennis Conahan, an Irish-born infantry man who eventually joined a San Patricio unit, also linked romance with his desertion. When later apprehended and court-martialed by the Americans, Conahan testified that after the battle of Monterrey he was spending the night with a Mexican woman ". . . and was captured by the Rancheros and carried across the river."[2] He claimed that the Mexicans would not let him return to his outfit, but he may have wanted to stay near his sweetheart.

Being drunk was the excuse most frequently given by deserters, who then added that, while intoxicated, they had strayed away or been captured by Mexicans. Some seem to have survived, either as wanderers or prisoners of war; others claimed that they had immediately been pressed into Mexican service; and still others said that they had joined the Mexican army "to avoid starvation." Of seventy-two San Patricios who were captured by Americans and brought to trial near Mexico City, twenty-nine claimed drunkenness as their excuse for being absent without leave.

Defense statements offered by two defectors were typical examples of the plea of drunkenness. Private John Daly, who admitted that he was intoxicated while his company was on the march to Matamoros, said that he threw himself on the road and refused to go farther. His lieutenant then attempted to force him along and even dragged him a short distance, but finally he left him on the road. Daly said that he was soon surrounded and carried off by Mexican lancers. Private James Spears testified, "There were three of us out drinking at Monterrey on the opposite side of the river. We got a little high there and got into a little scuffle with the Mexican rancheros, and they took us off; four of them took three of us off . . . to Saltillo."[3]

Other captured soldiers said that they left the American service because of harsh treatment for violation of military regulations. Their testimony and other sources indicate that barbarous punishments were often inflicted on soldiers for even minor offenses. Besides demotion and forfeiture of pay, a culprit might be forced for five consecutive days to wear a crude sign and stand on a barrel every alternate two hours from reveille to sundown. An offender could have his hands tied behind his back, weights put on his feet, and be mounted on a wooden horse on the parade ground for one or more days, or he could be spread-eagled against a cannon or wagon wheel for hours under the hot sun. One man was placed in a hole in the ground with a rustic door over him and kept there thirty days, being given only three crackers and water daily—this was because he had run past the sentry without obeying prescribed military form.[4]

Private William Keech of Company F, Fourth Artillery, was one of the soldiers who apparently defected to the San Patricios because of harsh punishment in the United States Army. At his court-martial in September 1847, Keech's sergeant testified:

On the 26th of May on the march from Perote to Puebla in Mexico, the prisoner fell out of the company, and came up sometime after we had halted. He was punished for this that evening & he declared that no man in the army would have an opportunity of tying him up again. The next day he fell behind the company & I have never seen him since until today.[5]

One of the commonest forms of punishment during the Mexican War was called the buck and gag. A recipient of this discipline was tied up in a sitting position, then a gag was put in his mouth, and he was left there for as long as his company officer desired. DeWitt Loudon of the First Regiment of Ohio Infantry wrote the following description in his diary:

This process of bucking being something new [to me] I must describe it for the benefit of "posterity." The patient is seated—his latter end resting upon his parent earth. His heels are then drawn up until they come in contact with his posterious. His hands are then taken forward of his knees and tied with a handkerchief—a rope should be used when the patient shows violent symptoms. The job is then finished by running a stick under his knees and over his arms.[6]

In his published reminiscence of service in Mexico, Samuel Chamberlain related how he and six buddies were all bucked on the same pole. The seven soldiers had refused to carry out orders from "the meanest officer in the service" to flog a disabled veteran accused of illegally selling liquor to servicemen. To illustrate the account in his journal, Chamberlain painted a picture showing the seven dragoons bucked and gagged.[7]

Military authorities put soldiers accused of serious offenses under strong guard while they were awaiting a court-martial. Those charged with moderate offenses were confined together, and those accused of heinous crimes were put in small cells, some measuring only eight-feet long, three-feet wide, and three-feet high. If the court-martial judges found a prisoner guilty, he was sentenced to any or all of the following: imprisonment with hard labor; fifty lashes on the bare back; or being branded with various letters such as "HD" for habitual drunkard, "W" for worthlessness, or "D" for deserter. Some offenders were drummed out of the service to the tune of the "Rogue's March," but others received capital punishment. Indeed, one complaining soldier asserted that "More persons have been shot or hung for various crimes by the American officers in Mexico during the past two years than would be capitally executed in the whole United States in the ordinary course of justice during ten years."[8]

Irish-born Patrick Maloney was one of those soldiers who was court-martialed by the Americans and soon defected to the Mexican army. While based in Puebla, Mexico, as a private in the Fifth-Infantry Regiment, Maloney was accused and tried on June 28, 1847, for attacking his sergeant. Found guilty, he was ordered to forfeit six months' pay and carry a thirty-pound iron ball from reveille to retreat every day for a month. On August 6 he deserted and joined the San Patricios where he became a lieutenant.[9] Military punishments during the Mexican War seem cruel to us today, but they reflected the brutality and criminal justice of the period when whipping-posts, stocks, and pillory were familiar sights in many American towns.

Harsh treatment of soldiers not only affected their morale and led to desertions, but also caused some of them to attack tyrannical officers. In one case more than a hundred soldiers and several officers mutinied against Colonel Robert Treat Paine, whose North Carolina regiment was then encamped in northern Mexico. One of the lieutenants reported that the colonel was an unjust disciplinarian who frequently arrested staff officers for "the most trivial circumstances." He reportedly struck a private who did not entirely remove his cap but only touched it in a salute. He verbally abused and gave a saber blow to a soldier for having his hands in his pockets. He also ordered another soldier beaten with a heavy stick "without any provocation." The colonel's conduct led to a demonstration during which soldiers threw stones at him, his own men refused to obey his orders, and all except two of his company officers signed a petition calling on him to resign. The mutiny, which was finally quelled with the death of one soldier shot by the colonel, was evidence of the hostility generated by excessive discipline.[10]

In their letters and other wartime records, a number of American soldiers complained about the brutality of their officers. Private Lachlin McLachlin of the Sixth Infantry said that he deserted on account of being ill-treated by one of the lieutenants of his company, who abused him and threatened to take his life, even though he was soldiering as well as he knew how. Another soldier, William Tomlinson of the Tenth Infantry, who was then stationed near Matamoros, wrote to a friend: "We are under very strict discipline here. [Some of] our officers [are] very good men but the balance of them are very tyrannical and brutal toward the men . . . They strike the men with swords and abuse them in the most brutal manner possible for a human being to be treated. . . . I wish a man of good standing would inform them men in Washington of the brutality of these officers now in Mexico, but there is no use of a soldier writing to them as no notice would be taken of it. . . ."[11]

George Ballentine, a former British soldier who served in the United States Army in Mexico, reported in his *Autobiography:*

I have frequently seen foolish young officers violently strike and assault soldiers on the most slight provocations, while to tie them up by the wrist, as high as their hands would reach, with a gag in their mouths, was a common punishment for trivial offenses. In fact, such a bad state of feeling seemed to exist between men and officers throughout the service, that I was not surprised that it would lead to numerous desertions.[12]

Severe and unjust discipline, inflicted by overly-strict officers, led many soldiers to abandon their military unit, and, for some, their country. An anonymous soldier composed the following ditty, which soon spread throughout the army:

> *Come all Yankee soldiers, give an ear to my song,*
> *It is a short ditty, it will not keep you long;*
> *It is of no use to fret, on account of your luck.*
> *We can laugh, drink, and sign yet in spite of the buck.*
>
> *Sergeant, buck him and gag him, our officers cry,*
> *For each trifling offense which they happen to spy,*

Till with bucking and gagging of Dick, Pat and Bill,
Faith, the Mexican's ranks they have helped to fill.

The treatment they give us, all of us know,
Is bucking and gagging for whipping the foe;
They buck and gag us for malice or spite,
But they're glad to release us when going to fight.

A poor soldier's tied up in the sun or the rain,
With a gag in his mouth till he's tortured with pain;
Why I'm blessed if the eagle we wear on our flag,
In its claws shouldn't carry a buck and a gag.[13]

Illness was another problem that plagued the United States Army in Mexico and may have caused some soldiers to desert or to stray away from their outfit. Ignorance of the ways by which diseases were transmitted, coupled with unsanitary camp facilities, resulted in epidemics of dysentery, influenza, smallpox, measles, cholera, typhoid, and other ailments. When the army moved farther into tropical Mexico, malaria and the *vómito* (yellow fever) became serious health problems. Private William Keech said that on the march to Puebla he "was taken sick and fell behind the company and was taken up by 12 or 14 [Mexican] Lancers and carried into the country. I was abused and dragged round like a dog and brought to Mexico [City]."[14] It is not known how many soldiers deserted as a result of illness or of seeing their comrades sicken and die.

A related problem was the unavailability of religious solace or the sacrament of last rites for Catholic soldiers who were ill. Almost half the American enlisted men who soldiered in Mexico were foreign-born, and a large number of them were Roman Catholics. Irishmen totaled about one-fourth of the rank and file. In contrast, virtually all officers were native-born Americans, nearly all of them Protestants. Major General Winfield Scott's army of ten thousand men had only one chaplain, an Episcopalian, Dr. John McCarty. Taylor had no commissioned chaplain with him, but as will be seen later, two civilian Catholic priests did accompany his force for several months in 1846. By contrast, each of the twelve Mexican infantry regiments had two chaplains, and the nine cavalry regiments had one apiece.[15] The absence of Catholic chaplains in the United States Army gave priests in Mexico an unusual opportunity to influence Catholic soldiers who were in American forces. During the war those soldiers who wanted to attend mass or receive the sacraments were given permission to visit Mexican churches where some of the men talked with the multilingual clerics, many of whom had been born in Europe. The overwhelming majority of the priests in Mexico did not try to persuade the United States soldiers to desert, but a few of them were accused of such tactics.

In the northern city of Monterrey some Catholic priests definitely were involved with attempts to induce Americans to desert. One report said that priests there "succeeded in persuading some fifty more men to desert."[16] At his court-martial hearing for desertion, John A. Meyers, a German-born American soldier, stated that in Monterrey a Dutch priest took him to a Mexican colonel, who sent him on to join the Mexican army. Another German-born soldier, Auguste Morstadt, testified under oath that on November 3, 1846, when he crossed the river at Monterrey to get some corn, he was captured by a priest and two Mexican lancers who sent him to central Mexico where he was "compelled to take service with the Mexicans." After the battle of Monterrey an American captain wrote that "On the 5th [of November 1846] a priest was detected inducing our men to desert. . . . The reverend gentleman was placed in confinement and was shipped to Camargo. If he gets his deserts, he should be hung, spite of his sanctity."[17]

Farther south in the region of Jalapa, Veracruz, a parish curate was reported to be part of "an organization now existing among Mexicans, whose object is to corrupt the rank and file of the American army by money and promises of promotion in their army." Seven deserters were apprehended with the priest, Rafael Ignacio Cortez, who was charged with "seducing American soldiers to desert and harboring them in his house at Naolinco." A military commission brought the priest to trial, but after three days of hearings, the proceedings against him were suspended because of difficulty in proving that he was seducing soldiers to desert. Bolstered by Captain John Kenly, his court-appointed counsel, Father Cortez claimed that he was offering sacraments and sanctuary to men who sought religious succor.[18]

J. Jacob Oswandel, an American soldier who was stationed in Jalapa and Puebla for many months, later published his wartime notes in which he accused Mexican priests of soliciting deserters. He wrote:

In fact, there are a great many of our soldiers deserting; even at Jalapa city, the Mexicans held out inducements of great promise to our men, (and particularly to the Catholic portion), to desert and join their cause . . . but I am glad to say that they were only successful among the Catholic portion of our army who were persuaded by priests that it was wrong and sinful to fight against their church and religion.[19]

Father Eugene McNamara, an Irish priest, was named as a principal conspirator in an attempt to wean American soldiers from Scott's army as they made their way from Jalapa to Puebla. A native of Ireland, McNamara was an apostolic missionary who had been in Mexico for at least two years before the Mexican-American War. During those years he visited Alta California and proposed a scheme to settle ten thousand Irish immigrants in the Sacramento Valley of that state. Despite approval by the governor and other officials, however, this proposal was set aside because of the outbreak of war. In the spring of 1847, he was back in Mexico City where he plotted with the Mexican foreign minister on a scheme to entice Yankee soldiers to defect, "offering them lands in California if they desert," according to an American captain who investigated the charges. Although some American officers called for MacNamara's apprehension and execution, he seems to have eluded the net set for him and returned to Great Britain.[20]

Just before the end of the war, another Catholic priest was accused of seducing American soldiers to defect. Arrested with thirteen others near the town of Guadalupe, all fourteen men were charged with promoting desertion and were confined in the government palace. The *American Star* reported that "the Priest gave his name as Pasqual Pastrato, but the name which he signed to the passports given the American soldiers to take them to Querétaro was Antonio Triate."[21] The outcome of this case was not reported in any of the Mexico City newspapers; probably the charges were dropped.

Although official records show no Catholics serving as commissioned chaplains in the United States Army between 1781 and 1849,[22] two American priests did serve for a short time as civilian "acting chaplains" with General Taylor's forces in northern Mexico. In May, 1846, the secretary of war informed Taylor that President Polk had invited two Jesuits, Father John McElroy and Father Anthony Rey to serve in this capacity.

[They were told] to attend to the army under your command and to officiate as chaplains. Although the President cannot appoint them as chaplains, yet it is his wish that they be received in that character by you and your officers, be respected as such and be treated with kindness and courtesy—that they should be permitted to have intercourse with the soldiers of the Catholic Faith—to administer to them religious instruction, to perform divine service for such as may wish to attend whenever it can be done without interfering with their military duties, and to have free access to the sick and wounded in hospitals or elsewhere.[23]

The two priests arrived in Matamoros in July, 1846. Father Rey accompanied Taylor's troops to Monterrey and participated in that city's capture. Then, four months later, in January, 1847, while returning to Matamoros he was brutally killed by a party of Mexican guerrillas. Meanwhile, Father McElroy served at Matamoros for ten months, principally ministering to hospitalized soldiers. He attended some six hundred men, of whom he baptized eighty-five. In May, 1847, he returned to Washington on account of illness.[24] They were the only Catholic priests delegated by the government to serve wartime American troops at home bases or in Mexican territory from California to Mexico City.

Polk's designation of the two Jesuits as acting chaplains was also an attempt to correct Mexican misapprehension about American religious practices. The Secretary of War's letter, cited above, also stated:

The President has been informed that much pains have been taken to alarm the religious prejudices of the Mexicans against the U.S. . . . It is confidently believed that these gentlemen in their clerical capacity will be useful in removing the false impression of the Mexicans in relation to the U.S., and in inducing them to confide in the assurance you have already given that their religious institutions will be respected. . . .[25]

Acting on suggestions from Washington, the two American generals who commanded the largest occupation forces in Mexico issued proclamations to the Mexican people guaranteeing their religious institutions. Taylor's message read, in part:

Your religion, your altars and churches, the property of your churches and citizens, the emblems of your faith and its ministers, shall be protected and remain inviolate. Hundreds of our army and hundreds of thousands of our people are members of the Catholic Church. In every State, and in nearly every city and village of our Union, Catholic churches exist, and the priests perform their holy functions in peace and security, under the sacred guarantee of our constitution.[26]

Upon the fall of Veracruz, General Scott ostentatiously attended mass in the cathedral, then he ordered publication of his address to the Mexicans, in which he said:

We are the friends of the peaceful inhabitants of the country we occupy, and the friends of your holy religion, its hierarchy, and its priesthood. The same church is found in all parts of our country, crowded with devout Catholics, and respected by our government, laws and people.[27]

These proclamations also served to counteract claims in the United States that the war was a Protestant crusade to overthrow Catholicism in Mexico. One example of such a charge was an editorial in the New York *Express* that referred to American Catholics and said: "They cannot but see and feel that the conquests we are making are Protestant conquests . . . [American soldiers] are Protestant volunteers, and that the inevitable consequence of such invasion is the subjection of the Mexican religion to the Protestant religion of the invaders."[28]

The decade before the Mexican War was one of intense nativism and anti-Catholicism in the United States. Opposition was particularly virulent toward Irish immigrants, most of whom were Catholics and whose numbers increased by over one-half million between 1836 and 1846. As immigration of Catholics increased, so did harassment of the newcomers and hysteria of a vocal segment of old-timers. Editors of publications such as *Protestant Magazine* boasted that they would expose "those doctrines and practices of Roman Catholicism which are contrary to the interests of mankind." Similar vocal and written attacks led to anti-Irish and anti-Catholic riots in Boston, Philadelphia, and St. Louis, where mobs set fire to Catholic church property and private houses. Anti-foreign organizations sprang up. One was the Native American Association founded in Washington in 1837; another was the American Protective Association. At the same time American nativist political parties emerged: the Know Nothings and the American Republicans, for example.[29]

Nativist prejudice, which frequently was combined with contempt for Roman Catholicism, was widespread in the American army. Foreign-born soldiers were taunted— Irishmen were disparagingly called "micks" or "potato heads"—and discriminated against, often being passed

162   SHAMROCK AND SWORD

over for promotion. Although immigrants constituted the
bulk of recruits for the infantry, they generally were ex-
cluded from elite units such as dragoons and engineer
companies. While based in Mexico, a number of Protestant
officers and soldiers disparaged the Catholic Church there,
calling its rituals "absurd" and "flummery." Some Americans robbed chapels or churches, others stabled their
horses in religious buildings, and a few disrupted religious
processions.[30] These outrages, along with crimes perpe-
trated against Mexican civilians by unruly Yankee soldiers,
were cited by Mexican propagandists who tried to persuade foreign-born Catholic soldiers to desert from the invading army.

Assessing the importance of religion as a stimulus to
army desertion during the Mexican War is difficult. None
of the captured turncoats testified to defection because of
religion. Nevertheless, a number of those who wrote about
the war maintained that the San Patricio turncoats defected for religious reasons. For example, a biographer of
Mexican General José Joaquín Herrera said that the group
". . . was largely made up of Irish Catholics who had deserted during the Mexican War to fight for Mexico and
Catholicism." And an illustrated history of the Mexican
Army stated: "The Battalion of San Patricio formed a part
of the North American army that invaded Mexico in 1847.
These Irish forces professed the Catholic faith, and on
realizing that the great majority of the Mexican people was
deep-rooted in its religion, deserted from the Yankee
troops and prepared to defend the just cause of Mexico."[31]

Several Mexican generals considered religion a critical
issue, for they disseminated English-language handbills directed to Catholic soldiers, urging them to desert "from
the service of a heretic country." One of Santa Anna's leaflets, directed to Catholic Irish soldiers in the invading
army, proclaimed:

Irishmen! Listen to the words of your brothers, hear the ac-
cents of a Catholic people. . . . Is religion no longer the strongest

of human bonds? . . . . Can you fight by the side of those who put fire to your temples in Boston and Philadelphia? Did you witness such dreadful crimes and sacrileges without making a solemn vow to our Lord? If you are Catholic, the same as we, if you follow the doctrines of Our Saviour, why are you seen sword in hand murdering your brethren? Why are you antagonistic to those who defend their country and your own God?

Are Catholic Irishmen to be the destroyers of Catholic temples, the murderers of Catholic priests, and the founders of heretical rites in this pious nation? . . .

Come over to us; you will be received under the laws of that truly Christian hospitality and good faith which Irish guests are entitled to expect and obtain from a Catholic nation. . . .

May Mexicans and Irishmen, united by the sacred tie of religion and benevolence, form only one people![32]

Besides such appeals based on religion and ethnicity, the Mexican surrender leaflets also alleged foreign condemnation of the aggressive United States. Mexican General José Urrea issued several printed proclamations aimed at the invading troops. One of them read as follows:

Soldiers and volunteers of the American army! The war which you wage on Mexico is the most unjust and barbarous conceivable; civilized people detest it and they do not see you as defenders of the rights of an enlightened nation, but as simple instruments of a man [President Polk] without foresight, without reckoning, and to obtain undeserved acclaim, has not feared to compromise seriously the interests of a great people. . . .

Americans! Stop appearing before the world in such hateful and miserable character; no longer serve the whims of a man without good sense or virtue; abandon your ranks because they are not honorable ones; embrace the Mexican nation which, magnanimous and merciful, will forgive your offenses. Here you will find land to cultivate. . . .[33]

Undoubtedly, one of the most important factors for desertion was the Mexican government's promise of land bonuses for those who would abandon the American flag. Deserters understood that in order to be eligible for land grants they would have to join the Mexican army. In September, 1846, a Mexican presidential commission formulated regulations to encourage desertions from the American forces, especially by those men who had not been born in the United States. The five-man committee worked out the following points:

1. The number of acres of land and the terms that the government would grant to individuals who, not having been born in the United States, would abandon the North American lines and pass over to ours.
2. Designation of the vacant or uncultivated lands that the government could assign for this purpose, in any of the states.
3. Specification of financial means with which the government could assist the said individuals [after the war], be it for bringing their families here, if they have them, or to provide tools and other items necessary for cultivation.[34]

In addition to authorizing land grants and distributing propaganda leaflets aimed at enemy soldiers, the Mexican government employed several agents to persuade American soldiers to desert. An Englishman named Nicholas Sinnot worked in the north, where he promised large land grants to deserters. The amount of land to be granted varied with a man's rank, as shown in table 3.

Although none of the deserters who were later caught and court-martialed admitted that land bonuses played a part in their desertion, the offer was likely to have been a significant factor. In the mid-nineteenth century, when so many people made their living by agriculture or raising livestock, and when land ownership conferred social and economic status, the promise of land must have been very tempting to poor, immigrant soldiers. Undoubtedly, the Mexican scheme influenced the United States Congress to enact in February, 1847, a land bonus of 160 acres for any honorably discharged veteran who had served at least twelve months.[35]

Another Mexican inducement for desertion was the

TABLE 3.
Land Grants Promised to Deserters

Rank	Acres	Extra per Year of Service
Private	200	100
Corporal	300	150
Sergeant 2d Class	400	200
Sergeant 1st Class	500	250
2d Lieutenant	750	375
1st Lieutenant	1200	600
Captain	2000	1000
Major	3000	1500
Lt. Colonel	5000	2500
Colonel	8000	4000

SOURCE: Wilfred H. Callcott, *Church and State in Mexico, 1822–1857*, 198; Smith, *War with Mexico*, 1:507.

promise or expectation of military promotion. One American enlisted man, who was sent across the lines as a spy, returned to report that a Mexican commander had offered him a commission as a captain if he would raise a company of deserters who would switch sides. Records show that John Riley, Patrick Dalton, Patrick Maloney, and others deserted from the United States Army as privates and became officers in the Mexican army. Furthermore, defectors were assured by General Santa Anna that they could serve together in the Mexican army "under the immediate command of their own officers."[36] Defecting to the Mexican army was, for some soldiers, a way to gain promotion despite the great risk involved.

Some causes for desertion were those common to soldiers in wars, or even in peacetime. These would include dissatisfaction with the regimentation of military life, or resentment of harsh punishment inflicted for violation of the rules. The Mexican War had some additional factors, however, including: the unpopularity of the war; the religious issue, in which some men may have placed sectarian faith above patriotism; and economic enticements offered

by Mexicans. Although there are many reasons why some
soldiers may have deserted or defected to the Mexican
army, there would be a difficulty to be certain about the
actual motive that impelled a particular man to go over the
hill. In the absence of specific data, only an educated guess
is possible as to why almost two hundred soldiers left the
United States Army to join the Saint Patrick's Battalion.

CHAPTER 9

Myths and Realities

THE UNITED STATES – MEXICAN WAR had a tremendous impact on the history of both countries. North of the Rio Grande the war was divisive, exacerbated by the slavery issue and politics. President Polk and his cabinet had to contend with factious opposition in Congress where many members tried to direct foreign policy, sometimes through control of the war chest. Politics also played a crucial role in the military field because the Democratic executive and cabinet were reluctant to give top command to Whig generals, whom they may have viewed as opponents or possible political successors. Nevertheless, both Scott and Taylor became Whig presidential candidates after the war, the latter being elected in 1848 in large measure because he was a war hero.

War guilt haunted many Americans during and after the war. Some citizens regarded it as unjustified aggression against a weak neighbor; others envisioned a plot of slaveholders to extend their territory; and still others blamed commercial interests or New England merchants and shippers. The enormous financial outlay of the war, estimated at more than seventy-five million dollars, was another negative factor that had an impact long after the fighting stopped. So did the cost in blood and lives; more than 5,100 Americans were killed in battle, and 10,000 soldiers died from sickness. A nineteenth-century historian added: "This was not all, however. Many on their way to join their regiments in Mexico fell sick and died, without having appeared on the rolls of the actual force. Many died after being mustered out of service. It may therefore be said with truth that the loss of life was not less than 25,000 men. . . ."[1]

Some unpleasant aspects of the war were offset in the United States by the exhilarating effect of triumphs and heroism. This was the nation's first foreign war fought almost entirely on foreign soil; it involved the first large-scale amphibious landing of troops; it provided the first experience for occupying a foreign capital; it was the first time American military government was established for an alien civilian population; it was the first war to be extensively covered by war correspondents; and the two-year conflict was marked by a string of military victories. One long-range effect was that the brilliant wartime performance of West Pointers, mostly junior officers, stimulated congressional support of the professional training of army officers at the Military Academy at West Point. Before the war, there had been proposals to abolish the Academy.

A number of military officers in the Mexican War were destined to wield power and gain renown in later years. Four of them became presidents: Zachary Taylor, Franklin Pierce, Ulysses Grant of the United States, and Jefferson Davis of the Confederacy. Two were presidential candidates, but not elected: Winfield Scott and John Fremont. The war also proved to be a training ground for leaders on both sides in the American Civil War when many army commanders had already served in Mexico. Twenty-six Union generals and seventeen Confederate generals had been junior officers in the Mexican War.[2]

The Mexican War made the United States a continental power stretching from the Atlantic to the Pacific. This expansion engendered a two-ocean navy as well as a large military establishment to patrol the vast western territories. When the Treaty of Guadalupe Hidalgo transferred to the United States more than half a million square miles of former Mexican land, an area larger than France, Spain, and Italy combined, it stimulated a western land rush. The discovery of rich gold and silver deposits in California and Nevada was an unexpected bonanza that greatly contributed to the national economy and to the westward movement. Although this new territory provided room for expansion and fine ports on the Pacific coast, it also upset the balance between free and slave states, which helped bring on the catastrophe of the Civil War.

During the Mexican War a great number of people of both belligerent nations were exposed to each other's culture. Thousands of American soldiers and sailors stationed or camped at bases from Alta California to southern Mexico experienced life in an exotic climate with strange foods and alien customs. The Mexicans—with whom they billeted, or purchased food or horses, or had other dealings—had an opportunity to observe some aspects of American life and manners. This interchange diminished the narrow parochialism of some people, but it probably reinforced the stereotypes and prejudices of others. Yet, because the two nations were at war, there was a natural hostility that was hard to overcome.

For Mexico the war was a series of tragedies. Besides the thousands of military and civilian deaths directly attributable to battles, the war left tens of thousands of orphans, widows, and cripples. Artillery shelling and small arms gunfire caused extensive destruction to buildings in various cities and ports, and the land war and naval blockade severely affected the economy. Internal and external trade was disrupted for two years; that, along with the massive conscription of peasants, caused a steep decline in agricultural production. The small industrial sector was in similar disarray. The war also ruined political careers and destroyed many citizens' faith in democracy. Indeed, the political instability during and immediately after the war led to a new despotic regime headed by none other than General Santa Anna, who styled himself His Most Serene Highness.

Although they may blame the United States for provoking the war, many Mexican historians recognize that the threat could have been parried better if there had been less financial irresponsibility and political chaos in Mexico at this time. A modern Mexican writer summarized some of the problems:

> While the United States came together to win the war, and there was unity of command in each campaign, Mexico disintegrated into anarchy: President Paredes was imprisoned; the form of government and the Constitution were changed; there were seven presidents; six generals successively directed the campaign against Taylor; insurrections continued; and only seven of the nineteen states which then formed the Mexican federation contributed men, arms, and money to the national defense.[3]

Frequent changes in the Mexican cabinet were another indication of political instability. For example, ten different men served as minister of foreign relations during the two war years.[4]

Probably the most lasting effect of the war on Mexicans was psychological. A tragic loss of soldiers and battles, the humiliation of having their capital and much of their country occupied by enemy troops, and the ignominy of a peace treaty that alienated half of the national territory (counting Texas) was a blow. It shattered a sense of national honor and dignity, and it engendered a deep feeling of resentment towards Yankees. In the first years after the war, hundreds of Americans, crossing Mexico on their way to the goldfields of California, encountered a war-born hostility against *gringos*. A. C. Ferris recalled that his group of mounted men was threatened in Jalapa by a mob, but the well-armed Americans escaped with a wild ride out of town. He added: "Through the villages of the country parts we were received by the *señoras* and *señoritas* with kindness, but by the males with frowns and threats, and with the significant gesture of a finger drawn across the throat. In no place were we safe from attack except in groups which commanded safety and respect. To them in their ignorance we were still Yankees and *soldados* [soldiers]."[5]

Unlike their neighbors to the north, the Mexicans have

not forgotten the war of 1846–48, which they often call the "American Intervention." Nor have they forgotten the lost territory; some still talk or dream about Texas and their eventual reconquest of "the Left Bank," and others refer to California as "Occupied Mexico." In 1985, two Mexican historians concluded: "The trauma of the Mexican–U.S. War of the last century . . . is still very much alive. However, from the point of view of the United States, this same historical event is as dead and irrelevant to the present as the French and Indian war of the mid-eighteenth century."[6]

Historians of the two countries have quite different views about the war. In her part of a recently published book the prominent Mexican historian, Josefina Z. Vásquez, wrote, "The terms of the Treaty of Guadalupe Hidalgo are among the harshest imposed by a winner upon a loser in the history of the world."[7] But a number of respected American historians have judged the treaty terms as mild, considering the United States military forces had severely trounced and decimated the Mexican army, occupied the capital and great parts of Mexico, and could have annexed the entire country, or most of it. Historian Justin Smith claimed, "But we gave back much of what we took, and paid for the rest more than it was worth to the Mexicans." Nor did the triumphant Yankees loot Aztec sculpture, colonial paintings, or other booty to embellish their museums, public squares, or homes. Noting that the Americans tempered victory with humanity, Cadmus Wilcox added: "No cities were sacked, no domain plundered. Scott's act in halting his troops after the battle of Churubusco at the gates of the City of Mexico, and, instead of imposing humiliating terms, inviting the Mexicans to listen to propositions of peace, is without parallel in military annals."[8]

Unquestionably, the Mexican War was a significant watershed in relations between the neighboring republics, but what about the importance of the Saint Patrick's Battalion? How has it fared in written history and folklore of the two countries? Books and legends in both countries perpetuate myths and a great deal of misinformation about the San Patricios. Some errors are obviously due to inaccessability of official records, but some stories may have been created by people with definite prejudices. To better understand the story of the "Irish Volunteers" in Mexico, and to judge their significance, one needs to look beyond the mere fact of their existence and their participation in some of the major battles of the Mexican War.

First, the Saint Patrick's Battalion was unique; it was unlike other foreign legions. It can not be compared to the Royal Irlandais, an Irish brigade that fought with the French at the battle of Malplaquet in 1709; nor to the Irish regiments of Irlanda, Waterford, and Ultonia that formed a part of the Spanish Army in the eighteenth century; nor to the Irish battalion formed in 1803 that fought with Napoleon Bonaparte; nor to the Irish Legion of several thousand men that aided Simón Bolívar in his liberation of South America.[9] Those contingents were composed of Irish volunteers, but the men were not deserters from the enemy army, as were most of the San Patricios.

Some authors who have written on the subject said that the San Patricios deserted en masse—the entire battalion at once, but it did not happen that way. Nor did they all desert early in the war on the Rio Grande, as suggested by others. In contradiction to a biography of General Scott, which claimed that "the majority of them had come from Taylor's Army of the North,"[10] apparently the majority came from Scott's Army of the South. Of the seventy-two San Patricios who were captured and court-martialed, only thirty were from Taylor's forces; the rest had been in Scott's expeditionary army.

Because Scott's invasion began a year later than Taylor's incursion into Mexican territory, many desertion dates were surprisingly late in the war, as can be seen in table 4. All those between March and August, 1847, were from Scott's army. What is astonishing is that thirty-two of the men deserted near Mexico City only a few weeks before they were captured by the Americans; thus, their time in a

TABLE 4.
Desertion Dates of Captured San Patricios

Date	Number of Desertions
Nov. 1845	1
Apr. 1846	5
Oct. 1846	4
Nov. 1846	15
Dec. 1846	1
Jan. 1847	1
Feb. 1847	3
Mar. 1847	7
Apr. 1847	1
May 1847	2
Jun. 1847	8
Jul. 1847	19
Aug. 1847	5

SOURCES: court-martial records, USNA/RG 153, EE 525 and EE 531; U.S. Army service in USNA/RG 94, Registers of Enlistments, 1840–48.

San Patricio unit was extremely short. The average length of service that the seventy-two men spent in the United States Army before deserting was eleven months and twenty-eight days.[11]

Although army desertion during the Mexican War was known to be high, it comes as a surprise to find that the rate was the highest of any American foreign war and double that of the Vietnam War. Apparently there has been no previously published comprehensive comparison, so the figures in table 5 will interest military historians as well as general readers.

The extent of desertion by Irish-American soldiers in the Mexican War has been exaggerated. Because some "sons of the Green Isle" defected, several writers about that war have incorrectly imputed a general lack of patriotism on the part of Irish soldiers. True, some Irish-Americans deserted, as did soldiers of other ethnic or national backgrounds, but the overwhelming majority remained loyal to

TABLE 5.
U.S. Army Desertion Rates in Foreign Wars

Engagement	%
U.S.-Mexican War	8.3
Spanish-American War	1.6
World War I	1.3
World War II	5.3
Korean War	1.9
Vietnam War	4.1

SOURCES: Mexican War figures in Francis B. Heitman, *Historical Register and Dictionary of the United States Army*, 2:282; Spanish-American War in U.S. War Dept., *Annual Reports, 1914*, 1:276; World War I in typescript prepared by Major H. K. Loughry, et al, "Present Desertion Rates," Individual General Staff Memoranda, The Army War College, 1926; others in U.S. Bureau of the Census, *Statistical Abstract of the United States, 1974*, 317.

their adopted country. Army records for the year 1845 verify the enlistment or re-enlistment of 2,135 natives of Ireland; to this figure must be added those Irish-born soldiers whose terms had not expired. Then, during the two years of the Mexican War, an additional 2,664 Irish-born men joined the regular army, and 1,012 enlisted for a shorter period. They not only enlisted individually, but there were seventeen Irish companies including the Emmett Guards from Albany, the Jasper Greens of Savannah, the Mobile Volunteers of Alabama, and the Pittsburgh Hibernia Greens.[12] Thus, the Irish-born renegades who crossed over to the Mexican lines were a minute percentage of the total number of Irishmen who served in the American army.

The Irish composition of the Saint Patrick's Battalion has likewise been overstated in many accounts. For example, Mexican historian José María Roa Bárcena in his *Recuerdos* (*Recollections*) said that "all the San Patricio companies were Irish"; the *Reminiscences* of an American veteran, Amasa Clark, described the men as "a band of renegade Irishmen who had deserted from the American ranks"; and the *Know-Nothing Almanac*, for 1856, said that the battalion was "composed of Irishmen, deserters from

our ranks." Actually, only about two-fifths of the San Patricios were from Ireland, and most others had been born
in the United States, Great Britain, or on the European
continent. The roster in the Appendix at the end of this
book gives the birthplace of more than one hundred of the
men; that data is summarized in table 6.

The story of the Saint Patrick's Battalion highlights the
little-known fact that the Mexican War marked the apex
for the number of executions of American army deserters
in any foreign war. Detailed comparative statistics on desertion and executions seem not to have been previously
published by the United States government, perhaps because the subject was negative and it reflected badly on
military practices. Nevertheless, scattered references give
the scope, if not precise details. Desertion was widespread
during the long Revolutionary War; one author found
that forty soldiers were punished with death for the crime.
During the War of 1812 six soldiers were executed for mutiny and one for desertion.[13] The exact number of soldiers
executed for desertion during the Mexican War is unknown, but it was at least fifty-four. Curiously, the official
Adjutant General's report about military forces and casu-

TABLE 6.
Birthplace of 103 San Patricios

Country	No.	%
Ireland	40	39
United States	22	21
German states	14	13
Scotland	7	7
Mexico	7	7
England	4	4
Great Britain	3	3
Canada	2	2
France	1	1
Italy	1	1
Spanish Florida	1	1
Poland	1	1

alties during that war, printed by Congress one and one-half years after the close of the war, concluded that thirty-four men were "executed by sentence of a court-martial." That figure is erroneous, and probably should be doubled, since it includes executions for all capital offences including desertion, murder, mutiny, and rape. We know that fifty San Patricios were hanged for desertion, and there were other soldiers who received the death penalty for the same offence. A quick perusal of Army Enlistment Records revealed the following names of men who were court-martialed and executed for desertion: Dennis Sullivan, shot by a firing squad in Mexico City on January 10, 1848, and John Collins, James Hale, and Samuel Sanford, who were executed at Camargo, Mexico, on March 13, 1848.[14]

Army executions for desertion and other crimes were very high during the Civil War, but they decreased thereafter. There were no executions in the course of the brief Spanish-American War; indeed, the Fifth Army Corps, numbering twenty thousand men, recorded not a single court-martial. Among twenty-eight soldiers who were executed for capital crimes during World War I, not one was for desertion. Private Edward Slovik was the only man executed for desertion in World War II. Vietnam War desertions were high, but apparently there were no executions for that offense. Moreover, on September 16, 1975, President Gerald Ford announced an amnesty and clemency program for draft evaders and deserters.[15] In retrospect, the Mexican War hangings represented a macabre peak.

Although John Riley, the Irish-born founder of the San Patricios, escaped the hangman's noose, his postwar career has received some imaginative treatment by historians and writers. His role in the aborted military coup d'etat of July, 1848, has been generally ignored, as has his subsequent two years of military duty in Veracruz and Puebla, where he served with the permanent rank of major. Although Riley was honorably discharged in the summer of 1850, and undoubtedly left Mexico for Ireland, the principal

Mexican biographical dictionary stated that he remained in Mexico and died there. Sam Chamberlain maintained that after the war the Irishman married a wealthy Mexican *señora* and lived in his adopted country, respected by the Mexicans. On the other hand, a story in *Smithsonian* said that Riley "was asked to leave the country," and an article in *The Americas* said that he was expelled from Mexico in the postwar era.[16]

Virtually every article about the Saint Patrick's Battalion has repeated the false story that after the war Riley returned to the United States where he was the plaintiff in a lawsuit against the United States government. The first mention of this court action appears to have been in Jacob Oswandel's *Notes of the Mexican War*, published in 1885:

> Riley . . . returned to the United States and entered suit in the United States District Court of Cincinnati, Ohio, for $50,000 damages, for flogging and branding him in Mexico. After a week's trial, the jury returned a verdict of not guilty, and put the cost of the suit on Col. Riley. So ended one of the most singular suits that has ever been brought before any court in the United States, or in the world, to obtain damages for deserting his country's flag and going over to the enemy to fight against his country.[17]

The story of Riley's lawsuit is a complete fabrication. No such legal action is listed in the printed court records, and staff members at the Federal Records Center in Chicago, which houses the original Cincinnati District Court records of that era, were unable to find any documentary evidence of such a suit by Riley or other defectors. Furthermore, the lawsuit was supposed to have been instigated in 1849, but during that entire year John Riley was on duty in the Mexican army.

Strong circumstantial evidence suggests that Riley left Mexico in the summer of 1850, to return to Erin, but whether he ever arrived in his homeland is not known. During that season there was a terrible cholera epidemic in Veracruz and other parts of Mexico, and there were sev-

Plaque Honoring San Patricio Battalion

eral shipwrecks in the Atlantic Ocean. A check of post-1850 records in Ireland failed to turn up any John Riley of County Galway. His name does not appear in any of the following: *Index to Prerogative Inventories, 1810–1860; Ireland Court Records; Surname Index of the Registry of Deeds, 1855–1859;* and the *Surname Index to Griffith's Valuation Lists, 1848–1864* (names of tenants, lessees, and owners of property). The variant name of John Reilly, "lessor of a house," is listed in Griffith's 1855 valuation of the town of Clifden. However, there is no evidence that this man was the San Patricio veteran. At the Registrar General's Office in the Dublin Custom House, one may request a copy of civil records of marriages, births, and deaths after 1864, but one needs the date of the event, and there is no master index by name. John Riley seems to have disappeared into the same historical mists of Ireland out of which he first emerged. It would be interesting to know what happened to Riley after he was discharged from the Mexican army, but that is beyond the scope of this book, which essentially is a history of the Saint Patrick's Battalion.

More than a hundred years after the Mexican–American War, a Mexican sculptor etched Riley's name, along with those of seventy other American deserters, on a memorial commemorating the San Patricios. Sculptor Lorenzo Rafael, son of Patricia Cox who wrote a novel about the San Patricios, designed the marble plaque, which was erected on a wall facing the San Jacinto plaza in Mexico City's suburb of San Angel. (Since 1931 the official name of this charming town has been Villa Obregón, but the old name persists.) An escutcheon at the top of the plaque depicts an Irish Celtic cross protected by the outstretched wings of the Mexican Aztec eagle. Below that, the Spanish inscription reads (in translation): IN MEMORY OF THE IRISH SOLDIERS OF THE HEROIC SAN PATRICIO BATTALION, MARTYRS WHO GAVE THEIR LIVES FOR THE CAUSE OF MEXICO DURING THE UNJUST AMERICAN INVASION OF 1847. Names of the seventy-one soldiers are listed in three columns, and at the bottom appears the phrase: With the Gratitude of Mexico,

112 Years after Their Sacrifice.[18] It is a splendid piece of stone and a touching sentiment, but the plaque gives an erroneous impression, and it contains numerous errors.

Belying the inscription, fewer than half of the men listed were Irish. Of the seventy-one men, whose names correspond to those who were court-martialed by the Americans in San Angel and Tacubaya, only twenty-nine had been born in Ireland. Of the rest, nineteen were born in the United States, thirteen were natives of German states, eight were non-Irish British subjects, and there was one each from France and Sicily. Of the Irish-born San Patricios mentioned on the plaque, nineteen were hanged. Nearly a third of the soldiers listed on the plaque were not martyrs—that is, they did not die for Mexico during the war of 1846–48. All of them were deserters from the United States Army, and all except two subsequently joined the San Patricio units of the Mexican army to fight against the Yankees. But after their capture by American forces in August 1847, and their subsequent court-martial for desertion, only fifty of the men were hanged; the rest had their death sentences remitted, as was pointed out in Chapter Five. Two of the men never joined the San Patricios: one was Lewis Pieper (or Prefier), declared at his court-martial to be insane, and the other was Abraham Fitzpatrick, whose record of service in the Mexican War deserves further elucidation.

Born in King's County, Ireland, in 1818, Fitzpatrick emigrated with his parents, who settled in upstate New York. As a young man he enlisted in the United States Army, and, by the beginning of the Mexican War, he was a sergeant in the Eighth Infantry Regiment. After fighting in the battles of Palo Alto, Resaca de la Palma, and Monterrey, he deserted or disappeared from his unit in October, 1846. He later testified that, after a drinking spree near Monterrey, he was captured by Mexican lancers who sent him south. By June, of 1847, he was in Mexico City, where John Riley urged him to join the Foreign Legion, but he refused, even after he was offered a commission as an offi-

San Patricio Commemorative Medal (reverse)

cer. On August 28, during the two-week armistice, Fitz-patrick turned himself in to American authorities. Court-martialed at Tacubaya, he was sentenced to be shot to death, but in consideration of his prior good conduct and of hav-ing surrendered himself, his sentence was remitted. Re-duced to the rank of private, he rejoined his American outfit on September 7, 1847, and the very next day fought in the battle of Molino del Rey where he received severe wounds, which led to his death the following month.[19] Thus, Fitzpatrick was an American martyr, not a Mexican

182 SHAMROCK AND SWORD

one! Virtually every writer about the San Patricios has erroneously included the names of Fitzpatrick and Pieper in the unit roster.

Having said that some of the names on the commemorative stone should not be there, an appropriate suggestion is that other names should be engraved on any memorial to the Saint Patrick's Battalion. These names would include Lieutenant Camillo Manzano and twenty-one other San Patricios who were killed at the battle of Buena Vista (Angostura), plus the thirty-five San Patricios who died in action at Churubusco. Names of those fifty-seven San Patricios who lost their lives while fighting for Mexico are not on the plaque in San Angel, nor on any other monument in Mexico. Instead, their names are buried in the Mexican National Defense archives, where many historians are unable to retrieve them.

Twice a year since 1959, when the memorial plaque was unveiled in San Angel, the plaza of San Jacinto has been the scene of colorful ceremonies honoring the San Patricios. On the September 12 anniversary of the hangings and on every Saint Patrick's Day, a crowd has convened in the small triangular park that has been especially decorated with flowers and bedecked with the tricolors of Mexico and Ireland. Regular guests have included civic officials, Mexican military units, Irish diplomatic personnel, members of the Irish Society of Mexico, and students from the nearby public elementary school named "*Batallón de San Patricio*" (San Patricio Battalion).[20]

The San Patricio commemorative events of September 12, 1983, were typical. First, there was a special mass at the parish church of San Jacinto, adjacent to the plaza. Then, outside, school children placed floral wreaths on the paving stones under the plaque; the Mexico City Symphonic Band played the national anthems of Mexico and Eire; units of the Mexican armed forces rendered military honors; Irish Ambassador Tadgh O'Sullivan paid tribute to those who died for their adopted country; a Villa Obregón (San Angel) official eulogized the fallen warriors, saying that twenty Irishmen had been executed on that spot [actually, there were only sixteen]; Stephanie Counahan de Rafael, wife of the sculptor of the plaque, recited the seventy-one names on the memorial stone; and after each name, the crowd shouted, *"Murió por la patria"* (He died for the nation).[21]

Lorenzo Rafael, father of the sculptor of the marble plaque, also designed a commemorative medal honoring the San Patricios. Pictured on the face of the medal are the Mexican eagle, a Celtic cross, and the legend *Al Heróico Batallón de San Patricio, 1847* (To the Heroic Battalion of San Patricio, 1847). The reverse shows a military officer in front of the Churubusco convent. His right hand wields a raised sword, and his left hand points to a cannon. In 1960 the government mint issued five thousand of the silver medals, which measured about one and one-half inches in diameter. Later that year Casa Barón, a numismatic firm, provided gold, silver, and bronze editions of the San Patricio medals.[22]

With medals, memorial plaques, annual ceremonies, and public schools honoring them, clearly the San Patricios are treated as heroes in Mexico. The story of their colorful outfit, often exaggerated, is well-known there. Not only are there frequent newspaper articles about the "Irish Volunteers," but they also appear in official histories as well as in popular literature. The Secretariat of Education even co-published a series of substantial booklets on Mexican history, illustrated in comic-book form, one of which highlights the exploits and martyrdom of the San Patricios. Pages fifty-nine to sixty-one of this widely-distributed booklet related how the entire battalion of Irish San Patricios deserted from the United States Army at Puebla, and two days later joined the Mexican army in Mexico City, just in time to fight the battle of Churubusco.[23] Of course, there never was such a battalion in the American army; nevertheless, that erroneous version of the origin of the San Patricios has become legendary in Mexico.

Unfortunately, the printed brochure that accompanied

the San Patricio medals issued in 1960 perpetuated several
myths about the origin of the group. A translation of part
of the leaflet says: "The San Patricio Battalion was com-
posed of Irish Catholics who fled Protestant persecution in
Ireland and settled in San Patricio, Texas. . . . After the
Mexican War began, the Irishmen were forced by Stephen
Austin to take arms against Mexico. When the invading
troops came into contact with the Mexicans at the city of
Matamoros, the San Patricio Battalion went over to the
Mexican Army." This story, which has been repeated in
various books and newspaper accounts, is completely false.
Furthermore, Stephen Austin died in 1836, a decade be-
fore the Mexican War began.[24] Yet, through the distribution of these handsome medals, the story of the San Patricio Battalion has been diffused in Mexico.

North of the Rio Grande, by contrast, the story of the
Saint Patrick's Battalion is hardly known. Occasionally
there is a passing reference, often erroneous, in United
States history books. Surprisingly, there is not even a mention of it in some college textbooks of Mexican history. As
for the individual San Patricios—at least those who deserted from the United States Army—they have always
been regarded by North Americans as traitors. Yankee
writers invariably have maintained that those defectors
who were caught, court-martialed, and punished deserved
their fate. From most any viewpoint the story of the San
Patricios is a tragedy. It is not, as it has often been depicted
in Mexico, a romantic tale of gallant Catholic Irishmen
whose conscience and religious persuasion obliged them to
switch allegiance and uniforms in the midst of the Mexican
War. Rather, as detailed in these pages, it is a woeful story
of naive and bewildered young men from varied national
and religious backgrounds, many of whom were tempted
by alcohol and opportunism. There should also be a note
that all of the San Patricio defectors had been privates in
the United States Army, where several of them had been
troublemakers. For example, George Jackson, Patrick Maloney, Andrew Nolan, and Richard Parker deserted from

different American military camps, yet each defected after escaping from the guardhouse where he had been confined and under sentence. Lachlin McLachlin, whose sergeant said, "he was always in the guardhouse," had previously been charged with mutiny, among other things. John Sheehan first deserted near Reynosa, but after his apprehension, he was permitted to rejoin his outfit. Nevertheless, he deserted again at Monterrey and defected to the Mexican army.[25] Clearly, those San Patricios who were deserters seem not to have realized the fatal step they were taking when they donned the Mexican uniform.

The tale of the Saint Patrick's Battalion is a colorful episode in the history of relations between the United States and Mexico. It is also a good story with strong characters who portray various aspects of human behavior. In addition, many points of interest transcend the narrative itself and relate to matters of concern today: ethnic minorities in Anglo-American society, "unpopular" wars, religious or ideological objections to war, wartime versus peacetime desertion, amnesty and pardon, the role of military chaplains, and abuse of drugs such as alcohol. Truly, this saga has elements of universality and timelessness.

Appendix: Roster of Known San Patricios

An asterisk indicates San Patricio commissioned officers; a cross designates those men hanged in September, 1847.

Name	U.S. Army Unit	Age	Enlistment Date	Birthplace	Desertion Date
Akles, Hezekiah W.	Co. H, 3d Art.	28	May 4, 1846	Winchester, Va.	March 21, 1847
Aloif, C.					
*Alvarez, Ignacio				Mexico	
†Antison, Patrick	Co. E, 4th Inf.	24	Dec. 25, 1845	Londonderry, Ireland	Nov. 14, 1846
†Appleby, John	Co. D, 2d Art.	25	July 20, 1846	Donegal, Ireland	June 24, 1847
*Arce, C. D. N.					
*Bachelor, Ramón B.				Mexico	
*Bachiller, Michael					
Bartley, John	Co. H, 3d Art.	23	Sept. 8, 1846	New York, N.Y.	March 21, 1847
†Benedick, John	Co. F, 6th Inf.	23	Nov. 1846	Hamburg, Germany	June 19, 1847
Bingham, George					
Bowers, John	Co. H, 3d Art.	22	Aug. 21, 1846	England	March 21, 1847
Brooke, John	Co. F, 6th Inf.	[16]	Jan. 13, 1847	Somerset, Pa.	July 20, 1847
Burke, Richard				Ireland	
Burns, Michael	Co. A, 6th Inf.	28	Sept. 23, 1846	Wicklow, Ireland	Apr. 11, 1847
*Calderón, José M.				Mexico	
†Casey, Patrick	Co. F, 4th Inf.	21	Nov. 4, 1846	New York, N.Y.	Aug. 3, 1847
Cassady, Thomas	Co. I, 8th Inf.	25	Sept. 4, 1846	Dundalk, Ireland	July 15, 1847
†Cavanaugh, John	Co. E, 8th Inf.	23	Nov. 26, 1845	Dublin, Ireland	Oct. 19, 1846
Chambers, John				England	
†Conahan, Dennis	Co. I, 7th Inf.	27	Jan. 26, 1845	Londonderry, Ireland	Oct. 4, 1846
†Cuttle, John	Co. B, 2d Inf.	23	Apr. 25, 1846	Ireland	Nov. 29, 1846
*†Dalton, Patrick	Co. B, 2d Inf.	21	Aug. 2, 1845	Co. Mayo, Ireland	Oct. 23, 1846

Name	Company	Enlisted	Age	Place of Birth	Date
†Dalwig, George	Co. K, 2d Art.	Oct. 4, 1844	22	Bremen, Germany	July 18, 1847
Daly, John	Co. F, Mtd. Rif.	July 16, 1846	27	Co. Cork, Ireland	Dec. 10, 1846
†Delaney, Kerr	Co. D, 4th Inf.	Aug. 13, 1845	23	Tipperary, Ireland	Nov. 14, 1846
Donaley, Thomas				Ireland	
*Doyle, Matthew					
*Duhan, Roger	Co. F, 6th Inf.	Nov. 24, 1846	21	Roscommon, Ireland	Jan. 23, 1847
Eglen, William					
Ellis, Edward	Co. I, 2d Drag.	[not sworn in]			June 17, 1847
*Fany, Carlos					
Fitz-Henry, Henry				Great Britain	
Fischer, William	Co. D, 1st Art.	Oct. 29, 1846	26	Machias, Maine	Nov. 1, 1847
†Fogal, Frederick K.	Co. K, 2d Drag.	May 13, 1846	24	Germany	July 10, 1847
†Frantius, Marquis T.	Co. K, 3d Inf.	April 3, 1846	32	Rockland, N.Y.	July 23, 1847
†Fritz, Parian	Co. F, 6th Inf.	Aug. 21, 1846	22	Cumoree, Pa.	July 20, 1847
†Garretson, Robert W.	Co. H, 3d Art.	Feb. 5, 1845	22	Messina Prov., Italy	June 13, 1847
Geary, August				Great Britain	
Green, Joseph					
Groot, Othon de				Prussia, Germany	
Hamilton, John					
†Hanley, Richard	Co. A, 2d Art.	March 18, 1844	26	Limerick, Ireland	July 17, 1847
†Hart, Barney	Co. K, 2d Art.	March 24, 1846	21	Ireland	June 7, 1847
†Hogan, Roger	Co. I, 4th Inf.	Nov. 23, 1846	24	Tipperary, Ireland	July 21, 1847
Hoginn, John					
Horacs, John					
*Humphrey, James				Scotland	
Hynes, John				Ireland	

Name	U.S. Army Unit	Age	Enlistment Date	Birthplace	Desertion Date
†Jackson, George W.	Co. H, 1st Art.	21	June 1, 1846	Philadelphia, Pa.	Feb. 14, 1847
†Keech, William H.	Co. F, 4th Art.	26	Sept. 9, 1845	Tompkins, N.Y.	May 27, 1847
Kelley, James	Co. C, 3d Inf.	30	Aug. 10, 1844	Cork, Ireland	Nov. 15, 1845
†Kenney, Harrison	Co. E, 4th Inf.	25	June 2, 1845	Berkeley, Va.	May 28, 1847
†Klager, John W.	Co. K, 2d Drag.	24	June 2, 1846	France	July 27, 1847
Linger, John					
Little, John	Co. C, 2d Drag.	25	Aug. 1, 1845	Kildare, Ireland	April 8, 1846
†Longenhamer, Henry	Co. F, 2d Drag.	25	May 18, 1846	Darmstadt, Germany	Aug. 6, 1847
†Lusk, Elizier S.	Co. C, 3d Inf.	26	Feb. 18, 1847	Albany, N.Y.	July 21, 1847
†Lydon, Martin	Co. D, 7th Inf.	25	Dec. 13, 1845	Galway, Ireland	Nov. 11, 1846
Lynch, John					
†McClellan, Hugh	Co. A, 8th Inf.	24	Aug. 27, 1844	Ireland	Nov. 13, 1846
McCornick, John					
†McDonald, John	Co. A, 8th Inf.	28	Aug. 25, 1846	Edinburgh, Scotland	July 22, 1847
†McDowell, Gibson	Co. A, 8th Inf.	31	Sept. 29, 1846	Wilmington, Del.	April 20, 1847
†McDowell, James	Co. K, 7th Inf.	24	Oct. 7, 1846	Galway, Ireland	March 31, 1847
McElroy, David H.	Co. E, 6th Inf.	16		New Orleans, La.	July 8, 1847
McFarland, James D.				Montreal, Canada	
McHerron, Edward H.	Co. G, 4th Art.	18	Feb. 10, 1847	Philadelphia, Pa.	July 21, 1847
McKee, Alexander	Co. H, 3d Art			Ireland	March 21, 1847
Macky, Laurence	Co. K, 3d Inf.	32	June 29, 1846	Dublin, Ireland	Nov. 12, 1846
†McLachlin, Lachlin	Co. F, 6th Inf.	24	Oct. 29, 1846	Scotland	Feb. 19, 1847
Mahon, James	Co. H, 8th Inf.	24	Sept. 4, 1846	Dublin, Ireland	June 27, 1847
*Maloney, Patrick	5th Inf.	23	Sept. 28, 1846	Ireland	Aug. 7, 1847
*Manzano, Camillo				Mexico	
Mauray,					

Name	Company	Age	Enlistment	Birthplace	Date
*Mejia, Enrique				Mexico	
*Mestard, Agustin					
†Meyers, John A.	Co. G, 5th Inf.	23	Jan. 8, 1846	Hanover, Germany	Nov. 7, 1846
Miles, Martin	Co. A, 8th Inf.	30	Nov. 8, 1846	Ireland	July 22, 1847
Miller, James	Co. F, 7th Inf.			Arkansas	August, 1845
†Millett, Thomas	Co. D, 3d Art.	23	Aug. 28, 1846	Lower Canada	March 25, 1847
Mills, James	Co. H, 3d Inf.	21	April 28, 1845	Oswego, N.Y.	April 4, 1846
Milord,					
*Moreno, Francisco R.				Spanish Florida	
†Morstadt, Auguste	Co. I, 7th Inf.	33	Jan. 27, 1846	Baden, Germany	Nov. 3, 1846
Murphy, John	Co. C, 8th Inf.	28	Dec. 9, 1845	Co. Mayo, Ireland	April 6, 1846
†Neil, Peter	Co. B, 4th Inf.	32	Nov. 6, 1845	Galway, Ireland	Nov. 19, 184b
Neuer, Henry	Co. D, 4th Art.	19	May 18, 1846	Germany	Aug. 5, 1847
†Nolan, Andrew	Co. G, 4th Art.	22	Sept. 22, 1845	Down, Ireland	Nov. 20, 1846
O'Brien, Peter				Ireland	
†O'Conner, Francis	3d Inf.	30	Dec. 7, 1846	Co. Cork, Ireland	March 8, 1847
†O'Conner, William C.	Co. K, 1st Art.	25	Aug. 14, 1845	Philadelphia, Pa.	Nov. 21, 1846
O'Connor, Thomas				Ireland	
†Ockter, Henry	Co. D, 4th Art.	27	Nov. 29, 1846	Osnabruck, Germany	Aug. 6, 1847
*O'Leary, Santiago [or Saturnino]				New York	
O'Sullivan, Michael				Ireland	
†Outhouse, William	Co. I, 2d Inf.	28	Feb. 12, 1847	Portland, Maine	June 18, 1847
†Parker, Richard	Co. K, 5th Inf.	25	July 1, 1845	Dublin, Ireland	Nov. 8, 1846
*Peel,				Ireland	
Popes, Henry					
†Price, John	Co. F, 2d Inf.	21	Nov. 25, 1845	England	Feb. 20, 1847

Name	U.S. Army Unit	Age	Enlistment Date	Birthplace	Desertion Date
†Rhode, Francis	Co. I, 2d Drag.	23	Nov. 17, 1846	Stettin, Prussia	June 13, 1847
*Riley, John	Co. K, 5th Inf.	28	Sept. 4, 1845	Co. Galway, Ireland	April 12, 1846
Riley, Thomas	Co. H, 3d Inf.	24	July 13, 1845	Ireland	April 4, 1846
Rocher, Daniel					
Romero, Elizio				Mexico ?	
†Rose, John	Co. F, 6th Inf.	29	Oct. 5, 1846	Oldenburg, Germany	July 1, 1847
*Schafino, Francisco				Mexico	
†Schmidt, Herman	Co. D, 3d Inf.	26	Aug. 24, 1844	Hannover, Germany	Nov. 27, 1846
†Sheehan, John	Co. G, 5th Inf.	26	June 13, 1845	Ireland	Nov. 13, 1846
Smith, Charles	Ordnance	26	Sept. 6, 1846	Frankfort, Germany	Dec. 28, 1846
†Spears, James	Co. D, 7th Inf.	26	Dec. 21, 1844	Scotland	Nov. 12, 1846
*Stevenson, John	Co. H, 5th Inf.	32	Aug. 4, 1846	Armagh, Ireland	May 27, 1847
*Sutherland, John				Scotland	
Thomas, Samuel H.	Co. C, 6th Inf.	31	Jan. 30, 1847	Batavia, N.Y.	July 22, 1847
*Thompson, Henry				Scotland	
Vader, John					
†Venator, Henry	Co. I, 2d Drag.	27	April 16, 1845	Germany	June 13, 1847
Vinet,				Poland	
Vosbor, John					
†Wallace, William A.	Co. C, 3d Inf.	26	Jan. 13, 1847	Scotland	July 21, 1847
Ward, Edward					
†Wheaton, Lemuel N.	Co. A, 6th Inf.	20	Sept. 12, 1846	Ashtabula, Ohio	July 7, 1847
†Whistler, Henry	Co. E, 4th Art.	30	Jan. 15, 1847	Philadelphia, Pa.	July 17, 1847
Williams, Charles					
Wilton, John				England	
Winitt, Luis				Great Britain	

Notes

Abbreviations Used

CtY/BRBL	Yale University Library, New Haven, Beinecke Rare Book and Manuscript Library
CU-B	University of California, Berkeley, The Bancroft Library
GB/PRO FO	Great Britain, Public Record Office, Foreign Office
GB/PRO WO	Great Britain, Public Record Office, War Office
MEX/ADN	Mexico, Archivo de Defensa Nacional
OkU/WHC	University of Oklahoma Library, Western History Collections
TxU/BLAC	University of Texas Library, Austin, Benson Latin American Collection
TxU/BTHC	University of Texas Library, Austin, Barker Texas History Center
USNA/RG 59	United States, National Archives, Department of State, Record Group 59
USNA/RG 94	United States, National Archives, Department of War, Adjutant General's Office, Record Group 94
USNA/RG 153	United States, National Archives, Department of War, Judge Advocate General, Record Group 153

Notes

Chapter 1. Bloodshed on the Rio Grande

1. Riley to British Minister in Mexico, Puebla, Nov. 9, 1849, GB/PRO FO 204, 102:313; USNA/RG 94, Registers of Enlistments in the United States Army, 44:218.
2. Riley to Ewan Mackintosh, Puebla, July 14, 1849, and enclosures, GB/PRO FO 203, 94:110–15. See also Riley to Charles O'Malley, Mexico City, Oct. 27, 1847, USNA/RG 94, Mexican War, Misc. Papers, Box 7.
3. George L. Rives, *The United States and Mexico, 1821–1848,* chaps. 1–23; for a recent Mexican viewpoint, see Josefina Zoraida Vásquez and Lorenzo Meyer, *The United States and Mexico,* chap. 2.
4. Rupert N. Richardson, *Texas: The Lone Star State,* 48–51, 58, 70–71, 100.
5. Richardson, *Texas,* 100, 108, 114–15; Frederick Merk, *The Monroe Doctrine and American Expansionism, 1843–1849,* 140–42.
6. Gene M. Brack, *Manifest Destiny, 1821–1846,* 110; N[athan] C. Brooks, *A Complete History of the Mexican War,* 52–53. Annexation treaty vote in David M. Pletcher, *The Diplomacy of Annexation: Texas, Oregon, and the Mexican War,* 149.
7. Quoted in Polk's message to Congress, Dec. 8, 1846, Fred L. Israel, ed., *The State of the Union Messages of the Presidents, 1790–1966,* 1:679.
8. Among the authors who suggested that Polk deliberately provoked a war with Mexico are Jesse S. Reeves, *American Diplomacy Under Tyler and Polk;* and Richard Stenberg, "The Failure of Polk's Mexican War Intrigue of 1845," *The Pacific Historical Review* 4 (1935): 35–68. See also Charles Sellers, *James K. Polk, Continentalist, 1843–1846,* 407. Size of army in Justin Smith, *The War with Mexico,* 1:139, 143.
9. Pletcher, *The Diplomacy of Annexation,* 94–100, 307–308.
10. Allen Johnson and Dumas Malone, *Dictionary of American Biography,* s.v. "Taylor, Zachary"; Smith, *War with Mexico,* 1:140, 2:316; K. Jack Bauer, *Zachary Taylor: Soldier, Planter, Statesman of the Old Southwest.*
11. Justin Smith, *The War with Mexico,* 1:139–40, 143; Edward J. Nichols, *Zach Taylor's Little Army,* 33.
12. McCampbell, *Saga of a Frontier Seaport,* 8, 10–11.
13. Pletcher, *Diplomacy of Annexation,* 58.

14. Slidell's mission in Louis Sears, *John Slidell,* chap. 3; see also Pletcher, *The Diplomacy of Annexation,* 286–89, 355–56, 361, 365, 371.
15. Brack, *Mexico Views Manifest Destiny,* 117–18, 140–44; Allan R. Millett and Peter Maslowski, *For the Common Defense; A Military History of the United States,* 138, 140.
16. Brack, *Mexico Views Manifest Destiny,* 178; Philip R. Katcher, *The Mexican-American War, 1846–1848,* 19–20; Roswell S. Ripley, *The War with Mexico,* 1:89.
17. Ulysses S. Grant, *Personal Memoirs,* 1:168; Katcher, *The Mexican-American War,* 21.
18. London *Times,* Dec. 4, 1846, copied from the New York *Courrier and Enquirer,* n.d.
19. Cited in George W. Smith, and Charles Judah, eds., *Chronicles of the Gringos: The U.S. Army in the Mexican War, 1846–1848,* 277, 283.
20. Smith, *War with Mexico,* 1:148; John E. Weems, *To Conquer a Peace: The War Between the United States and Mexico,* 109; George Potter, *To The Golden Door; The Story of the Irish in Ireland and America,* 474.
21. Albert M. Carreño, *Jefes del ejército mexicano en 1847,* 141–54.
22. Ampudia's appeal of April 2, 1846, is printed in John Frost, *Life of Major General Zachary Taylor,* 48–49.
23. John Frost, *Pictorial History of Mexico and the Mexican War,* 200.
24. The appeal of April 20, 1846, in U.S. Congress, House, *Mexican War Correspondence,* H. Exec. Doc. 60, 30th Cong., 1st sess., 303–304. Arista's career in Carreño, *Jefes del ejército mexicano,* 44–57.
25. Horacio O. Ladd, *History of the War with Mexico,* 40.
26. James D. Richardson, ed., *A Compilation of the Messages and Papers of the Presidents, 1789–1897,* 4:442; Smith *War with Mexico,* 1:149–50; Mexican declaration in *Diario del Gobierno de la República mexicana* (hereafter cited as *Diario del Gobierno*), July 7, 1846.
27. Robert W. Johannsen, *To the Halls of the Montezumas: The Mexican War in the American Imagination,* 8, 10–11.
28. U.S. Congress, House, *Military Forces Employed in the Mexican War,* H. Exec. Doc. 24, 31st Cong., 1st sess., table 8-a; Russell F. Weigley, *History of the United States Army,* 182–83; Smith, *War with Mexico,* 1:139, 143.
29. Act of May 13, 1846, *Statutes at Large,* 9, chaps. 9–10; Millett and Maslowski, *For the Common Defense,* 141–42; Emory Upton, *The Military Policy of the United States,* 197.
30. Thoreau's essay and other contemporary protest articles in Archie P. McDonald, ed., *The Mexican War: Crisis for American Democracy.* See also Samuel E. Morison, Frederick Merk, and Frank Freidel, *Dissent in Three American Wars,* 33–63.
31. *Niles National Register* (Baltimore), Oct. 16, 1847.
32. James G. Randall, *Lincoln the President,* 1:16.
33. Leonard L. Richards, *The Life and Times of Congressman John Quincy Adams,* 186–90, 193, 202.

34. A primary example is Smith, *War with Mexico*, 2:318–319. Desertion figures in Francis Heitman, comp., *Historical Register and Dictionary of the United States Army*, 2:282. See comparative desertion rates in table 5 below, chap. 9.

35. Robert E. May, "Invisible Men: Blacks and the U.S. Army in the Mexican War," *The Historian* 49 (10 Aug. 1987):463–77.

36. Thomas M. Exley, *A Compendium of the Pay of the Army from 1785 to 1888*, 51; William A. Ganoe, *The History of the United States Army*, 183–84.

Chapter 2. Organizing the San Patricios

1. Carreño, *Jefes del ejército mexicano*, 74–222; *Enciclopedia de México*, s.v. "Bean, Ellis Peter"; Harris G. Warren, *The Sword Was Their Passport: A History of American Filibustering in the Mexican Revolution*, 146–72; José Enrique de la Peña, *With Santa Anna in Texas*, 128.

2. Manuel Balbontín, *La invasión americana, 1846 a 1847*, 72; [John A. Scott], *Encarnacion Prisoners*, 63; *Enciclopedia de México*, s.v. "Langberg"; Holzinger [Olzinger] mentioned in Ramón Alcaraz, et al, eds., *The Other Side; or Notes for the History of the War between Mexico and the United States*, 206.

3. USNA/RG 94, Registers of Enlistments in the United States Army, vol. 44:218; *North American* (Mexico City), Dec. 24, 1847; *Diccionario Porrúa de historia, biografía y geografía de México*, 2:2130–2131; Riley to Ewan Mackintosh, Puebla, Aug. 6, 1849, GB/PRO FO 203, vol. 94:124.

4. Riley to British Minister, Chapultepec, Mexico, Jan. 7, 1848, GB/PRO FO 204, 99:9; Riely to Ewan Mackintosh, Santiago Prison, Aug. 20, 1848, GB/PRO FO 203, 93:365–66; discharge of Juan Reeley in *Periódico Oficial*, Aug. 14, 1850.

5. Riley to Charles O'Malley, Mexico City, Oct. 27, 1847, USNA/RG 94, Mexican War, Misc. Papers, Box 7.

6. *Niles National Register*, Oct. 9, 1847, reprinted from the New York *Courier;* GB/PRO WO, Muster Books, 66th Reg. Foot, soldiers numbered 510 and 711. Riley's testimony in USNA/RG 153, EE 531, Case 27, John Reilly [Riley]; his supposed New York career repeated by B. Kimball Baker, "The St. Patricks Fought for their Skins, and Mexico," *Smithsonian*, 8:(1978):95; and Edward S. Wallace, "The Battalion of Saint Patrick in the Mexican War," *Military Affairs* 14 (1950):85.

7. O'Malley to Maj. Gen. Winfield Scott, Mackinac, Feb. 5, 1848, USNA/RG 94, Mexican War, Misc. Papers, Box 7. O'Malley was also County Clerk, Pioneer Society of Michigan, *Collections* 6(1884):349, 18(1892):625–26.

8. Riley's enlistment in USNA/RG 94, Registers of Enlistments, vol. 44:218; language of contemporary enlistment certificate from that of

Private Dennis Cohahan, in possession of his collateral descendant, Eugene Conahan, of Taos, N. Mex.

9. USNA/RG 153, EE 531, Case 27, John Reilly [Riley].
10. USNA/RG 153, EE 531, Case 27, John Reilly [Riley].
11. Nichols, *Taylor's Little Army*, 52; Smith, *War with Mexico*, 1:160.
12. Taylor to Adj. Gen., Matamoros, May 30, 1846, printed in U.S. Congress, House, *Mexican War Correspondence*, H. Exec. Doc. 60, 30th Cong., 1st sess., 303.
13. William S. Henry, *Campaign Sketches of the War with Mexico*, 73–74; see also Alfred H. Bill, *Rehearsal for Conflict: The War with Mexico, 1846–1848*, 90.
14. Riley to Mexican President, Aug. 20, 1848, GB/PRO FO 203, 93:367.
15. [George Ballentine], *Autobiography of an English Soldier in the United States Army*, 14.
16. Dalton's enlistment in USNA/RG 94, Registers of Enlistments, 44:68; his Irish birthplace in John Riley to Charles O'Malley, Mexico City, Oct. 27, 1847, USNA/RG 94, Misc. Papers, Box 7.
17. British San Patricios mentioned in GB/PRO FO 203, 93:105–106; 94:74–75; FO 204, 102:64, 71–72, 483.
18. Detmar H. Finke, "The Organization and Uniforms of the San Patricio Units of the Mexican Army, 1846–1848," *Military Collector and Historian* 9 (1957):37–38.
19. Brantz Mayer, *Mexico as It Was and as It Is*, 16–17.
20. John A. Perry, *Thrilling Adventures of a New Englander; Travels, Scenes and Sufferings in Cuba, Mexico, & California*, 28.
21. Manuel Dublán, and José María Lozana, eds., *Legislación mexicana*, 3:735. See also Katcher, *The Mexican-American War*, 30.
22. Samuel E. Chamberlain, *My Confession*, 124; Riley to Charles O'Malley, Mexico City, Oct. 27, 1847, USNA/RG 94, Mexican War, Misc. Papers, Box 7; *Niles National Register*, Mar. 13, 1847, 32.
23. New Orleans *Daily Picayune*, Sept. 9, 1847.
24. These facts cannot be verified because Mexican authorities refused to permit checking records in their military archives.

Chapter 3. Fighting Under the Shamrock Flag

1. Taylor to Adj. Gen., Matamoros, May 30, 1846, in U.S. Congress, House, *Mexican War Correspondence*, House Exec. Doc. 60, 30th Cong., 1st sess., 303; Riley to President of Mexico, Santiago Prison, Aug. 20, 1848, GB/PRO FO 203, 93:367. At his court-martial Riley claimed that he was imprisoned during the Matamoros fight, but this was refuted by other testimony.
2. K. Jack Bauer, *The Mexican War, 1846–1848*, 53–62.

3. USNA/RG 94, Registers of Enlistments, 44:149; 44:163; 44:167; 44:218; 44:217.

4. José María Roa Bárcena, *Recuerdos de la invasión norteamericana, 1846–1848*, 1:90. Riley's copy of his pay record shows him in Linares during the month of June 1846, GB/PRO FO 203, 94:114.

5. Asa B. Clarke, *Travels in Mexico and California*, 25.

6. An original copy of Ampudia's leaflet of Sept. 5, 1846, is in CtY/BRBL; the item was printed in *Diario del Gobierno*, Sept. 25, 1846.

7. Smith, *War with Mexico*, 1:494, note 11; Balbontín, *La invasión*, 38; David Lavender, *Climax at Buena Vista*, 101.

8. Smith, *War with Mexico*, 1:258, 505–506; capitulation terms in *Complete History of the Late Mexican War . . . by an Eyewitness*, 42–43.

9. Bauer, *The Mexican War*, 100.

10. Henry, *Campaign Sketches*, 223–24.

11. [Luther Giddings,] *Sketches of the Campaign in Northern Mexico*, 276.

12. [Giddings], *Sketches*, 277.

13. Henry, *Campaign Sketches*, 249; see also *Complete History of the Late Mexican War*, 49.

14. Oakah L. Jones, Jr., *Santa Anna;* Wilfrid H. Callcott, *Santa Anna, the Story of an Enigma Who Once was Mexico*, 243.

15. USNA/RG 153, EE 531, Case 6, Patrick Dalton.

16. *Diario del Gobierno*, Jan. 9, 1847; the church loan in *Diario del Gobierno*, Feb. 24, 1847; silver seizure in Smith, *War with Mexico*, 1:380.

17. Translated version in *Niles National Register*, Mar. 13, 1847, 32.

18. Roa Bárcena, *Recuerdos*, 1:143; Balbontín, *La invasión*, 60.

19. [Scott] *Encarnacion Prisoners*, 43–45.

20. John S. Jenkins, *History of the War Between the United States and Mexico*, 220–21.

21. Santa Anna to Minister of War, Feb. 27, 1847, printed in *Diario del Gobierno*, Mar. 21, 1847; Smith, *War with Mexico*, 1:386.

22. Bauer, *The Mexican War*, 211; Lavender, *Climax at Buena Vista*, 192, 226; John Muller, *A Treatise on Artillery*, 6–7; *Diario del Gobierno*, Aug. 18, 1847.

23. Muller, *Treatise of Artillery*, 48, 151, 155, 179; Lavender, *Climax at Buena Vista*, 226–28.

24. Chamberlain, *My Confession*, 118.

25. Chamberlain, *My Confession*, 124; Bauer, *The Mexican War*, 216; Smith, *War with Mexico*, 1:391.

26. Smith, *War with Mexico*, 1:397.

27. Mejía's report, *Diario del Gobierno*, Apr. 7, 1847; American losses in Bauer, *The Mexican War*, 217; Mexican losses, Balbontín, *La invasión*, 91; Capt. Moreno's report of San Patricio losses in Emilio del Castillo Negrete, *Invasión de los Norte-americanos en México*, 2:407; *Diario del Gobierno*, Aug. 18, 1847.

28. *Diario del Gobierno,* June 25, 26, 1847.

29. Letter from "El soldado de la Patria," *Diario del Gobierno,* Mar. 22, 1847. See also Smith, *War with Mexico,* 1:399.

30. *Diario del Gobierno,* Mar. 20, 1847.

31. Roa Bárcena, *Recuerdos,* 2:9–11; Vicente Riva Palacio, ed., *México a través de los siglos,* 4:714.

32. Smith, *War with Mexico,* 2:25–34; Bauer, *The Mexican War,* 232–52.

33. Johnson and Malone, *Dictionary of American Biography,* s.v., "Scott, Winfield."

34. *Diario del Gobierno,* March 31, 1847; see also Feb. 24, 1847. Church property issue in Vásquez and Meyer, *The United States and Mexico,* 45.

35. Santa Anna to Minister of War, April 6, 13, 1847, in "Letters of General Antonio López de Santa Anna Relating to the War Between the United States and Mexico, 1846–1848," ed. Justin Smith, *Annual Report of the American Historical Assoc. for 1917,* Washington, 1920. San Patricio participation in Riley to President of Mexico, Aug. 20, 1848, GB/PRO FO 203, 93:367; Riva Palacio, *México a través,* 4:714; Roa Bárcena, *Recuerdos,* 2:12.

36. Smith, *War with Mexico,* 2:50–53.

37. George W. Kendall, *The War Between the United States and Mexico,* 25.

38. Smith, *War with Mexico,* 2:58–59.

39. Report in *Diario del Gobierno,* June 14, 1847; Irish medics in Smith, *War with Mexico,* 2:347.

40. London *Times,* Aug. 6, 1847.

41. Jorge I. Rubio Mañé, "El Excmo. Sr. Dr. D. Martin Tritschler y Córdova, primer arzobispo de Yucatán," *Asbide, revista de cultura mexicana,* 5:9 (1941):587–90; Robert Anderson, *An Artillery Officer in the Mexican War, 1846–7,* 220–31.

42. Anderson, *An Artillery Officer,* 231–37.

43. An original copy of the broadside is in CtY/BRBL. Origin of the scheme in Guillermo Prieto, *Memorias de mis tiempos, 1828–1853,* 2:139, 173–74; José Fernando Ramírez, *Mexico During the War with the United States,* 127.

44. Supplement printed in *Diario del Gobierno,* Sept. 10, 1847, and *New York Herald,* Oct. 17, 1847.

45. Niceto de Zamacois, *Historia de Méjico desde sus tiempos más remotos hasta nuestros días,* 12:695–97; see also Sister Blanche M. McEniry, *American Catholics in the War with Mexico,* 82–83.

46. Bauer, *The Mexican War,* 270–71; desertions in USNA/RG 153, EE 525, and EE 531.

Chapter 4. The Place of the War God

1. William Preston, *Journal in Mexico*, 36–38.
2. W. C. S. Smith, *A Journey to California in 1849*, 6. The Aztec calendar stone, colonial buildings, and bronze statue of Charles IV are still tourist favorites.
3. London *Times*, May 10, 1847, 6.
4. London *Times*, Aug. 6, 1847, 6.
5. *Diario del Gobierno*, May 5, 8, 10, and July 2, 13, 1847.
6. London *Times*, Aug. 6, 1847.
7. An original copy of Santa Anna's decree in UC–B; it was published in *Diario del Gobierno*, July 15, 1847.
8. Dublán and Lozano, *Legislación mexicana*, 3:734–35; see also Katcher, *The Mexican–American War*, 26, 30, and color plates A and D.
9. Zamacois, *Historia de Méjico*, 13:743.
10. Larry Koller, *The Fireside Book of Guns*, 44–45; Lavender, *Climax at Buena Vista*, 220, 224.
11. Lavender, *Climax at Buena Vista*, 221, 224.
12. *Diario del Gobierno*, Aug. 18, 1847. A translation of the contract printed in New Orleans *Picayune*, Sept. 28, 1847, and reprinted in McEniry, *American Catholics*, 160–61.
13. Legion officers listed in *Diario del Gobierno*, July 21, 1847. Story about O'Leary in St. Louis, Mo., *Republican*, Nov., 1847, copied and enclosed in a letter from S. G. Hopkins to Justin H. Smith, June 1, 1917, in Justin Smith corresp. file, Box 2J9, Earl Vandale Collection, Tx U/ BTHC. James Humphrey also said that O'Leary was an American, GB/PRO FO 204, 102, (64).
14. USNA/RG 153, EE 525, Case 6, Marquis Frantius.
15. USNA/RG 153, EE 531, Case 24, Hezekiah Akles; Case 29, John Bowers.
16. Sundry deserters to Ewan Mackintosh, H. B. M. Consul General, Mexico City, June 23, 1847, GB/PRO FO 203, 93:105–106; see also numbers 66, 107–108, 115.
17. Charles W. Elliott, *Winfield Scott, the Soldier and the Man*, 495–99; Bauer, *The Mexican War*, 282–85.
18. Law of April 20 in Dublán and Lozana, *Legislación mexicana*, 5:268; see also *Diario del Gobierno*, Apr. 21, 1847.
19. Ethan Allen Hitchcock, *Fifty Years in Camp and Field; Diary of Major-General Ethan Allen Hitchcock*, ed. W. A. Croffut, 259, 263–65, 316; uniform described in Katcher, *The Mexican-American War*, 40, and plate F. See also John R. Kenly, *Memoirs of a Maryland Volunteer*, 461–62.
20. The San Patricios were at El Peñón between Aug. 9–16, USNA/ RG 153, EE 531, Case 29, John Bowers.
21. Original copy of the surrender leaflet in UC–B.
22. Undated manuscript, Box 2E 288, George W. Kendall Collection,

TxU/BTHC. Internal evidence and Riley's rank as major suggest it was written about Aug. 17, 1847.
23. *Diario del Gobierno,* Aug. 17, 1847.
24. *Diario del Gobierno,* Aug. 13, 1847.
25. Movement of San Patricios in USNA/RG 153, EE 531, Case 29, John Bowers.
26. *Diario del Gobierno,* Aug. 20, 24, 1847; Smith, *War with Mexico,* 2:109–10; Elliott, *Winfield Scott,* 511–13; Bauer, *The Mexican War,* 295. The cannons are now on display at the U.S. Military Academy, West Point, N.Y.
27. *Enciclopedia de México,* s.v. "Churubusco."
28. Defenses at Churubusco described in Gen. Rincón's post–battle report, *Diario del Gobierno,* Aug. 31, 1847; also in Mexico, Instituto Nacional de Antropología e Historia, *Churubusco en la acción militar del 20 de agosto de 1847,* 32–47.
29. Cited in Nathan C. Brooks, *Complete History of the Mexican War,* 378–79.
30. Recapitulation of defense posture in Santa Anna's letter to Minister of War, Tehuacán, Nov. 19, 1847, printed in *El Correo Nacional,* Dec. 7, 1847.
31. Rincón's report, *Diario del Gobierno,* Aug. 31, 1847; Santa Anna's report in *El Correo Nacional,* Dec. 7, 1847. Cf. G. T. Hopkins, "The San Patricio Battalion in the Mexican War," *Cavalry Journal* 24 (1913):280; Edward S. Wallace, "Deserters in the Mexican War," *Hispanic American Historical Review* 15 (1935):379–80; Dennis Wynn, *The San Patricio Soldiers; Mexico's Foreign Legion,* 4.
32. Worth's report of actions on Aug. 20 in U.S. Congress, Senate, *Message from the President . . . ,* S. Exec. Doc. 1, 30th Cong., 1st sess., 1847, 315–22.
33. *Complete History of the Late Mexican War,* 85.
34. Rincón's report, *Diario del Gobierno,* Aug. 31, 1847.
35. Kendall, "War Between the United States and Mexico," 718–19, typescript of unpublished ms in Fayette Copeland Collection, OkU/WHC.
36. Kendall, "War Between the United States and Mexico," 725, Fayette Copeland Col., OkU/WHC; Maj. Gen. Gideon J. Pillow's dispatch in *North American* (Mexico City), Dec. 24, 1847.
37. Alacaraz, *The Other Side,* 299.
38. Davis, *Autobiography,* 203; U.S. Congress, Senate, *Message from the President,* S. Exec. Doc. 1, 30th Cong., 1st sess., 1847, 324–25.
39. *Diario del Gobierno,* Aug. 31, 1847. Riley's injury in GB/PRO FO 203, 93:367. The exact number of San Patricios who defended Churubusco is unknown—estimates range from 200 to 260; see Potter, *To the Golden Door,* 486; Elliott, *Winfield Scott,* 528.
40. *El Correo Nacional* (Mexico City), Oct. 11, 1848.

41. U.S. Congress, Senate, *Message from the President*, S. Exec. Doc. 1, 30th Cong., 1st sess., 1847, 319, 331.

42. Alcaraz, et al, *The Other Side*, 295; Fairfax Downey, *Texas and the War with Mexico*, 127.

43. Scott's report in *American Star* (Mexico City), Dec. 15, 1847; also in U.S. Congress, Senate, 30th Cong., 1st sess., S. Exec. Doc. No. 1 : 314.

44. Raphael Semmes, *Service Afloat and Ashore during the Mexican War*, 428; Arthur D. Smith, *Old Fuss and Feathers; The Life and Exploits of Lt. General Winfield Scott*, 313; Santa Anna's letter in Hitchcock, *Fifty Years*, 340; articles of the armistice in *Complete History of the Late Mexican War*, 85–88.

Chapter 5. Trials and Punishment

1. USNA/RG 153, EE 525, "Proceedings of a General Court Martial convened at Tacubaya, Mexico, 43 cases;" EE 531, "Proceedings of a General Court Martial convened at San Angel, Mexico, 29 cases."

2. USNA/RG 153, EE 531, Case 6, Patrick Dalton.

3. Court-martial records in USNA/RG 153, EE 525 and EE 531.

4. Wilton's background in USNA/RG 153, EE 531, Case 1, Henry Venator; his release in USNA/RG 94, Orders and Circulars, 1797–1910, Maj. Gen. W. O. Butler, General Orders 116, Mexico City, June 1, 1848. O'Connor's background in EE 531, Case 27, John Riley.

5. USNA/RG 153, EE 531, Case 16, Martin Lydon; EE 525, Case 42, John McDonald.

6. USNA/RG 153, EE 525, Case 3, Henry Longenheimer.

7. USNA/RG 153, EE 531, Case 6, Patrick Dalton.

8. USNA/RG 153, EE 531, Case 29, John Bowers; Case 25, John Bartley.

9. USNA/RG 153, EE 525, Case 1, Frederick Fogal.

10. USNA/RG 153, EE 531, Case 14, James McDowell.

11. USNA/RG 153, EE 531, Case 24, Hezekiah Akles. See also EE 525, Case 43, Abraham Fitzpatrick, another deserter who refused to join the Mexican army.

12. USNA/RG 153, EE 525, Case 38, Thomas Millett; EE 531, Case 29, John Bowers; Case 19, Henry Ockter.

13. USNA/RG 153, EE 531, Case 27, John Riley.

14. USNA/RG 153, EE 531, Case 27, John Riley.

15. USNA/RG 153, EE 531, Case 27, John Riley.

16. USNA/RG 153, EE 525, Cases 24, 33, 41, 43.

17. *American Star*, Sept. 20, 1847; *Niles National Register*, Oct. 16, 1847; Roa Bárcena, *Recuerdos*, 3 : 58.

18. New Orleans *Picayune*, Sept. 9, 1847.

19. USNA/RG 94, Misc. Papers, Box 7, no. 3.

20. Humphrey's service in GB/PRO FO 204, 102 : 71–72; Suther-

land's experience in FO 204, 102:451, 453; Tracy and others in [Scott] *Encarnacion Prisoners*, 58, 65; data on Smith in Martin A. Haynes, *Gen. Scott's Guide in Mexico: A Biographical Sketch of Col. Noah F. Smith.*

21. Smith, *Old Fuss and Feathers*, 311; Elliott, *Winfield Scott*, 9.

22. Davis, *Autobiography*, 228–29; USNA/RG 94, Orders and Circulars, 1797–1910, General Orders 281 and 283, Headquarters of the Army in Mexico; USNA/RG 94, Register of Enlistments, 21, 44:80, Abraham Fitzpatrick, and 21, 44:190, Henri Neuer.

23. USNA/RG 94, Hq. of Army in Mexico, General Orders 281 and 283, Tacubaya, Mexico, Sept. 8, 11, 1847; orders summarized in *American Star*, Sept. 25, 1847.

24. Abolition of flogging, Act of Aug. 5, 1861, *Statutes at Large* 12, ch. 54, sec. 3:317; branding abolished, Act of June 6, 1872, *Statutes at Large* 17, ch. 316, sec. 2:261.

25. Nugent's letter, dated at Mexico City, Oct. 23, 1847, M–M 1700: 199, UC–B.

26. Davis, *Autobiography*, 224–26.

27. Davis, *Autobiography*, 226–27; Amasa G. Clark, *Reminiscences of a Centenarian*, 14.

28. *American Star*, Sept. 20, 1847; *Diario del Gobierno (Alcance)*, Sept. 10, 1847; *Niles National Register*, Oct. 16, 1847. The double branding mentioned in Riva Palacio, *México a través de los siglos*, 4:714, and verified in Riley's letter to the President of Mexico, Aug. 20, 1848, GB/PRO FO 203, 93:367.

29. Davis, *Autobiography*, 227–28; another eyewitness described the gallows, Clark, *Reminiscences*, 14.

30. Davis, *Autobiography*, 228; *American Star*, Sept. 20, 1847.

31. Francisco Fernández del Castillo, *Apuntes para la historia de San Angel*, 129–30; Hopkins, "The San Patricio Battalion," 281; Tom Mahoney, "50 Hanged and 11 Branded, the Story of the San Patricio Battalion," *Southwest Review* 32 (1947):376.

32. W. S. Harney, *Official Correspondence of Brig. Gen. W. S. Harney, U.S. Army, and First Lt. Geo. Ihrie*, 3–8; Chamberlain, *My Confession*, 226–27.

33. "General Harney" [obituary] in *Journal of the United States Cavalry Association* 3 (1890):1–8; Edward D. Mansfield, *The Mexican War*, 280–81; Chamberlain, *My Confession*, 227.

34. James Reilly, "An Artilleryman's Story," *Journal of the Military Service Institution* 33 (1903):443–44; *American Star*, Sept. 20, 1847.

35. Semmes, *Service Afloat and Ashore*, 428.

36. *North American*, Jan. 6, 1848.

37. Reprinted in *North American*, Jan. 7, 1848; see also Brooks, *A Complete History*, 401.

38. Mansfield, *The Mexican War*, 280.

39. [Scott] *Encarnacion Prisoners*, 85; Ramírez, *Mexico During the War*, 160; Prieto, *Memorias de mis tiempos*, 173–74.
40. Supplement to *Diario del Gobierno*, Sept. 10, 1847; an English translation in *Niles National Register*, Oct. 16, 1847. Santa Anna's decree in *Diario del Gobierno*, July 13, 1847.

Chapter 6. In and Out of Prison

1. *Diario del Gobierno*, Sept. 7, 1847.
2. Alcaraz, *The Other Side*, 348. See also Smith, *War with Mexico*, 140–47, 403; Balbontín, *La invasión americana*, 126–29.
3. Smith, *The War with Mexico*, 2:405–11; Bauer, *The Mexican War*, 311–18. Names of prisoners captured at Chapultepec (and other places) in *El Correo Nacional*, Mar. 16, 20, 30, 1848; see also Roa Bárcena, *Recuerdos*, 103–104.
4. *The Eagle: The Autobiography of Santa Anna*, ed. Ann F. Crawford, 108–109.
5. *American Star*, Sept. 20, 1847. See Lota M. Spell, "The Antlo-Saxon Press in Mexico, 1846–1848," *American Historical Review* 38 (1932): 22, 25–27.
6. *American Star*, Sept. 23, 1847; also in Davis, *Autobiography*, 260–61.
7. Hopkins, "The San Patricio Battalion," 281; Wallace, "Deserters in the Mexican War," 382; and Wallace, "The Battalion of Saint Patrick," 90.
8. Santa Anna's letter describing his exit from the capital in *El Correo Nacional*, Dec. 10, 1847; reorganization of the government in this same new official newspaper, Oct. 18, Nov. 11, 1847, and Jan. 11, 1848.
9. Henry A. Wise, *Los Gringos*, 251.
10. *El Monitor Republicano*, Oct. 8, 1847.
11. *North American*, Dec. 7, 1847; see also issues for Oct. 2, 4, 1847.
12. *North American*, Dec. 24, 1847.
13. O'Malley eventually sent Riley's letter to Gen. Winfield Scott; the original is now in USNA/RG 94, Mexican War, Misc. Papers, Box 7.
14. USNA/RG 153, EE 619, "Proceeding of a General Court Martial held in the City of Mexico on the 6th of December 1847."
15. USNA/RG 96, Register of Enlistments, 45:63; Duhan's promotion in *El Correo Nacional*, Jan. 11, 15, 1848, and *American Star*, Jan. 15, 1848.
16. *American Star*, Nov. 10, 1847; *El Monitor Republicano*, Nov. 8, 1847.
17. *El Monitor Republicano*, Nov. 11, 13, 15 and Dec. 22, 23, 1847.
18. Riley to H. B. Minister, Chapultepec, Jan. 7, 1848, GB/PRO FO 204, 99:9.
19. Lord Palmerston to Charles Bankhead, London, Aug. 30, 1847,

GB/PRO FO 203, 91:130. Doyle to Riley, Mexico City, Jan. 15, 1848, GB/PRO FO 204, 99:12.

20. Reorganization in *El Correo Nacional,* Dec. 18, 25, 29, 1847; Dublán and Lozana, *Legislación mexicana,* 5:300–303, 323. See also Rives, *The United States and Mexico,* 2:586, 592.

21. *El Correo Nacional,* Jan. 3, 1848.

22. *El Correo Nacional,* Dec. 23, 1847; Jan. 21, Feb. 15, Mar. 7, 9, 1848.

23. The *North American* (Mexico City), Jan. 27, Feb. 8, 1848; see also Ramón Alcaraz, et al, *Apuntes para la historia de la guerra,* 368–69.

24. Dennis Berge, ed. and trans., *Considerations on the Political and Social Situation of the Mexican Republic, 1847,* 53.

25. Bauer, *The Mexican War,* 381–84.

26. Text of the treaty in Hunter Miller (ed.), *Treaties and Other International Acts of the United States of America, 1776–1863,* 5:207–36.

27. Mexico, Secretaría de Relaciones Exteriores, *Algunos documentos sobre el Tratado de Guadalupe y la situación de México durante la invasión americana,* 58; Smith, *War with Mexico,* 2:474.

28. Wise, *Los Gringos,* 267; *North American,* Mar. 17, 1848; *El Correo Nacional,* Mar. 10, 1848.

29. USNA/RG 94, Orders and Circulars, Major General W. O. Butler, General Orders 112, Mexico City, May 29, 1848; *American Star,* May 4, 30, 1848.

30. *El Siglo Diez y Nueve* (Mexico City), June 1, 1848.

31. USNA/RG 94, Orders and Circulars, Maj. Gen. W. O. Butler, General Orders, 1847–1848; Baker, "The St. Patricks Fought for their Skins," 100. Lyrics and music of the Rogue's March in Edward A. Dolph, *"Sound Off!" Soldier Songs from the Revolution to World War II,* 71.

32. Hitchcock, *Fifty Years,* 330, 334, 341.

Chapter 7. The Postwar Battalion

1. *El Siglo Diez y Nueve,* June 6–9, 21, 1848.

2. *El Siglo Diez y Nueve,* June 11, 1848.

3. Carlos Franco to Mariano Riva Palacio, Tlalnepantla, June 11, 1848, Doc. 2703, TxU/BLAC, Mariano Riva Palacio Archives.

4. Carlos Franco to Mariano Riva Palacio, Tlalnepantla, June 13, 1848, Doc. 2713, TxU/BLAC, Mariano Riva Palacio Archives.

5. Zamacois, *Historia de Méjico,* 13:191; Riva Palacio, *México a través de los siglos,* 4:713–14.

6. MEX/ADN, Expediente XI/481.3/2806 (microfilm, CU–B).

7. Mexico, Ministerio de Guerra y Marina, *Memoria, 1849* [for June–Dec. 1848], Table 10; pay in *El Correo Nacional,* July 18, 1848.

8. Riva Palacio, *México a través de los siglos,* 4:711–12; *El Monitor Re-*

publicano, June 16, 1848; Thomas E. Cotner, *The Military and Political Career of José Joaquín Herrera, 1792–1845,* 174–75.

9. Cotner, *Military Career,* 175, 178–79; plan of June 1 in *El Siglo Diez y Nueve,* June 19, 1848; Paredes' proclamation of June 12 in *El Siglo Diez y Nueve,* June 23, 1848; his manifesto of June 15 in *El Monitor Republicano,* June 21, 1848; and a letter of June 17 in *El Correo Nacional,* July 3, 1848.

10. Riva Palacio, *México a través de los siglos,* 1:712; *El Siglo Diez y Nueve,* Aug. 14, 1848; *Periódico Oficial* (Mexico City), July 4, 1849.

11. *El Correo Nacional,* July 20, 22, 1848; Cotner, *Military Career,* 181–83; Riva Palacio, *México a través de los siglos,* 4:712–13.

12. GB/PRO FO 204, 102:21, 64, 119, 483–91. Humphrey's court-martial in MEX/ADN, Expediente XI/481.3/3003.

13. *El Siglo Diez y Nueve,* July 24, 1848.

14. *El Siglo Diez y Nueve,* July 24, 1848.

15. Daniel Wadsworth Coit, *Digging for Gold Without a Shovel; The Letters of,* 47.

16. *El Monitor Republicano,* July 28, 1848; see also the official 17-page report, "Parte del Comandante del Batallón de San Patricio, José María Calderón, dando cuenta de la sublevación del mismo en la Villa de Guadalupe," Expediente XI/481.3/2877, MEX/ADN.

17. McFarland to British Minister, San Miguel de Allende, April 27, 1849, GB/PRO FO 203, 94:74–75.

18. *El Correo Nacional,* Sept. 16, 1848; see also Aug. 18, 1848.

19. GB/PRO FO 203, 94:138–39, 142, 257.

20. Wynn, *The San Patricio Soldiers,* 33–34; *El Monitor Republicano,* Aug. 3, 14, 1848.

21. GB/PRO FO 204, 101:619; 102:84, 119.

22. Arista to Minister of Foreign Relations, in GB/PRO FO 204, 102:453.

23. Riley to Ewan Mackintosh, Santiago prison [Mexico City], Aug. 20, 1848, GB/PRO FO 203, 93:365.

24. Riley to President of Mexico, GB/PRO FO 203, 93:367.

25. Perry, *Thrilling Adventures,* 22. Riley's release from Santiago prison in *El Monitor Republicano,* Sept. 6, 1848; his transfer to Puebla in MEX/ADN, Expediente XI/481.2/3039.

26. Manuel Toussaint, *La catedral y las iglesias de Puebla,* 21.

27. Mayer, *Mexico as It Was,* 23–24.

28. E. Turnbull and A. Robeschultze to Ewan Mackintosh, Puebla, July 13, 1849, GB/PRO FO 203, 94:108–109.

29. Riley to Mackintosh, Puebla, July 14, 1849, and enclosures, GB/PRO FO 203, 94:110–15.

30. Riley to Mackintosh, Puebla, July 14, 1849, and enclosures, GB/PRO FO 203, 94:110–15.

31. Riley to Mackintosh, Puebla, Aug. 6, 1849, GB/PRO FO 203, 94:124.

32. Riley to H. B. M. Minister, Puebla, GB/PRO FO 204, 102:313.

33. *Periódico Oficial,* Aug. 14, 1850.

34. The author visited Taxco and Pachuca in 1974 and again in 1984 in an unsuccessful attempt to locate traces of the San Patricios.

35. John F. Finerty, *John F. Finerty Reports Porfirian Mexico, 1879,* ed. Wilbert H. Timmons, 199–200.

36. Finerty, *John F. Finerty Reports,* 200.

Chapter 8. Why They Defected

1. Chamberlain, *My Confession,* 147, 180, 212–16, 224, 237.

2. USNA/RG 153, EE 531, Case 13, Dennis Conahan.

3. USNA/RG 153, EE 531, Case 12, James Spears; EE 525, Case 11, John Daly.

4. Smith and Judah, *Chronicles of the Gringos,* 423–24.

5. USNA/RG 153, EE 531, Case 17, William Keech.

6. DeWitt Clinton Loudon, manuscript Diary, entry for Aug. 27, 1846, CU–B.

7. Chamberlain, *My Confession,* 192–95.

8. Quoted in Otis Singletary, *The Mexican War,* 146; Ganoe, *History of the Army,* 174–75.

9. USNA/RG 94, Registers of Enlistments, 45:157; *The American Star No. 2* (Puebla), July 1, 1847.

10. Smith and Judah, *Chronicles,* 429–31. In another case, Captain Braxton Bragg, known as a severe disciplinarian, barely escaped assassination when a bomb exploded under his bed, *Niles National Register,* Oct. 9, 1847.

11. Smith and Judah, *Chronicles,* 423–24; USNA/RG 153, EE 525, Case 18, Lachlin McLachlin.

12. [Ballentine], *Autobiography,* 232–33.

13. [Ballentine], *Autobiography,* 247.

14. USNA/RG 153, EE 531, Case 17, William Keech.

15. Katcher, *The Mexican–American War,* 23, 28–29; George T. Davis, *Autobiography of the Late Col. Geo. T. M. Davis,* 186. Ethnic composition of army in Nichols, *Zach Taylor's Little Army,* 33; Robert B. Considine, *It's the Irish,* 180.

16. Wallace, "Deserters in the Mexican War," 374.

17. Henry, *Campaign Sketches,* 240. Meyers' testimony in USNA/RG 153, EE 531, Case 8; Morstadt's testimony, EE 525, Case 16.

18. Kenly, *Memoirs,* 381–82.

19. Oswandel, *Notes of the Mexican War,* 229–30.

20. Anderson, *An Artillery Officer,* 314–15; Hubert H. Bancroft, *His-*

tory of California, 5:217–18; Mexico, Secretaría de Relaciones Exteriores, *Lord Aberdeen, Texas y California* (Archivo histórico diplomático, 15).

21. *American Star* (Mexico City), May 5, 1848.

22. McEniry, *American Catholics*, 49, note 7; see also Roy J. Honeywell, *Chaplains of the United States Army*, 45. The first Catholic chaplain in the U.S. Navy was commissioned in 1888, Peter Karsten, *The Naval Aristocracy*, 97, note 52.

23. Sec. of War to Gen. Taylor, May 29, 1846, in Fr. John McElroy, "Chaplains for the Mexican War—1846," *The Woodstock Letters* 15 (1886):201.

24. McEniry, *American Catholics*, 50; "First Catholic Chaplains in U.S. Army and Navy," *The Woodstock Letters*, 70 (1941):466–67.

25. Sec. of War to Gen. Taylor, May 29, 1846, in McElroy, "Chaplains for the Mexican War," 201.

26. U.S. Congress, House, *Mexican War Corresp.*, House Exec. Doc. 60, 30 Cong., 1st sess., 1847–48, 286–87.

27. U.S. Congress, House, *Mexican War Corresp.*, H. Exec. Doc. 60, 30th Cong., 1st sess., 1847–48, 937.

28. Quoted in McEniry, *American Catholics*, 1.

29. Ray Allen Billington, *The Protestant Crusade, 1800–1860*, 57–59; Carleton Beals, *Brass-Knuckle Crusade*, 98–100; Potter, *To the Golden Door*, 133–34.

30. Smith and Judah, *Chronicles*, 410–11, 465 note 60; [Ballentine], *Autobiography*, 212–13.

31. Cotner, *The Military Career*, 181; Carlos D. Neve, *Historia gráfica del ejército mexicano*, 12.

32. Supplement to Santa Anna's broadside of April, 1847, published in *Diario del Gobierno*, Sept. 10, 1847, and reprinted in *New York Herald*, Oct. 17, 1847.

33. *Diario del Gobierno*, Sept. 10, 1847; the proclamation was dated at Tula de Tamaulípas, Aug. 12, 1847.

34. *Diario del Gobierno*, Sept. 8, 1846; Dublán and Lozana, *Legislación mexicana*, 5:161. John Black, U.S. Consul in Mexico City, also reported the new policy, USNA/RG 59, "Despatches from U.S. Consuls in Mexico City," letters of Sept. 12 and Oct. 8, 1846.

35. Act of Feb. 11, 1847, *Statutes at Large* 9, ch. 8, sec. 9:125. A previous Act of July 5, 1838, had granted 160 acres to any enlisted man who served continuously for ten years.

36. Santa Anna's proclamation from Orizaba, April 1847, was printed in *Diario del Gobierno*, Sept. 10, 1847; an original copy of the broadside in CtY/WAC. The spy story is in Philip N. Barbour and Martha I. Barbour, *Journals of the Late Brevet Major Philip Norbourne Barbour*, 30.

Chapter 9. Myths and Realities

1. Hubert H. Bancroft, *History of Mexico*, 5:544; financial cost in Millett and Maslowski, *For the Common Defense*, 150.

2. Army commanders listed in Oliver L. Spaulding, *The United States Army in War and Peace*, 225.

3. *Enciclopedia de México*, 1978 ed., s.v., "Guerra de E.U. a México."

4. Ministers with dates of service listed in Luis Zorilla, *Historia de las relaciones entre México y los Estados Unidos de América, 1800–1858*, 2:187.

5. Ferris, "To California in 1849 through Mexico," *Century* 42 (1891):671.

6. Vásquez and Meyer, *The United States and Mexico*, 2.

7. Vásquez and Meyer, *The United States and Mexico*, 49.

8. Wilcox, *History of the Mexican War*, 2; Smith, *War with Mexico*, 2:323.

9. Sir Charles Petrie, *King Charles III of Spain*, 101–102; *Encyclopædia Britannica*, 1954 ed., "Malplaquet"; B. H. Liddell Hart, ed., *The Letters of Private Wheeler*, 32; Alfred Hasbrouck, *Foreign Legionaries in the Liberation of Spanish South America*, 164–89.

10. Smith, *Old Fuss and Feathers*, 311, note.

11. Desertion data compiled from court-martial records, USNA/RG 153, EE 525 and EE 531; U.S. Army service in USNA/RG 94, Registers of Enlistments, 1840–48.

12. Potter, *To the Golden Door*, 474–75.

13. Allen Bowman, *The Morale of the Revolutionary Army*, 89; James Parton, *Life of Andrew Jackson*, 2:277–80; R. Ernest Dupuy, *Where They Have Trod: The West Point Tradition in American Life*, 68.

14. U.S. Congress, House, *Military Forces Employed in the Mexican War*, H. Exec. Doc. 24, 31st Cong., 1st sess., 1849–50, Table 8–A; *American Star* (Mexico City), Jan. 8, 1848; USNA/RG 94, Registers of Enlistments, 44:44, 45:104 and 226.

15. Victor Hicken, *The American Fighting Man*, 194–97; William B. Huie, *The Execution of Private Slovik*, 12–13; *New York Times*, Sept. 17, 1974, 1.

16. *Diccionario Porrúa*, 2:2130–2131; Chamberlain, *My Confession*, 226; Baker, "St. Patrick's Fought for their Skins," 100; Richard B. McCornack, "The San Patricio Deserters in the Mexican War," *The Americas* 8 (Oct. 1951):139.

17. J. Jacob Oswandel, *Notes of the Mexican War, 1846–47–48*, 427–28.

18. Data about the memorial stone and its designer in "Mexico Hails its Ill-fated Irish Battalion," *Los Angeles Times* (Calif.), March 17, 1980.

19. USNA/RG 153, EE 525, Case 43, Abraham Fitzpatrick; his death from wounds occurred in Mexico City, Oct. 29, 1847, USNA/RG 94, Registers of Enlistments, 44:80.

20. The school is located at Calle M8 L32, Colonia Lomas de los Angeles, Tepelpan.

21. *News* (Mexico City), Sept. 13, 1983 and Sept. 11, 1983.

22. Data about the medals in Frank W. Grove, *Medals of Mexico*, 2:144–45.

23. Jorge Fernández Tomás, et al, *Ahí vienen los del norte; La invasión norteamericana de 1847*, 59–61.

24. Erroneous myth in Carlos D. Neve, *Historia gráfica del ejército mexicano*, text accompanying plate 8; (Mexico City) *Novedades*, Sept. 13, 1974; (Mexico City) *News*, Sept. 10, 1974 and March 13, 1988. John B. Flannery, *The Irish Texans*, 68, affirms there was no connection between the San Patricio colony and the battalion.

25. Conduct of the deserters in testimony during their courts-martial, USNA/RG 153, EE 525, EE 531.

Bibliography

1. Manuscripts

Great Britain Public Record Office
  Foreign Office, 50. Diplomatic Correspondence, Mexico
  Foreign Office, 203. Embassy and Consular Archives, Mexico
  Foreign Office, 204. Embassy and Consular Archives, Mexico
  War Office, 12. Army Muster Books and Pay Lists
  War Office, 25. Army Deserters
  War Office, 97. Army Service Records
United States National Archives
  Department of State, RG 59. Despatches from U.S. Consuls in
    Mexico
  Department of War, RG 94. Adjutant General's Office
    Correspondence, File No. 27932
    General Orders, Headquarters, Mexico, 1847–48
    Miscellaneous Papers Relating to the Mexican War, Box
    No. 7
    Registers of Enlistments in the U.S. Army, 1840–1848
  Department of War, RG 153. Judge Advocate General's Office
    Proceedings of General Court Martial at Tacubaya, Mexico,
    1847
    Proceedings of General Court Martial at San Angel, Mex-
    ico, 1847
University of California, Berkeley, The Bancroft Library
  Guía del Archivo Histórico Militar de México, 1848–1855, MSS
  DeWitt Clinton Loudon MSS Diary, 1846–1847
  Thomas Carr Nugent MSS
University of Oklahoma Library, Western History Collections
  Fayette Copeland Collection. George Wilkins Kendall manu-
    script, "War Between the United States and Mexico."
University of Texas Library, Austin, Barker Texas History Center
  George W. Kendall Collection
  Earl Vandale Collection. Justin H. Smith Correspondence

University of Texas Library, Austin. Benson Latin American Collection
Mariano Riva Palacio Archives

2. Printed Documents

Mexico. Instituto Nacional de Antropología e Historia. *Churubusco en la acción militar del 20 de aosto de 1847*. Mexico: INAH, 1947.

Mexico. Laws. *Legislación mexicana*. Edited by Manuel Dublán and José María Lozana. 19 vols. Mexico: Edición oficial, 1876–89.

Mexico. Secretaría de Defensa Nacional *Guía del archivo histórico militar de México*. Vol. 1 (1821–47). Mexico: Taller Autográfico, 1948.

Mexico. Secretaría de Guerra y Marina. *Memoria* [1848]. Mexico: Imprenta de Vicente García Torres, 1849.

Mexico. Secretaría de Relaciones Exteriores. *Algunos documentos sobre el tradado de Guadalupe Hidalgo y la situación de México durante la invasión americana*. (Archivo histórico diplomático, 31). Mexico, 1930.

————. *Lord Aberdeen, Texas y California* (Archivo histórico diplomático, 15). Mexico, 1925.

United States. Congress. House. *Mexican War Correspondence*. H. Exec. Doc. 60, 30th Cong., 1st sess., 1847–48.

United States. Congress. Senate. *Message from the President*. S. Exec. Doc. 1, 30 Cong., 1st sess., 1847.

United States. Congress. House. *Military Forces Employed in the Mexican War*. H. Exec. Doc. 24, 31st Cong., 1st sess., 1849–50.

United States. Congress. *Statutes at Large*. Vols. 9, 12, 17. Act of May 13, 1856; Act of Feb. 11, 1847; Act of Aug. 5, 1861; Act of June 6, 1872.

United States. Department of Commerce. Bureau of the Census. *Statistical Abstract of the United States, 1974*. Washington, D.C.: Government Printing Office, 1974.

United States. War Department. *Annual Reports, 1914*. 3 vols., Washington, D.C.: Government Printing Office, 1914.

Yale University. Beinecke Rare Book and Manuscript Library Broadside issued by Gen. Pedro de Ampudia, Monterrey, Sept. 15, 1846.

Broadside issued by Gen. Antonio L. de Santa Anna, Orizaba, Apr. 1847.

3. Newspapers

Baltimore, *Niles National Register*
London, *The Times*
Los Angeles Times
Mexico City, *The American Star*
Mexico City, *Diario del Gobierno de la República mexicana*
Mexico City, *El Correo Nacional*
Mexico City, *The News*
Mexico City, *The North American*
Mexico City, *Novedades*
Mexico City, *Periódico Oficial*
New Orleans, *Picayune*
New York Times
Puebla, *The American Star No. 2*
Querétaro, *Correo Nacional*

4. Accounts of Participants and Eyewitnesses

Anderson, Robert. *An Artillery Officer in the Mexican War, 1846–
7:Letters of Robert Anderson, Captain 3rd Artillery, U.S.A.* New
York: G. P. Putnam's Sons, 1911.
Balbontín, Manuel. *La invasión americana, 1846 a 1847.* Mexico:
Gonzalo A. Esteva, 1883.
[Ballentine, George]. *Autobiography of An English Soldier in the
United States Army, Comprising Observations and Adventures in
the States and Mexico.* New York: Stringer & Townsend, 1853.
———. *The Mexican War, by An English Soldier.* New York: W. A.
Townsend & Co., 1860.
Barbour, Philip N., and Martha I. Barbour. *Journals of the Late
Brevet Major Philip Norbourne Barbour, Captain in the 3rd Regi-
ment, United States Infantry, and His Wife, Martha Isabella Hop-
kins Barbour.* Edited by Rhoda van Bibber Tanner Double-
day. New York: G. P. Putnam's Sons, 1936.
Carpenter, William W. *Travels and Adventures in Mexico.* New
York: Harper & Bros., 1851.
Chamberlain, Samuel E. *My Confession.* New York: Harper &
Bros., 1956.
Clark, Amasa G. *Reminiscences of a Centenarian, as Told by Amasa*

Gleason Clark, Veteran of the Mexican War, to Cora Tope Clark. Edited by J. Marvin Hunter, Sr., Bandera, Tex.: n.p., 1930.

Clarke, Asa B. *Travels in Mexico and California.* Boston: Wright & Hasty's, 1852.

Coit, Daniel Wadsworth. *Digging for Gold Without a Shovel: The Letters . . . from Mexico City to San Francisco, 1848–1851.* Edited by George P. Hammond. Denver: Old West Pub. Co., 1967.

Complete History of the Late Mexican War, Containing an Authentic Account of All the Battles Fought in That Republic . . . by an Eyewitness. New York: F. J. Dow, 1850.

Davis, George T. *Autobiography of the Late Col. Geo. T. M. Davis, Captain and Aide-de-Camp Scott's Army of Invasion (Mexico).* New York: [Jenkins & McCowan], 1891.

Ferris, A. C. "To California in 1849 Through Mexico," *Century* 42 (1891):666–79.

[Giddings, Luther]. *Sketches of the Campaign in Northern Mexico by an Officer of the First Regiment of Ohio Volunteers.* New York: George P. Putnam & Co., 1853.

Grant, Ulysses S. *Personal Memoirs of U. S. Grant.* 2 vols. New York: C. L. Webster & Co., 1885–86.

Harney, William S. *Official Correspondence of Brig. Gen. W. S. Harney. U.S. Army, and First Lt. Geo. Ihrie, Late U.S. Army, with the U.S. War Department, and Subsequent Personal Correspondence* [Washington, D.C., n.p., 1861].

Henry, William S. *Campaign Sketches of the War with Mexico.* New York: Harper & Bros, 1847.

Hitchcock, Ethan A. *Fifty Years in Camp and Field; Diary of Major General Ethan Allen Hitchcock, U.S.A.* Edited by W. A. Croffut. New York: G. P. Putnam's Sons, 1909.

Kendall, George W. *The War Between the United States and Mexico: Drawings by Carl Nebel.* New York: D. Appleton & Co., 1851.

Kenly, John R. *Memoirs of a Maryland Volunteer; War with Mexico in the Years 1846–7–8.* Philadelphia: J. B. Lippincott & Co., 1873.

McElroy, John. "Chaplains for the Mexican War—1846," *The Woodstock Letters* 15 (1886):198–202; 16 (1887):33–39.

Oswandel, J. Jacob. *Notes of the Mexican War, 1846–47–48.* Philadelphia: n.p., 1885.

Perry, John A. *Thrilling Adventures of a New Englander; Travels,*

Scenes and Sufferings in Cuba, Mexico, & California. Boston: Redding & Co., 1853.

Preston, William. *Journal in Mexico . . . Nov. 1, 1847 to May 25, 1848.* Paris: Privately printed, n.d.

Prieto, Guillermo. *Memorias de mis tiempos, 1828 a 1853.* 2 vols. Mexico: Editorial Patria, 1948.

Ramírez, José Fernando. *Mexico During the War with the United States.* Edited by Walter V. Scholes. Translated by Eliott B. Scherr. Columbia, Mo.: University of Missouri Press, 1970.

Reilly, James. "An Artilleryman's Story," *Journal of the Military Service Institution* 33 (1903): 438–46.

Santa Anna, Antonio López de. *The Eagle: The Autobiography of Santa Anna.* Edited by Ann Fears Crawford. Austin: Pemberton Press, 1967.

———. "Letters of General Antonio López de Santa Anna Relating to the War Between the United States and Mexico, 1846–1848." Edited by Justin H. Smith. *Annual Report of the American Historical Assoc. for the Year 1917.* Washington, D.C.: Government Printing Office, 1920.

[Scott, John A.] *Encarnacion Prisoners, Comprising an Account of the March of the Kentucky Cavalry from Louisville to the Rio Grande.* Louisville: Prentice & Weissinger, 1848.

Semmes, Raphael. *Service Afloat and Ashore During the Mexican War.* Cincinnati: William H. Moore & Co., 1851.

Smith, W. C. S. *A Journey to California in 1849.* [Napa, Calif.?, 1925?]

Wise, Henry Alexander. *Los Gringos; Or an Inside View of Mexico and California.* New York: Baker and Scribner, 1849.

5. Monographs and Secondary Sources

Alcaraz, Ramón, et al (eds.). *Apuntes para la historia de la guerra entre México y los Estados Unidos.* Mexico: M. Pyno, 1848.

———. *The Other Side; or Notes for the History of the War Between Mexico and the United States.* Translated by Albert C. Ramsey. New York: J. Wiley, 1850.

Baker, B. Kimball. "The St. Patricks Fought for their Skins, and Mexico." *Smithsonian* 8 (1978): 94–101.

Bancroft, Hubert H. *History of California.* Vol. 5, 1846–1848. (Vol. 22 of *Works.*) San Francisco: The History Co., 1886.

————. *History of Mexico.* Vol. 5, *1821–1861.* San Francisco: A. L. Bancroft Co., 1885.

Bauer, K. Jack. *The Mexican War, 1846–1848.* New York: Macmillan Co., 1974.

Bauer, K. Jack. *Zachary Taylor: Soldier, Planter, Statesman of the Old Southwest.* Baton Rouge: Louisiana State University Press, 1985.

Beals, Carleton. *Brass-Knuckle Crusade.* New York: Hastings House, 1960.

Berge, Dennis E., ed. and trans. *Considerations on the Political and Social Situation of the Mexican Republic: 1847.* Southwestern Studies, Monograph 45. El Paso: Texas Western Press, 1975.

Bill, Alfred H. *Rehearsal for Conflict: The War with Mexico, 1846–1848.* New York: Alfred A. Knopf, 1947.

Billington, Ray A. *The Protestant Crusade, 1800–1860.* New York: Rinehart & Co., 1938.

Bloom, John Porter. "With the American Army into Mexico, 1846–1848." Ph.D. diss., Emory University, 1956.

Bowman, Allen. *The Morale of the American Revolutionary Army.* Washington, D.C.: American Council on Public Affairs, 1943.

Brack, Gene M. *Mexico Views Manifest Destiny, 1821–1846; An Essay on the Origins of the Mexican War.* Albuquerque: University of New Mexico Press, 1975.

Brooks, N[athan] C. *A Complete History of the Mexican War: Its Causes, Conduct, and Consequences; Comprising an Account of the Various Military and Naval Operations, from its Commencement to the Treaty of Peace.* Philadelphia: Grigg, Elliot & Co., 1849.

Callcott, Wilfrid H. *Church and State in Mexico, 1822–1857.* Durham: Duke University Press, 1926.

————. *Santa Anna: The Story of an Enigma Who Once Was Mexico.* Norman: University of Oklahoma Press, 1936.

Carreño, Alberto M. *Jefes del ejército mexicano en 1847: biografías de generales de división y de brigada y de coroneles del ejército mexicano por fines del año 1847.* Mexico: Secretaría de Fomento, 1914.

Castillo Negrete, Emilio del. *Invasión de los Norte-Americanos en México.* 4 vols. Mexico: n.p., 1890–91.

Considine, Robert B. *It's the Irish.* New York: Doubleday & Co., 1961.

Cotner, Thomas E. *The Military and Political Career of José Joaquín Herrera, 1792–1854*. Austin: University of Texas Press, 1949.

Cox, Patricia. *Batallón de San Patricio*. Mexico: Editorial Stylo, 1954.

Diccionario Porrúa de historia, biografía y geografía de México. 3 vols. Mexico: Editorial Porrúa, 1986. S.v. "O'Reilly, Juan; San Patricio (Battallón de)."

Dolph, Edward A. *"Sound Off!" Soldier Songs from the Revolution to World War II*. New York: Farrar & Rinehart, 1942.

Downey, Fairfax. *Texas and the War with Mexico*. New York: American Heritage Pub. Co., 1961.

———. "Tragic Story of the San Patricio Battalion," *American Heritage* 6 (1955): 20–23.

Dupuy, R. Ernest. *Where They Have Trod: The West Point Tradition in American Life*. New York: Frederick A. Stokes, 1940.

Elliott, Charles W. *Winfield Scott, The Soldier and the Man*. New York: Macmillan Co., 1937.

Enciclopedia de México. 1978 ed. S.v. "Guerra de E.U. a México."

Encyclopædia Britannica. 1954 ed. S.v. "Malplaquet."

Exley, Thomas M., ed. *A Compendium of the Pay of the Army from 1785 to 1888*. Washington, D.C.: Government Printing Office, 1888.

Fernández del Castillo, Francisco. *Apuntes para la historia de San Angel y sus alrededores*. Mexico: Museo Nacional de Arqueología, Historia y Etnología, 1913.

Fernández Tomás, Jorge, et al. *Ahí vienen los del norte; la invasión norte-americana de 1847*. (*México: historia de un pueblo*, no. 8.) Mexico: Secretaría de Educación Pública y Editorial Nueva Imagen, 1980.

Finerty, John F. *John F. Finerty Reports Porfirian Mexico, 1879*. Ed. Wilbert H. Timmons. El Paso: Texas Western Press, 1974.

Finke, Detmar H. "The Organization and Uniforms of the San Patricio Units of the Mexican Army, 1846–1848." *Military Collector and Historian* 9 (1957): 36–38.

"First Catholic Chaplains in U.S. Army and Navy," *The Woodstock Letters* 70 (1941): 466–67.

Flannery, John B. *The Irish Texans*. San Antonio: University of Texas, Institute of Texan Cultures, 1980.

Frost, John. *Life of Major General Zachary Taylor: With Notices of the War in New Mexico, California, and in South Mexico; and Bio-

graphical Sketches of Officers who have Distinguished Themselves in the War with Mexico. New York: D. Appleton & Co., 1847.

———. *Pictorial History of Mexico and the Mexican War.* Philadelphia: Thorne, Cowperthwait & Co., 1849.

Ganoe, William A. *The History of the United States Army.* New York: D. Appleton & Co., 1942.

Grove, Frank W. *Medals of Mexico,* Vol. 2, *1821–1971.* [San Antonio: Almanzar's Coins], 1972.

[Harney, William S.] "General Harney" [obituary], *Journal of the United States Cavalry Association* 3 (1890): 1–8.

Hasbrouck, Alfred. *Foreign Legionaries in the Liberation of Spanish South America.* New York: Columbia University Press, 1928.

Haynes, Martin A. *Gen. Scott's Guide in Mexico: A Biographical Sketch of Col. Noah F. Smith.* Lake Village, N.H.: Lake Village Times, 1887.

Heitman, Francis B., ed. *Historical Register and Dictionary of the United States Army from its Organization, September 29, 1789, to March 2, 1903.* 2 vols. Washington, D.C.: Government Printing Office, 1903.

Henry, Robert S. *The Story of the Mexican War.* Indianapolis: Bobbs Merrill Co., 1950.

Hicken, Victor. *The American Fighting Man.* New York: MacMillan Co., 1969.

Honeywell, Roy J. *Chaplains of the United States Army.* Washington, D.C.: Department of the Army, Office of Chief of Chaplains, 1958.

Hopkins, G. T. "The San Patricio Battalion in the Mexican War," *U.S. Cavalry Journal* 24 (1913): 279–84.

Huie, William B. *The Execution of Private Slovik.* New York: Duell, Sloan & Pearce, 1954.

Israel, Fred L., ed. *The State of the Union Messages of the Presidents, 1790–1966.* 3 vols. New York: Chelsea House, 1967.

Jenkins, John S. *History of the War Between the United States and Mexico.* Philadelphia: J. E. Potter, [1848].

Johannsen, Robert W. *To the Halls of the Montezumas: The Mexican War in the American Imagination.* New York: Oxford University Press, 1985.

Johnson, Allen, and Dumas Malone, eds. *Dictionary of American Biography.* New York: Charles Scribner's Sons, 1928–1944. S.v. Winfield Scott and Zachary Taylor.

Jones, Oakah L., Jr. *Santa Anna.* New York: Twayne Publishers, 1968.

Karsten, Peter. *The Naval Aristocracy; The Golden Age of Annapolis and the Emergence of Modern American Nationalism.* New York: The Free Press, 1972.

Katcher, Philip R. *The Mexican-American War, 1846–1848.* London: Osprey Pub., 1976.

Koller, Larry. *The Fireside Book of Guns.* New York: Simon & Schuster, 1959.

Krueger, Carl. *Saint Patrick's Battalion.* New York: Dutton & Co., 1960.

Ladd, Horatio O. *History of the War with Mexico.* New York: Dodd, Mead & Co., 1883.

Lavender, David. *Climax at Buena Vista: The American Campaign in Northeastern Mexico, 1846–47.* Philadelphia: J. B. Lippincott Co., 1966.

Liddell Hart, B. H., ed. *The Letters of Private Wheeler, 1809–1828.* London: Michael Joseph, 1951.

McCampbell, Coleman. *Saga of a Frontier Seaport.* Dallas: South-West Press, 1934.

McCornack, Richard B. "The San Patricio Deserters in the Mexican War," *The Americas* 8 (1951): 131–42.

McDonald, Archie P., ed. *The Mexican War: Crisis for American Democracy.* Lexington, Mass.: D. C. Heath & Co., 1969.

McEniry, Sister Blanche M. *American Catholics in the War with Mexico.* Washington, D.C.: Catholic University of America, 1937.

Mahoney, Tom. "50 Hanged and 11 Branded, The Story of the San Patricio Battalion," *Southwest Review* 32 (1947): 373–77.

Mansfield, Edward D. *The Mexican War: A History of its Origin, and a Detailed Account of the Victories which Terminated in the Surrender of the Capital.* New York: A. S. Barnes, 1849.

May, Robert E. "Invisible Men: Blacks and the U.S. Army in the Mexican War," *The Historian* 49 (Aug. 1987): 463–77.

Mayer, Brantz. *Mexico as It Was and as It Is.* Philadelphia: G. B. Zieber & Co., 1847.

Merk, Frederick. *The Monroe Doctrine and American Expansionism, 1843–1849.* New York: Alfred A. Knopf, 1966.

Miller, Hunter, ed. "Treaty of Guadalupe Hidalgo," vol. 5. *Treaties and Other International Acts of the United States of America,*

1776–1863. Washington, D.C.: Government Printing Office, 1937.

Miller, Robert R. *Mexico: A History*. Norman: University of Oklahoma Press, 1985.

Millett, Allan R., and Peter Maslowski. *For the Common Defense: A Military History of the United States of America*. New York: Free Press, 1984.

Muller, John. *A Treatise of Artillery*. Reprint. Ottowa: Museum Restoration Service, 1965.

Neve, Carlos D. *Historia gráfica del ejército mexicano*. Cuernavaca: Manuel Quesada Brandi, 1967.

Nichols, Edward J. *Zach Taylor's Little Army*. Garden City: Doubleday & Co., 1963.

Parton, James. *Life of Andrew Jackson*. 3 vols. Boston: Ticknor & Fields, 1866.

Peña, José Enrique de la. *With Santa Anna in Texas: A Personal Narrative of the Revolution*. Translated and edited by Carmen Perry. College Station: Texas A & M University Press, 1975.

Petrie, Sir Charles A. *King Charles III of Spain: An Enlightened Despot*. London: Constable, 1971.

Pioneer Society of the State of Michigan. *Collections of the Pioneer Society of the State of Michigan* 6 (1884): 349; 18 (1892): 694.

Pletcher, David M. *The Diplomacy of Annexation: Texas, Oregon, and the Mexican War*. Columbia: University of Missouri Press, 1973.

Potter, George W. *To the Golden Door: The Story of the Irish in Ireland and America*. Boston: Little, Brown & Co., 1960.

Power, Wally. "The Enigma of the Patricios," *An Cosantoir* (Irish Ministry of Defense) 21 (1971): 7–12.

———. "Facets of the Mexican War," *The Recorder* (American Irish Historical Society) 36 (1975): 135–43.

Randall, James G. *Lincoln the President*. Vol. 1. New York: Dodd, Mead & Co., 1945.

Reeves, Jesse S. *American Diplomacy under Tyler and Polk*. Baltimore: Johns Hopkins Press, 1907.

Richards, Leonard L. *The Life and Times of Congressman John Quincy Adams*. New York: Oxford University Press, 1986.

Richardson, James D., ed. *A Compilation of the Messages and Papers of the Presidents, 1789–1897*. Vol. 4. Washington, D.C.: Government Printing Office, 1897.

Richardson, Rupert N. *Texas: The Lone Star State*. Englewood Cliffs: Prentice-Hall, Inc., 1958.

Ripley, Roswell S. *The War with Mexico.* 2 vols. New York: Harper & Bros., 1849.

Riva Palacio, Vicente, ed. *México a través de los siglos.* 5 vols. Mexico: Ballesca y Cía., 1887–89.

Rives, George L. *The United States and Mexico, 1821–1848.* 2 vols. New York: Charles Scribner's Sons, 1913.

Roa Bárcena, José M. *Recuerdos de la invasión norteamericana (1846–1848).* 3 vols. Mexico: Editorial Porrúa, 1947.

Rubio Mañé, Jorge I. "El Excmo. Sr. Dr. D. Martín Tritschler y Córdova, primer arzobispo de Yucatán," *Asbide, revista de cultura mexicana* 5:9 (1941):587–90.

Sears, Louis M. *John Slidell.* Durham: Duke University Press, 1925.

Sellers, Charles. *James K. Polk, Constitutionalist, 1843–1846.* Princeton: Princeton University Press, 1966.

Singletary, Otis A. *The Mexican War.* Chicago: University of Chicago Press, 1960.

Smith, Arthur D. *Old Fuss and Feathers: The Life and Exploits of Lt.-General Winfield Scott.* New York: Greystone Press, 1937.

Smith, George Winston, and Charles Judah, eds. *Chronicles of the Gringos: The U.S. Army in the Mexican War, 1846–1848; Accounts of Eyewitnesses & Combatants.* Albuquerque: University of New Mexico Press, 1968.

Smith, Justin H. *The War with Mexico.* 2 vols. New York: MacMillan, 1919.

Spaulding, Oliver L. *The United States Army in War and Peace.* New York: G. P. Putnam's Sons, 1937.

Spell, Lota M. "The Anglo-Saxon Press in Mexico, 1846–1848," *American Historical Review* 38 (1932):20–31.

Stenberg, Richard R. "The Failure of Polk's Mexican War Intrigue of 1845," *Pacific Historical Review* 6 (1935):35–68.

Stinson, Byron. "They Went over to the Enemy," *American History Illustrated* 3 (1968):30–36.

Sweeny, William M. "The Irish Soldier in the War with Mexico," *American Irish Historical Society Journal* 26 (1927):255–59.

Toussaint, Manuel. *La catedral y las iglesias de Puebla.* Mexico: Editorial Porrúa, 1954.

Upton, Emory. *The Military Policy of the United States.* Washington, D.C.: Government Printing Office, 1917.

Vásquez, Josefina Zoraida, and Lorenzo Meyer. *The United States and Mexico.* Chicago: University of Chicago Press, 1985.

224   SHAMROCK AND SWORD

Wallace, Edward S. "The Battalion of Saint Patrick in the Mexican War," *Military Affairs* 14 (1950):84–91.

———. "Deserters in the Mexican War," *Hispanic American Historical Review* 15 (1935):374–83.

Warren, Harris G. *The Sword was their Passport: A History of American Filibustering in the Mexican Revolution.* Reprint, Port Washington, N.Y.: Kennikat Press, 1972.

Weems, John E. *To Conquer a Peace: The War Between the United States and Mexico.* Garden City: Doubleday & Co., 1974.

Weigley, Russell F. *History of the United States Army.* New York: Macmillan [1967].

Wilcox, Cadmus M. *History of the Mexican War.* Edited by Mary Rachel Wilcox. Washington, D.C.: Church News Publishing Co., 1892.

Wynn, Dennis J. *The San Patricio Soldiers: Mexico's Foreign Legion.* Southwestern Studies, monograph 74. El Paso: Texas Western Press, 1984.

———. "The San Patricios and the United States–Mexican War of 1846–1848." Ph.D. diss., Loyola University of Chicago, 1982.

Zamacois, Niceto de. *Historia de Méjico desde sus tiempos más remotos hasta nuestros días.* 18 vols. Mexico: J. F. Parres y Cía., 1877–82.

Zorrilla, Luis. *Historia de las relaciones entre México y los Estados Unidos de América, 1800–1858.* 2 vols. Mexico: Editorial Porrúa, 1965.

Index